Kitchen in the Clouds

Karen Alexander, M.A.

Published by
Windover Press
967 E. Parkcenter Boulevard., Suite 306
Boise, Idaho 83706-6700
(800) 359-4492

Illustrated by Suzanne Wood
Cover and book design by Vicki Marsh

The information contained in this book is written with the understanding that the reader accepts complete responsibility for his or her own health. Each human body responds uniquely to any intervention. The results of any health plan cannot always be anticipated and are never guaranteed. The author and publisher are not responsible for any adverse effects or consequences resulting from the use of any of the information included in this book. Please include a physician who is trained in nutrition, natural health professionals, and your own inner wisdom as you make choices about your health.

Library of Congress Cataloging-in-Publication Data
Alexander, Karen.
2001-131636

First Edition
Printed in the United States of America

A book comes into being through many contacts, sources and experiences. But ultimately, it arrives because its writer has support, encouragement and inspiration. My deepest gratitude to Jim and Savanna Acee who expanded my heart and showed me the power of conviction. My thanks to Andi Saucerman who encouraged my dreams and contributed to the book's contents. Finally, to my husband Rick, I offer this work as a manifestation of the love, belief, energy and time you have given me over our years together. May it serve others and give hope where there has been despair, love where there has been emptiness, and healing where it is most needed.

Contents

Recipes 69

Appendix 254

Recipe Index 293

Kitchen in the Clouds

The Essential Vegan Guidebook

A resource to nourish and inspire body, mind and soul

Karen Alexander, M.A.

Illustrations by Suzanne Wood

Preface

The sun shines not on us but in us.

John Muir

There is a place that exists in the center of your heart. Here your body and mind are perfectly formed, designed to be just as they need to be for this passage through time on Earth. In each of your trillions of cells, a mystical force resides—the alchemical union of spirit and matter that can heal all suffering. That power remains suspended outside of time and space, only waiting for an invitation to enter into the realm of matter. Its birthing place is that still, sweet temple called the human heart.

Wherever human consciousness awakens, there is hope. Wherever the spell of industry is broken, there is hope. Wherever there is courage to step past the limits of sensory perception, there is hope.

In the ceaseless rhythm of the oceans, a shimmering drop of dew, a child's tears, the mists in the forest, the trickle of a stream, in these things beat the heart of the universe. And when you hold a child in your arms, when you feel your lover's heart beat with your own, when the light shines through the clouds in a particular way, then you cannot help but remember. You have a place in the divine order. You are as important as the totality of all that is.

And there is good news reverberating from every corner of our planet. As people begin to awaken, more and more emphasis is being given to the importance of wholeness, of unity, of healing. Whether we look outward into the heavens, or inward to the deepest corners of our hearts and minds, the answer is the same. We cannot ignore nature if we wish our bodies to survive. Our health and vitality during our lifetime on Earth depend upon our ability to harmonize with the laws governing all of nature. By doing so, we rejoin the stream of all creation—our only place to heal.

Old patterns of thought are rapidly falling apart and a new vision of reality is revealing itself in our innermost being, as it is in scientific laboratories around the world. The shimmering energy body of the cosmos is coming into view, revealing an undeniable unity behind all that exists. The vision spoken about in the mystical branch of every religious tradition of the world is emerging once again.

Physicists have broken down the illusion that anything exists separately from anything else. The ancient view that everything exists as one interconnected whole is being supported by all branches of science. Researchers admit that their investigations are overlapping with what used to be the province of philosophy and religion. This has enormous implications, both scientifically and spiritually.

Medicine can no longer ignore the emerging view of reality. Writers like Deepak Chopra, Andrew Weil, and Bernie Siegel have opened our eyes to a different way to see ourselves. The illusion that the physical body is separate from the mind and heart of the person is giving way; we are leaving behind the notion that our brain is the only part of us that can think or feel, and that our bodies are just long for the ride. Countless studies point to the elaborate intelligence contained in every cell of our bodies. Patients are no longer willing to be regarded as defective machinery in for repair. Increasingly, they are unwilling to passively submit themselves to their doctors, and a fate that is issued to them by the medical profession.

It is an exciting time; a time in which all of the great branches of human inquiry at last join together in celebration, as that which has appeared separate and contrary is at last united. With the advent of the new millennium, we stand on the threshold of perhaps the greatest of all ages—the age of healing.

A thousand unseen hands
Reach down to help you from their
Peace-crowned heights,
And all the forces of the firmament
Shall fortify your strength. Be not afraid
To thrust aside half-truths and grasp
The whole.

Ralph Waldo Trine

Chapter One

Who would believe that so small a space
could contain the images of all the universe?

Leonardo da Vinci
speaking about the human body

To heal the body, we must accept the fact that it is not a machine. Many of us are more comfortable with the biomechanical way of viewing ourselves—a belief that gives us a feeling of control. After all, a machine can be explained and fixed. When something goes wrong with it, one simply has to find a person who can diagnose the problem and fix it. In our culture, the physician is that person. He or she is the modern day shaman — the only person who can hold off death. In his or her hands lies the capacity to keep our machine running. Many are afraid that once the body is gone, so are we.

In recent years, the biomechanical viewpoint has come face to face with a disturbing and exciting challenge, which paradoxically, it created for itself. With increasingly sophisticated medical technology, more and more people were resuscitated after "being dead". Survivors reportrd that they had experienced a transpersonal realm—a place outside of the way we usually define ourselves. The personal self, based on life experience and biology, seemed to disappear. Instead, the individual merged with a vast intelligence and compassion that encompassed the entire universe. From their new perspective, survivors could see that their ordinary, everyday self was only a partial expression of life.

Near death survivors described a universal community that was filled with unending love. They experienced a deep sense of being valued; it was clear that each person was essential to all of creation. People were not simply the sum of their personality traits and accomplishments on Earth. Human beings had an inalterable membership in an unbroken, divine web that lay hidden behind ordinary reality. The transpersonal realm seemed to be our true home, and our ultimate destination. Eerily, the content from near-death experiences corresponded closely with ancient religious texts from all across the world.

The near death survivors reported being permanently changed by their experiences. Once they stepped outside of their own limited everyday self, it was impossible to return to such an eclipsed view. They could see that identification with the limited self separates us from knowing our own true nature, each other, and the greater cosmos. They experienced first hand the fundamental unity to which everything belongs.

Healing is what happens when we come to our edge, to the unexplored territory of mind and body, and take a single step beyond into the unknown, the space in which all growth occurs.

Stephen Levine

Most people behave as though life is a straight line. It begins at birth and ends at death. We rush from one place to the next, driving our cars past magnificent days and perfect opportunities to be intimate with one another. In the quiet of the night, when the television is turned off and the demands on our energy are at bay, many of us lie awake wondering what the point of living is. The years sweep by, the wrinkles in our faces provide evidence that time is running out. We hide from each other, from age—many of us are terrified of death.

What if death does not really exist? Perhaps, as ancient cultures believed, everything is woven together, and all manifest and unmanifest life is related and alive—inhabited by one sacred essence. Perhaps the universe is one organic, alive and transcendent being in which humanity, the Earth, and all of life resides. Could it be that our consciousness has become trapped in the illusion of a separate self—a self destined to die when the body ends?

Certainly, the experiences of near death survivors would validate this viewpoint. Once their body failed, membership in an unbroken whole revealed itself. Could it be that healing occurss not in the busy thoughts of the ordinary self, but in the vastness of the transpersonal, undivided self? Perhaps healing happens in the realm of what we truly are, and not in our desperation to become what we think we should be. In fact, forgetting our true nature, and devoting our lifetime to the ordinary self may be what lies behind the manifestation of illness and pain.

We think of our bodies as solid and stable, but if we had the perspective of a molecule, we would see something entirely different. The profound intelligence within each of our cells makes us more like a constantly communicating assembly of angels, rather than a biomechanical object which relies on a computer-like brain to tell it what to do.

Our thoughts, beliefs, and emotions have a constant effect on every cell within our system. Specific chemicals or neurotransmitters are formed in response to thoughts and feelings, both in the brain and in all the cells of the body. These chemicals spark profound changes in cellular communication. They transmit or transmute pain, form our sensory experiences, create disease or allow for spontaneous healing.

But chemistry only serves to facilitate the human body's true nature—it is an electrical storm of incomprehensible complexity—and its electrical communication is not limited to its own boundaries, but extends outward into its environment. Some scientists even speculate that our electrical impulses never end, but wind their way through the cosmos, affecting worlds our brains have only begun to dream of. For centuries, mystics from all religious traditions have spoken about human electrical fields. It seems we have abandoned our true nature, and invested in only a small part of our consciousness.

It has been estimated that the actual atomic matter that makes up the human body would fit into a teaspoon. Perhaps it is time to begin to consider what exists in the empty space between the atoms—the place where consciousness really resides.

Thou seest no beauty save thou make it first
Man, Woman, Nature, each is but a glass
Where the soul sees the image of itself,
Visible echoes, offsprings of itself.

James Russell Lowell

I am only one...
But still I am one.
I cannot do everything...
But still I can do something.
And because I cannot do everything
I will not refuse to do
The something that I can do.

E.E. Hale

Chapter Two

The probability that human consciousness and our infinitely complex universe could have come into existence through the random interactions of inert matter has aptly been compared to that of a tornado blowing through a junkyard and accidentally assembling a 747 jumbo jet.

Stanislav Grof

The biomechanical viewpoint is a recent development in human history. It has dominated our beliefs about the human body for a mere gasp in the breath of time. It is a bizarre aberration—a distortion of catastrophic proportions. It has cost us millions of lives and unspeakable suffering.

For thousands of years, nature—the divine feminine—was the central source of physical, spiritual and psychological renewal for humanity. From about 40,000 BCE to about 5,000 BCE, the feminine was honored as the connection between this world, and the invisible realm of the spirit. Through instinct, emotions, and the shimmering imagination of our own hearts, we could know the place of the soul—that essence which lies behind the mask of matter.

The sacred pathway given by the feminine allowed for our descent into a world that is unseen when logic and intellect are used alone. By following the divine feminine into the realm of the heart, we could know our deepest selves, and even pass beyond the local self and into the transcendent dimension of the whole. We were intimately aware that an invisible temple waited for our arrival—the energy and love that was there for us could not be explained or measured by the rational mind. Yet, our deepest heart knew that there could be no healing except by spirit.

The divine feminine ignited the energy required to act on behalf of life. Her values were wisdom, instead of acquired knowledge, justice instead of law, beauty instead of perfection, harmony instead of compliance, compassion instead of judgment, and wholeness instead of fragmentation. She reminded us that spirit could only be found with imagination, profound attention, receptivity, an unwavering sense of wonder, and a remarkable humility.

She was a sacred guide who allowed us to inhabit her luminous body—Earth.

In recent history, humanity has subjugated the feminine, and replaced her with a one-sided, masculine image of god—one that has often been portrayed as angry, jealous and, very far away. The results of this shift have been disastrous for our planet. The god of our own creation has catapulted us out of paradise, and into a place of fragmentation, exploitation, self-obsession, and violence. The values of power, control, and conquest have dominated. Cut off from our soul, unaware of our membership in the divine community, we are left alone with an intellect unworthy of our worship.

Our fascination with the mind and its technology has caused us to abandon the pathway to spirit. Without the sustaining power of the divine, life is exhausting. There is an ever present, underlying fear that we are alone in the universe, that no one cares, that ultimately life has no meaning at all. Life itself becomes an enemy—something whose processes we struggle to control. We have forgotten our understanding about how to live on Earth—something that is pliable, ever changing, and beautifully rhythmic.

Our physical selves have not been passive bystanders to this tragedy of human consciousness. The 20th century has seen an ever-accelerating incidence of degenerative disease. We cannot be at war with nature, and simultaneously have healthy bodies.

When we act in accordance with nature's principles, we bring back a way of life that upholds all of creation as sacred and interconnected. We support the health of the planet, and all forms of life. When we let go of the idea that human beings are somehow exempt from nature, we rejoin the whole, and can reap the benefits of membership in the universal.

An intimate relationship with Mother Nature provides the rhythms for our being—emotionally, physically, and mentally. Nothing about her should go unnoticed—the whisper of a breeze, a coming storm, the diminishing light in the fall, the return of the sun in the spring. Our plague of modern illnesses is only a reminder to come back into alignment with nature.

These are changes that must be made in human consciousness. Although we turned our backs on nature when we engaged in the industrial revolution, she has never abandoned us. It is we who have withdrawn our hearts and our awareness. These acts of free will have led our planet to the very brink of destruction.

Now it is time to let go of the exaggerated pride that plagues humanity. Preventing harm to any part of the divine creation—including ourselves—is an obligation that arrives with our very first breath. We cannot turn away from the fact that all of our actions have consequences.

How can you return to a deep connection with Mother Earth? How can you regain the optimal health that was intended for you?

Begin with something simple.
Begin with what you eat.

Chapter Three

Come forth into the light of things.
Let Nature be your teacher.
William Wordsworth

All around us, a quiet sacrament is occurs without notice—one in which the energy of the cosmos becomes integrated into our own physical form. Plants provide the meeting place between these energies and our world. They alone have the ability to collect and store energy from the sun. All food is ultimately derived from plants, which do the primary work of energy transformation that makes all other life forms possible. Without plants, we would have sunlight, water, and air but no food.

When we eat in harmony with nature's principles, our body stays in balance. We do not have to wait for symptoms to appear to remind us that we have gone too far in one direction or another. The natural cycles of the Earth sustain our health and inspire our souls. Eating plants becomes a sacred act of transmutation through which we bring the heavens to Earth.

Science now provides the evidence for what our deepest instincts have never forgotten; the plants around us provide the perfect support for our health and well being. When we consume whole fruits, vegetables, grains, and legumes, we partake of a sacred brew that does not exist by accident and cannot be created artificially.

The body is a miraculous community of living cells, some 30 trillion strong. Cells communicate through chemical reactions. Billions of reactions take place every minute of every day. The body must have a very precise blend of elements in order to effectively communicate with itself and complete the chemical reactions that insure our good health. Doctors cannot create a potion for perfect health. We cannot find that magic in a collection of vitamin bottles. The answer will not be found in a scientific laboratory. What your body needs in order to create perfect health already exists in the world of plants.

Molecules of everything that we eat end up in each of our cells; food provides a constant infusion of either positive or negative substances. The plant world contains millions of biologically active chemicals which are essential to our well being.

Our food has a powerful effect on the body both chemically and psychologically. The food we eat changes our mood, our spiritual awareness, our appearance, and our vitality. Food can provide a fertile breeding ground for a host of disease processes, or it can act to eliminate the factors that lead to illness.

Food can provide elements that tear through the defense systems of our cells, damage their

DNA, and create the opportunity for diseases to develop. Food can send natural warriors throughout our system that heighten the cells' ability to protect themselves. Substances in food can turn up our natural detoxification system, eliminating environmental pollutants. They can stop and even reverse cellular damage. Food compounds can inhibit the growth of tumors, or actually shrink existing ones. Natural substances can change the internal chemistry of the body so that wandering cancer cells no longer have the right conditions under which to attach and grow.

In short, food can help to make us sick, or it can help us to heal. The answer to our health care crisis is living in our gardens and fields just waiting to be prepared in our kitchens.

Recent statistics show that 30 percent of all Americans will contract some kind of cancer. New evidence indicates that up to 90 percent of all cancers have their origins in environmental factors. Millions of other Americans will fall to heart attacks, strokes, and a host of other degenerative diseases. Most of those illnesses can be prevented by changes in diet and health habits. That means that we have much more control over our destiny than many of us realize. We can change how we behave, and we can change what we eat.

Early symptoms tell us to change our diet, our lifestyle, our relationships, or our environment. Our medical system has helped us rationalize those symptoms away with the excuse that we are getting older or that we have too much stress. In fact, most of us exist in a chronic state of ordinary unwellness.

Appearance is one of the most obvious indications of the health status of the body. The next time you're in a public place, take a look at the people around you. Many are overweight. Their complexion is muddy, and their skin sags. There are bags and discoloration under their eyes. Their hair is dull and lifeless. They seem be in a fog of fatigue, their eyes don't sparkle, and they lack vitality. What you are seeing is the overt evidence of a poor diet, leading to poor circulation, inadequate oxygen in the system, and the inability to eliminate waste products.

Take a few minutes, and honestly answer some questions for yourself:

Are you happy with the way you feel both physically and mentally? When you wake up in the morning, do you have a clear head and plenty of energy to meet your day? When you look in the mirror, is your hair lustrous, your skin radiant, are your eyes bright? As the hours pass by, are you alert, can you concentrate, is your memory good? Do you digest your food without heartburn, stomachaches, or excess gas? Do you sleep at night? And one more thing-how's your sex life?

Maybe it's not yourself you're worried about. Is your husband or your wife carrying extra pounds around the middle—the kind that doctors say predict a heart attack? Does your child suffer from constant colds or allergies? Do you have a friend who has been diagnosed with cancer?

Take the self-test below. How many symptoms are you suffering? How about the people you love?

excess weight
exhaustion
irritability
headaches
insomnia
digestive problems
skin rashes, pimples
poor concentration
joint pain
trembling
heartburn
lack of coordination
hemorrhoids
frequent colds
lack of sexual desire
allergies
cold hands and feet
muddy complexion,
spider veins
varicose veins
dizziness
feeling "spacey"
muscle cramps
rapid pulse
bloating and intestinal gas
depression
forgetfulness
irregular heart beat
frequent anxiety

Were you surprised at how many symptoms applied to you?

Chapter Four

The art of medicine consists of amusing the patient while nature cures the disease.

Voltaire

Physicians' offices are flooded with people with vague, non-acute symptoms. Patients complain that they feel tired, can't sleep, have headaches, backaches, chronic constipation, pain in their joints, a lack of sexual desire, and difficulty concentrating.

Symptoms are intended by nature to serve as early warnings that something is going wrong with the body. Our medical system teaches people to ignore or deny their symptoms until they become unbearable or ripen into a medically definable illness.

The idea that people should live their life at optimal health is very new. The concept that each person is largely responsible for creating the conditions under which optimal health can flourish is just beginning to take hold. Although it is changing, we are still a society oriented to illness and its treatment, and not prevention. Although the word prevention is used, what most doctors mean by this term is regular medical examinations and tests. Diagnosing a disease early in its development is not the same as preventing it from happening.

Until the last few years, our health information was almost completely controlled by the American Medical Association. Yet, medical schools concentrate almost exclusively on the diagnosis, surgical intervention, or treatment of diseases that are already present in the patient. The vast majority of physicians have not been adequately trained in human nutrition. According to statistics compiled by EarthSave, out of the 125 medical schools in our country, only 30 require any training in nutrition at all. The average doctor has received about three hours of education about nutrition. This is not surprising when you consider the enormous amount of information an aspiring doctor must learn in order to diagnose and treat existing illness. Medical

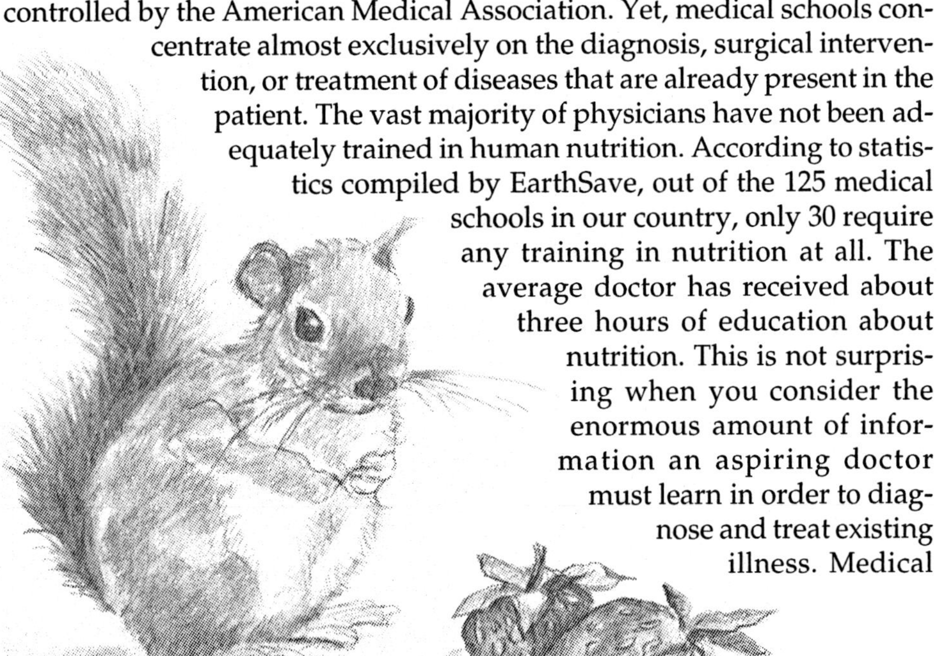

schools may have to expand their training an additional year just to be able to keep up with the rapid pace of technological development. However, their ignorance about nutrition is completely unrecognized by the public, and often by the physicians themselves. Their lack of knowledge combined with the public's assumption that a doctor is an expert is everything relating to human health has proved dangerous for millions of Americans.

Let's look at some of the basic assumptions in medical education:

- Nature is an enemy. It makes many mistakes, but through medical intervention, primarily drugs or surgery, many of those errors can be corrected.
- The physician's focus should be on the patient's disease, disability, and limitations. The primary aim of the physician is to alleviate or eliminate symptoms.
- Diseases are caused by inherent defects in individuals or by the invasion of the body by viruses or bacteria.
- A diagnosis must be made to identify the defect or infectious agent that is causing symptoms.
- The defects can be medically corrected and the contagious agents controlled through immunizations, surgeries, and drugs. Constant medical research and the development of new drugs and procedures are necessary to stem the tide of illness.
- Patients will expect a quick response to drugs or surgeries to eliminate their problems. Side effects from drugs and surgical intervention are to be expected and accepted.
- The patient will defer to the professional authority of the physician. He or she will accept the attitude, time restrictions, lack of personal attention, and lack of information that often characterize their brief contact with the physician.
- Diagnosis and treatment are the responsibility of the physician. The physician should not be expected to provide hope, encouragement, support or extensive information.
- The patient's perceptions about his or her illness, and treatment are unimportant. The attempts of the patient to educate himself about an illness and discuss that information with the physician is essentially irrelevant and a waste of the physician's valuable time.
- Technological, pharmaceutical, or surgical factors are valued in the treatment of disease. The effects of nutrition, exercise, stress management, and the spiritual component of human life are suspect or irrelevant.

A new model for medicine is just beginning to emerge. Its fundamental concepts are very different.

- Nature is wise, but people often make mistakes that interfere with nature. We can learn to avoid those mistakes.
- Many diseases are caused by the failure of our body's natural healing mechanisms. This failure is often the result of unhealthy choices. The person can be helped to become aware of better choices, and supported in learning new behaviors.
- The key to the elimination of many illnesses is to provide the body with what it needs nutritionally and/or environmentally, thereby allowing its natural healing systems to restore health.
- Physicians are often important in helping to restore health, but many other kinds of assistance, both professional, and nonprofessional, are also valuable and available.
- The purpose of diagnosis is to identify those nutritional, relational, spiritual, or environmental factors that contribute to the failure of the body's ability to heal itself.
- Treatment should focus on educating the patient, and encouraging the development and maintenance of behaviors that contribute to health. Intervention should aim at enhancing the natural ability of the body to heal itself.
- The responsibility to learn about and implement the factors that are necessary to restore health is the patient's.
- Drugs and surgery should be avoided as much as possible. They are seen as additional stressors to the body that further damage its ability to heal itself. However, some conditions may need pharmaceutical or surgical intervention.
- Most diseases have taken years to develop. It may take some time to restore health. Radical intervention may alleviate symptoms faster, but cannot restore lasting health.
- The side effects of any treatment should not be automatically accepted. They may be an indication that a particular treatment is contrary to how the body is trying to heal itself.
- It is the responsibility of all caregivers to encourage, support and continue to educate the patient so that he or she can take personal action that can result in healing.

We owe almost all our knowledge not to those who have agreed, but to those who have differed.

Charles Caleb Colton

It is tempting to make the medical establishment the enemy. Most of us have had encounters with doctors that left us angry, confused, or depressed. However, doctors shouldn't be excluded in our quest for health. As our nation continues to mature, we must be more adept at the inclusion of our alternatives, and not the polarization of our options. Many physicians have expressed a great sense of relief at the emergent focus on the responsibility of the patient for his or her own health. To be perceived as having all the answers, while knowing that you do not creates a great deal of stress and not a small measure of guilt for doctors who have been assigned responsibility for our care.

The doctor of the future will give no medicine, but instead will interest his patients in the care of the human frame, in diet, and in the cause and prevention of disease.

Thomas Edison

But physicians must recognize that health is more than the absence of disease. Patients must let go of the idea that they are helpless victims of disease—totally dependent on medical science to fight their battles and fix their problems. We need to stop owning our diseases like cherished pets, referring to "my cancer", or "my arthritis", or "my headaches." To talk about these problems with a sense of ownership makes them a permanent attribute, like "my arms", or "my legs". The body is meant to be well and function normally. Disease is not a weapon of nature; it is the most personal notification we have that nature has been thwarted. In order to restore radiant health, we will have to take responsibility for ourselves.

- We must develop the willingness to see that illness is something we can personally prevent and heal.
- We must learn that symptoms are early warning signs. There may be something that we are doing that is interfering with our body's natural ability to be well.
- We must have the personal motivation and determination to find out what it is in our environment or habits that is interfering with our natural ability to stay well. If we cannot determine this by ourselves, we need to consult with others to gain their information and insight. Although physicians are an important part of our community of assistants, they do not have all the answers.
- We need to be willing to educate ourselves about how our body works, and seek out information about all of the options available to help heal ourselves.
- We need to develop persistence in carrying out the changes necessary to eliminate the conditions for disease—be they nutritional, environmental, psychological, or spiritual.

The natural healing force within each one of us Is the greatest force in getting well.

Hippocrates

When we are suffering, it can be hard to remember that we are meant to enjoy ultimate, radiant health. It can seem as though we have been cast adrift on the Earth. But it is important to realize that our own free will is a tremendously powerful force. The decisions we make about how we live, what we eat, what habits we maintain do more to contribute to our health—excellent or poor—than any other force. Disease processes do not simply fall from the sky. We have a part in creating them by the choices we make.

Do we act to support our health, or do we choose to be passive? Do we even actively undermine our body's ability to heal? The only power that each of us has resides in our choices in the present moment. Only when we do all that we can to help ourselves can we take the luxury of wondering about what fate may bring. Many researchers believe that we are meant to easily live well past a hundred years. When supported and protected, our body is capable of carrying us through a long lifetime of abundant health.

One should die young—as late as possible
Ashley Montague

Chapter Five

I will sing of well-founded Earth, mother of all, eldest of all beings.
She feeds all creatures that are in the world,
All that go upon the goodly land, and all that are in the paths of the seas
And all that fly; all these are fed of her store.

Homer

Mother Nature and her kingdom of plants hold the keys to our health. The more willing we are to accept her gifts, the more vital and healthy we will be. When we embrace our membership in the universal body, when we let go of the idea that human beings are somehow separate and different from the rest of creation, then we become filled with peace and joy.

The anxiety of modern life has to do with trying to live out of one's true self, out of one's true element—trying to exist in a realm that is contrary to our true nature. There is no resting in the rhythm of life, but only endless movement in the squirrel's cage of the mind. It is the mind that convinces us that we cannot heal. It tells us that our limitations and impedements are permanent. It can even make us believe that we deserve to suffer. It drains our courage, inhibits our ability to find solutions, and leaves us with the sense that we are essentially alone in the universe.

It is the heart which experiences God and not the mind.

Pascal

Our bodies provide an inarguable testament to the fact that there can be no harm to others without harm to ourselves. Mother Earth holds everything we need to be healthy. But we cannot simply take her resources without thought. We cannot continue to act as though she exists for our exploitation. What our mind forgets, our body remembers—our disease statistics show this is graphic detail.

Our bodies are not our enemies. Their symptoms are an urgent call to return to our deepest origin—our membership in the divine—our rightful place in the arms of Mother Earth. How did we become so lost? How did we get so far away from what is best for our hearts and our health?

Beginning at the end of the 19th century, the industrial revolution brought unprecedented affluence. Suddenly people had the ability to eat whatever they wanted to;they were not limited to what they could catch or grow themselves. Consequently, there was an explosion in the consumption of former "luxury products", such as meat, dairy products, and sugar. At the same time, machines were developed that did much of the hard labor—exercise was dramatically reduced.

As the center of America's population migrated from the farm into the cities, people abandoned the practice of growing their own food. The last true intimate connection with Mother Earth was lost to the majority—an unprecedented event in human history. Additives became a regular component of our food supply, and refined flour and sugar consumption rose dramatically. Vitamin and mineral depletion began to play havoc with the human system, and the rate of degenerative diseases increased.

The fact that an opinion has been widely held is no evidence whatsoever that it is not utterly absurd.

Bertrand Russell

In 1956, the Department of Agriculture introduced "the four food groups"—dairy, meat, bread and vegetables. Millions of school children learned that one half of each day's intake of food should come from the flesh, milk, or eggs of animals. They received a strong message that there was a serious health risk if animal products were not consumed.

The promotion of the four food groups was directly funded by agribusiness. Food company advertising found a powerful new medium when television became a mainstay in every household. Americans relied on red meat, poultry, eggs, fish, cheese, milk, oil, white rice, refined flour, processed foods, salt, sugar, and a staggering number of additives for their nutrition. Visitors from other cultures reported that fat and salt were the predominant flavors in the American diet.

It is interesting to note that a generation earlier, the Department of Agriculture had promoted "the 12 food groups"—a model which included grains and beans. The surviving four groups were the result of political battles between competing groups within agribusiness.

While the four food groups continued to be vigorously promoted, numerous studies were already on record about the dangers of meat, eggs, and dairy products. In 1908, scientists had already observed that rabbits fed a diet of meat, whole milk and eggs developed fatty deposits on the walls of their arteries which constricted the flow of blood and led to heart attacks. In 1916, Cornelius de Langen, a physician working in Indonesia noticed that native people had much lower rates of heart disease than did the colonists living on the islands. Heart disease soared among Indonesians who left their native diet of plant foods and ate a European diet with lots of meat and dairy. Later, medical researchers in Denmark reported that deaths from heart disease had dramatically declined during World War II—a time when meat, dairy, and eggs had been scarce.

By 1959, medical and nutritional studies regularly appeared showing that meat and dairy products were highly associated with heart disease, strokes, and various forms of cancer. It had also been noted that people living in parts of the world where diets were centered around grains, beans, fruits, and vegetables lived longer and healthier lives. When those people came to live in the United States, and ate a diet consistent with our culture, their disease rates soon duplicated ours.

Studies from around the world consistently showed that the higher the consumption of meat and dairy in any culture, the more its people suffered from heart attacks, stroke, diabetes and cancers of the bowel, breast, prostate gland, and ovaries. Yet, the typical American was advised by the government and by the advertising of food companies to regularly send jolts of fat, protein, salt, and sugar through his body every few hours.

Increasingly it became impossible to ignore the fact that the four food groups could no longer be supported. The Physician's Committee for Responsible Medicine, along with countless other organizations, called for the adoption of a plant-based diet with dietary fat less than 15 percent. The recommendation that animal products be eliminated created a whirlwind of controversy. Agribusiness lobbyists began a vigorous and aggressive campaign, fueled by millions of dollars.

In 1992, the Department of Agriculture had to acknowledge the tidal wave of scientific evidence that the unlimited consumption of animal products was dangerous to human health. The food pyramid replaced the basic four. It called for Americans to consume a majority of their daily food as whole grains, fruits, and vegetables and substantially cut down on fats, oils, and sweets. However, meat and dairy interests made sure their products were still highly recommended for daily consumption.

Today we are reaping the terrible consequences of what we were conditioned to believe. What we learn when we are children is especially hard to change. The almost involuntary concern people display when the four food groups are challenged is a testament to that fact. Meanwhile, the food industry spends over 36 billion dollars a year reinforcing those entrenched beliefs.

Still, the scientific evidence continues to mount. A diet rich in fresh, whole foods, with no added fat and no added cholesterol, and as few processed and refined foods as possible is the best for human health.

Many eyes go through the meadow,
but few see the flowers in it.

Emerson

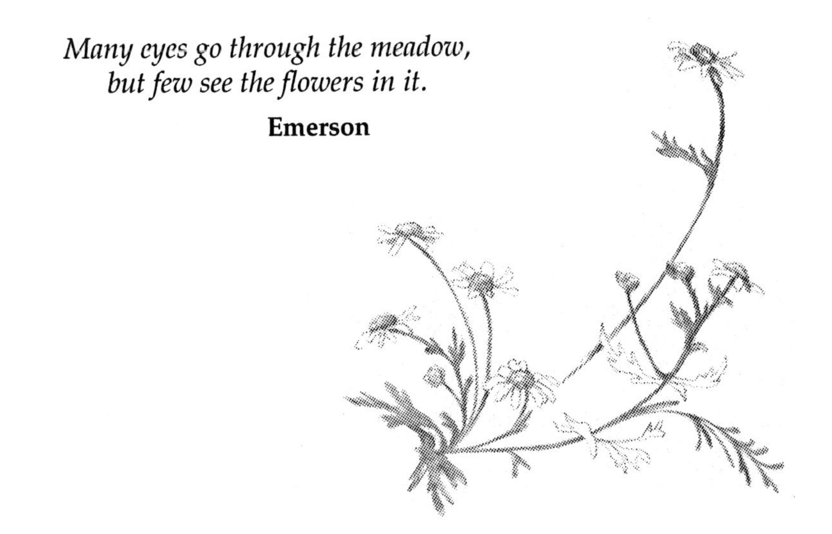

Just consider the following facts.
People who eat a natural, unrefined, plant-based diet have:

Lower mortality rates from coronary artery disease
Lower rates of breast cancer
Lower blood pressure
Lower rates of diabetes
Lower rates of colon cancer
Lower rates of prostate cancer
Lower rates of ovarian cancer
Lower rates of uterine cancer
Lower rates of pancreatic cancer
Fewer strokes
Lower incidence of arthritis
Lower rates of osteoporosis
Lower incidence of kidney stones
Lower incidence of gallstones
Lower rates of diverticular disease.
Lower weight and overall body fat
Lower serum cholesterol
Fewer problems with constipation and hemorrhoids
A measurably stronger immune system
Better circulation
Fewer varicose veins
Lower rates of heartburn, and indigestion
Fewer allergies
Fewer colds
Healthier complexions
Fewer problematic symptoms during menopause
Less difficulty with PMS
Healthier teeth and gums
Faster recovery from illness or surgery

Chapter Six

Sweep up the debris of decaying faiths
Sweep down the cobwebs of worn-out
Beliefs,
And throw your soul wide open to the light
Tune your ear
To all the wordless music of the stars
And to the voice of nature, and your heart
Shall turn to truth and goodness, as the plant
Turns to the Sun

Ralph Waldo Trine

How do plants perform these health miracles?

For a long time, we looked at food only in terms of the vitamins, minerals, and protein it could provide. Most of us are familiar with the "Recommended Daily Allowance" posted on vitamin bottles. We know that we have to meet a certain daily quota to avoid deficiencies. But the calories and vitamins that plants provide are just the beginning of what they have to offer.

In the last five years, researchers have flooded us with information about another class of active properties in food—properties that can save lives—phytochemicals. "Phyto" is simply the Greek word for plant. Phytochemicals make a powerful contribution to our health by interfering with damage at the cellular level.

Antioxidants are a particularly potent group of phytochemicals. These powerful agents oppose something called free radicals. A normal oxygen atom in the body contains four pairs of electrons. A free radical is a molecule that has lost one of its electrons. It becomes an unstable molecule that urgently works to replace its missing electron. In order to restore balance, it steals an electron from nearby molecules. When it does this, it sets off a chain reaction of cellular damage.

Free radicals spin out of control and rush through the body, attacking cells, turning their fats rancid, altering proteins, penetrating cell membranes, and corrupting the cell's genetic code. Cells either die or begin to mutate into forms that can be the precursors to cancer. Free radicals also affect blood proteins, hastening the buildup of plaque on arterial walls.

An antioxidant is capable of donating one of its electrons without becoming a free radical itself. By supplying the missing electron for a free radical, the molecule is restored to balance and stops creating damage to cells in the body.

Many researchers believe that many degenerative diseases such as cancer, heart disease, arthritis, and multiple sclerosis are different forms of the same process—accumulated cellular damage that was done by free radical attacks. Certianly free radical damage is a component of most degenerative diseases.

Antioxidants abound in plant foods—fruits, vegetables, grains, and legumes. Because of our diet, our internal universe is engaged in a harrowing battle against an army of free radicals that seek to destroy it. Our symptoms and appearance are major indicators about whether we are winning or losing that battle.

Antioxidants such as vitamins C, E, and beta-carotene may prove as potent as antibiotics and vaccines in fighting disease. The evidence is staggering.

Dr. Matthias Rath, Harvard University

Examples of Mother Nature's Magic

Asparagus, oranges, strawberries, peaches, potatoes, squash, cauliflower, and tomatoes contain powerful neutralizers of carcinogens.

Beans help to enhance our immune system

Blueberries, cranberries, grapes, citrus fruits help the body to eliminate potential cancer-causing chemicals.

Cabbage, broccoli, kale help to prevent excess estrogen from provoking hormone dependent tissues. This may reduce the risk of breast and ovarian cancer.

Chili peppers have anti-bacterial, and anti-fungal properties.

Garlic, onions, scallions and leeks help to increase the enzymes that dissolve carcinogens and make them easier to excrete.

Leafy greens, sweet potatoes, and other orange vegetables contain powerful antioxidants. They may reduce the risk of heart disease, and cancer, and stimulate the immune system.

Onions, shallots, broccoli and squash have anti-inflammatory, anti-bacterial, anti-fungal, and anti-viral properties.

Pumpkin, carrots, cantaloupe contain natural chemicals that can slow the growth of cancer cells, and enhance the immune system.

Soy products help to balance the hormonal system, and inhibit the growth of abnormal cells.

But plants have even more to offer. Glucose provides the energy all of the systems of the body require to function. Our level of glucose, or "blood sugar", is affected by anything that we eat. Simple carbohydrates cause the blood sugar level to shoot up. This causes the pancreas to secrete large amounts of insulin. Insulin quickly neutralizes the sugar, but that creates a rapid fall in available glucose. The result is intense food cravings, bursts of energy followed by fatigue, mood swings, and impaired fat metabolism. Chronic overtaxing of the pancreas is believed to be the cause of adult onset diabetes. The pancreas becomes exhausted and unable to provide necessary insulin, which must then be medically supplied.

When blood sugar is maintained within normal limits, it sustains mental and physical functioning—it helps us to have energy, stable moods, and good concentration. Because they take a long time to break down in the intestine, complex carbohydrates provide a slower release of glucose into the bloodstream.

A plant-based diet is high in fiber. Because certain parts of plants are resistant to being completely broken down in the body, they provide bulk that moves food easily and quickly through the digestive tract. The average American eats about 15 grams of fiber per day; we should eat at least 25 to 40 grams per day. In countries with a plant-based diet, 70-80 grams a day is typical.

Eating a high fiber diet has many benefits including: assisting weight loss, the prevention of appendicitis, high cholesterol, colon and colorectal cancer, constipation, coronary heart disease, diabetes, diverticular disease, gallstones, hemorrhoids, hypertension, and irritable bowel syndrome.

Fiber appears to offer wonderful benefits to people who suffer from adult onset diabetes. It often reduces insulin requirements, improves blood sugar stability, lowers cholesterol and triglyceride values, and promotes weight loss. In one study, a high-fiber diet led to a discontinuance of insulin therapy in 60 percent of diabetic subjects, and significantly reduced the dose in the other 40 percent.

Colon cancer is the major cancer of industrialized, sedentary western societies where the diet is high in meat consumption. The rates of colon cancer is inversely associated with the consumption of fiber; the more fiber, the less colon cancer. In the intestine, fiber appears to bind with carcinogens and excess hormones. It is able to escort these potentially dangerous substances out of the body before they have a chance to cause the mutations in cells that lead to cancer. People with high fiber diets have much lower rates of colon, breast, prostate, and ovarian cancer.

When you consume natural, unrefined plant-based foods, you are eating straight from nature. Nothing has been taken out and nothing added in. Vitamins, minerals, fiber, antioxidants, and other substances exist in a critical balance that we can never match by spraying highly refined foods with manufactured substances. Many of nature's ingredients have not even been identified by man, let alone reproduced.

The ability to simplify means to eliminate the unnecessary so that the necessary may speak.

Hans Hofmann

Chapter Seven

We become ill when the harmful elements of what we eat and how we live overwhelm our bodies ability to keep healthy. Heredity determines to a large extent what strengths and weaknesses our bodies possess and, therefore, where our systems may first fail under a particular strain. Of the two primary factors—diet and heredity—that produce disease, we must concentrate on the factors we have control over and disregard the ones that we cannot alter.

John McDougall, MD

There are two systems within your body that are particularly influenced by the food you eat and the environment in which you live—your immune system and your detoxification system. The AIDS crisis has raised our awareness about the importance of the immune system. This complex, delicately balanced defense system is difficult to maintain in a world filled with the environmental toxins we have little control over—smog, pesticides, heavy metal contamination, and polluted water present a constant challenge. However, your diet can contribute mightily to the health of your immune system. The phytochemicals contained in plant foods are a powerful force that helps to create and maintain cellular health.

A well-functioning immune system is essential to your health. It can save you from problems ranging from minor infections to cancer. While your genetic makeup influences your immune capability, your body's chemistry is profoundly affected by what you eat. The flood of compounds contained in fruits, vegetables, grains, and legumes are essential to the healthy functioning of your defense system. By making sure you bathe your cells regularly in natural phytotherapy, you are taking a powerful action to prevent diseases from ever getting started.

Your immune system involves several different kinds of cells. Lymphocytes are cells produced by the bone marrow, lymph nodes, and spleen. These circulate through your system helping to coordinate immune responses in the body. Cytotoxic cells help to remove virus infected cells from your body. Suppressor cells turn down your immune system when it becomes overactive. These systems are meant to coordinate with each other. They keep you protected from outside contaminants like bacteria and viruses. They also identify and remove cells within your body that have become defective.

An immune system can become unable to differentiate between its own cells and those of invading bacteria or viruses—autoimmune diseases result. An autoimmune disease is one in which the body no longer recognizes what cells or outside forces need to be controlled, and begins to attack healthy cells, treating them like an enemy. Researchers believe that autoimmune responses are initially triggered by environmental factors—toxins absorbed through the food supply is highly suspect, as are pharmaceuticals. When your immune system stops functioning, you quickly become subject to a host of illnesses.

When the immune system is sluggish or impaired, it lets many invaders pass through unchallenged. Many researchers hypothesize that cancer is the result of impaired immunity. Normally, cell division is a process under tight regulatory control by internal DNA. The essential difference between normal and cancerous cells is a loss of control over the process of cell division. Cancer cells are able to escape from the constraints that normally regulate cell division. Proliferation of a cell or group of cells in an uncontrolled way eventually gives rise to a growing tumor.

There is another system at work in your body—the detoxification system. Human beings are currently exposed to enormous numbers of environmental toxins. Our homes and offices are built and furnished with materials that emit large amounts of chemicals. Many of the cleaners we use contain ingredients that are harmful to both health and the environment. In our efforts to create energy-efficient housing, open windows no longer ventilate our interior spaces. Hazardous fumes are trapped, and can hang in the air for weeks.

In addition, we eat foods that are contaminated with an enormous variety of chemical agents. We are proud of the lack of spoilage and tremendous shelf-life of our food supply, a condition that demands the use of preservatives. People do not stop to consider that the shelf-life of a product is inversely proportional to its beneficial effects on your health. If bacteria doesn't want to consume certain foods, why should you?

Once we take toxins into our body, it immediately begins to try to neutralize them. In a complex process, the body changes many chemicals into different forms so that they may be safely excreted. Chemicals that cannot find a detoxification pathway out of the body are left in the system, and can create widespread damage. They poison enzymes, harm the membranes of cells, alter the DNA, and inhibit the regulatory processes that allow for normal cell division. As more chemicals come in, they begin to interact with those already there, forming combinations, or even mutations, that may be much more dangerous than the original components. The body's natural processes of elimination cannot rid itself of them. When the detoxification system has become sufficiently overloaded, a person becomes highly susceptible to a variety of disease processes.

...It will seem like every time you turn around you seem to have developed another ailment. You're afraid to tell your doctor since he hasn't figured out the causes of the first three complaints yet.

Sherry Rogers, MD

Each person has been exposed to years of environmental contaminants, chemicals in foods, and pharmaceuticals. Analysis of coronary artery plaque, and fat shows the presence of pesticides and common food additives. It seems that if the body cannot eliminate toxins, it attempts to contain them. So, we all carry an accumulated burden of toxins within our body. Our individual cells struggle to function normally in the face of continual chemical assault, both from the environment, and from contaminants already contained within the cells of the body. Researchers believe that many diseases are caused or at least facilitated by the overwhelming levels of toxins to which we are exposed.

How does the body continue to cope with the chemical contamination? First, it tries to eliminate a toxin by increasing the flow of mucus, and initiating an attack of white blood cells. That can result in colds or flu-like symptoms. Many people believe they suffer from allergies, but they may be reacting to food, and not the pollen in the air. When white blood cells rush to defend the body, chronic inflammation may be the result.

If your body cannot eliminate its enemy, it tries to contain it. That is the unfortunate job of the fat cells; they act as jailers to the toxins. So, when you decide you need to lose weight, your body views that as a decision to release years of stored toxins into your blood stream. It has a natural resistance to allowing the breakdown of fat. The body's solution is to prevent the weight loss. Many people turn to diet soda, reduced fat foods, and artificially sweetened foods when they try to lose weight. Those items are packed with chemicals. The body is forced to increase the fat cells in order to deal with all of those toxins. The result is weight gain, not loss.

Toxic overload is suspected in some mental symptoms. Scientists are beginning to investigate something they call "toxic brain syndrome." Patients report feeling spacey, dizzy, lethargic, confused, and depressed for "no reason". The brain is highly susceptible to toxins—a fact observed simply by watching someone who has been drinking. The explosion of diagnoses of depression and anxiety may be the result of altered brain chemistry due to chronic toxic overload.

Eating plant-based foods gives you the chance to avoid chemical additives. Although government safety boards study the individual chemicals that are added to our foods, the effects on the body of combinations of commonly found chemicals have not been studied. In addition, the companies who make the food being examined finance most studies about food product safety. If nature didn't make it, our body probably does not have the mechanisms by which to handle it properly.

When people return to a plant-based, natural way of eating, it is not at all uncommon to hear that symptoms suffered for a lifetime have disappeared. Energy becomes boundless, weight control is effortless, hair and complexions return to youthful beauty, vitality is restored, depression is lifted, and prescriptions are often no longer necessary.

Miracles are possible, but we have to be willing to prepare the way for their arrival. Take your health in your own hands. You will never know what can happen unless you try. Give yourself the gift of a month of eating a whole-foods, natural, plant-based diet. I think you will find that it was one of the best things you've ever done for yourself.

Something we were withholding made us weak Until we found out it was ourselves.

Robert Frost

How to improve your health:

- Eat a diet that is high in organic vegetables, fruits, grains, and legumes. These foods are naturally filled with toxin-fighting phytochemicals, nutrition, and fiber that all help to enhance both the immune and detoxification systems.
- Eat low on the food chain. The greatest concentrations of pesticides, herbicides, antibiotics, and growth hormones are found in animal products that are high on the food chain.
- Avoid processed foods with chemical additives such as preservatives, flavor enhancers, colorants, emulsifiers, artificial flavoring, or sugar substitutes.
- Consider including a well-designed program of vitamins, minerals, and antioxidants in your daily diet. Don't rely on supplements to replace natural foods, but use them to augment a healthy diet.
- Limit your intake of alcohol. Do not take any medications, including over-the-counter preparations without careful consideration. Understand that every drug you consume ends up in every cell of your body. Educate yourself thoroughly about the impact of any drug, particularly antibiotics.
- Use natural health-care and cosmetic products. There are increasing numbers of quality products on the market which are ethically manufactured, and do not include dangerous chemicals. Not only are these products better for your health, but they are better for our environment.
- Sweat regularly! The body uses its sweating mechanism to excrete heavy metals, pharmaceuticals, pesticides, and herbicides. Aerobic exercise is the best choice. Regular saunas can also be useful.
- Regularly open the windows in your office, car, and home. Energy efficient environments also trap chemical emissions from carpet, paint, adhesives, etc. Without even being aware of it, you can spend your days and nights in a chemical fog that can have profound implications for your health. Consider buying an air filter for any environment in which you spend significant time.
- Drink purified water.
- Use safe cleaning products—choose botanically based, and biodegradable options.
- Wear natural fiber clothing like cotton, linen or wool whenever possible—especially when clothing will be in direct contact with your skin. Use natural fiber sheets, and blankets. This is especially important for infants and people whose immune

systems are already compromised.

- Do not use pesticides, herbicides, fungicides, or synthetic fertilizers on your lawn or garden. No matter how careful you are, molecules of these substances go directly into your body; they are extremely difficult for your system to deal with. In addition, these chemicals end up in the water supply. There are wonderful organic products on the market that work just as well at controlling pests, and increasing yield. Fertilizer should have the effect of improving the long-term fertility of the soil, and not simply provoke a plant into an unnatural growth spurt. Organic additives like compost, manure, fish meal, etc. pay rewards that far exceed manufactured, non-organic chemicals.
- Don't douse your pets with chemicals. Not only is it unhealthy for them, but those chemicals end up in your environment, and thus, in your body.

Chapter Eight

Men dig their graves with their own teeth, and die more by those fated instruments than the weapons of their enemies.

Thomas Moffett

It is clear that the foods from the plant kingdom have astounding benefits to our health. But what about animal foods? Should you eat beef, chicken, fish, or eggs?

No one can tell you what to eat. Look at the evidence and then make the decisions for yourself. Keep in mind that food preferences are highly influenced by training. Anyone who has traveled can attest to the fact that other cultures regularly consume products that we might find distasteful, and vice versa. America's insistence on eating animal products is the result of conditioned beliefs created by agribusiness. The promotion of beef, chicken, fish, eggs, and dairy foods is fueled by billions of dollars.

The beef industry has contributed to more American deaths than all the wars of this century, all natural disasters, and all automobile accidents combined.

Neal Barnard, MD
President, Physician's Committee for Responsible Medicine

Researchers continue to find that eating animal products has a profoundly adverse effect on your immune and detoxification systems. Over time, your body buckles under the impossible burden of trying to cope with animal proteins, fats, and cholesterol. In addition, the pesticides, herbicides, and hormones contained in the food supply are all substances that the detoxification system must neutralize, and its capability is limited.

Anthropological evidence indicates that early man was primarily a vegetarian who had occasional feasts of animal flesh. His diet was low in fat and rich in fruits, herbs, seeds, nuts, grains, and vegetables. When animal protein was consumed, it was naturally low in fat. The animals were lean, not domesticated and raised to be fat. Furthermore, it was quite a job to catch that animal! Our ancestors had little time to rest; they worked continually just to survive.

Physical examination of the human body gives us strong evidence that we are meant to be herbivores. Our intestinal tract is very long, and highly convoluted; it is perfect for digesting plant materials that take a longer time than animal flesh to be broken down. Because plant material is naturally high in fiber, waste is efficiently eliminated after the body has absorbed the useful components of the food. A carnivore has a short intestinal tract because meat decomposes rapidly and contains little fiber. Fast digestion and rapid elimination are necessary, otherwise toxins accumulate in the bowel. Toxins held in the bowel are highly implicated in the development of intestinal and rectal cancer, and a host of other disease processes. The hydrochloric acid in our stomachs is approximately

20 times weaker than that found in carnivores; higher levels of stomach acid are required to break down muscle and sinew contained in animal flesh.

Carnivores have long teeth and claws for catching and holding their prey. Human beings have small mouths, jaws that can move from side to side, and flat teeth which can grind grains, seeds, nuts, and vegetables. Our dexterous hands serve to plant, tend and gather food. The majority of people have a natural aversion to the idea of eating raw, bloody meat. We have to disguise it by cooking before it seems appetizing.

Today's diet has at least six times the amount of fat, a much higher ratio of saturated to unsaturated fatty acids, less than a tenth of the optimal fiber, an almost inconceivable amount of sugar and salt, and few complex carbohydrates when compared to the diet that sustained mankind for thousands of years. Throughout the world, the adoption of such a diet has been accompanied by enormous increases in chronic and degenerative diseases, an epidemic of cancers, and skyrocketing heart disease. Attempting to live on the wrong kind of fuel overburdens our system beyond its capacity to cope.

If beef is your idea of 'real food for real people,' you'd better live real close to a real good hospital.

Neal Bernard, MD
Physician's Committee for Responsible Medicine

We can no longer afford to rely on our automatic ideas about the consumption of beef, chicken, fish, eggs, and dairy products. Consider the following facts:

- Animal flesh is high on the food chain. It holds dense concentrations of environmental contaminants, including pesticides and herbicides that are easily stored in the fatty tissues of the body. Meat is one of the most effective methods by which these poisons find their way into your system.
- Beef ranks third of all foods in insecticide contamination. According to the National Research Council, 99 percent of breastfeeding women who eat meat show insecticide residue in their milk. According to the National Research Council of the National Academy of Sciences, beef ranks second in pesticide contamination.
- Animals no longer run free in the pasture. Mass production practices make them highly susceptible to numerous illnesses; antibiotics are routinely administered, whether an animal is sick or not. Antibiotic residues of penicillin, sulfamethazine, streptomycin, tetracycline, and sulfaquinoxaline have been found in beef sold in supermarkets. Humans who eat meat often harbor antibiotic resistant strains of bacteria. As Dr. Jere Goyan writes, "Unless we take action now to curb the use of antibiotics in the livestock industry, we will not be able to use them to treat human disease."
- In information provided by EarthSave, we learn that 13 percent of staphylococci infection was resistant to penicillin in 1960. By 1988, the percentage of resistant bacteria was 91 percent.

- Animal flesh is subject to salmonella, e-coli, trichinella, worms, toxoplasmosis, parasites, hepatitis virus, and a host of other problems. According to the Centers for Disease Control, between 40 and 80 million people a year become sick due to food-borne contaminants—most of these are associated with animal products. A recent study revealed as many as 1 out of 3 carcasses are contaminated with e-coli.
- Although the Department of Agriculture gives the impression that animal products are carefully inspected, the reality is that federal meat inspectors examine less than 1 percent of the carcasses headed for consumption. Researchers have found animal hair, pieces of bone, fecal matter, and infectious material in meat being sent out for consumer use.
- Animal products are full of saturated fat and cholesterol. They contain no fiber and limited amounts of vitamins and minerals.
- When meat, poultry, or fish is cooked, substances called heterocyclic amines are created. These are powerful mutagens that stimulate free radicals. Cooking meat also leads to the formation of nitrsamines: chemicals that are implicated in almost every type of cancer.
- After eating meat, the body's white blood count increases. This suggests that the immune system is alerted when animal products are consumed. The body appears to regard them substances to be contained and eliminated.
- When meat is consumed, the red blood cells become sticky and create a kind of sludge in the small blood vessels. The capacity to dissolve dangerous blood clots becomes impaired—stroke and heart attacks become more likely.
- There are approximately 1.5 million heart attacks in America each year. About one third of them are fatal. The risk for having a heart attack for meat-eating American males is 50 percent. It is only 4 percent for vegetarian males.
- Medical literature is flooded with scientific studies that show a high correlation between red meat and heart disease, stroke, and cancers of the colon, breast and prostate.
- The American Heart Association, American Cancer Society, National Academy of Sciences, and the American Academy of Pediatrics are a few of the medical organizations that have recommended a dramatic reduction in the consumption of red meat and other animal derived foods.
- Populations that consume mostly plant foods and little or no meat, have very low rates of colon, breast, uterine, and prostate cancers. When those populations become westernized and their diets contain a lot of meat, their cancer rates soon match those of the west.

- Several studies have found that arthritis symptoms were alleviated in 9 out of 10 people when animal products were removed from the diet.
- The rate of colon cancer for people in meat eating cultures is ten times that of people in non-meat eating cultures.
- Countless studies show that vegetarians have strikingly lower blood pressure readings, regardless of age or weight.
- Health care costs attributable to meat consumption are from 28.6 to 61.4 billion dollars annually according to a study published in Preventive Medicine.

It's time to stop scratching our heads about the nation's exploding health care costs. We can cut those costs by eliminating subsidies for livestock feed and dairy products and scrapping out of date diet guidelines that encourage traditional, meat-based diets.

Neal Barnard, MD

There is something else to consider when you make decisions about eating animal foods. Many scientists are convinced that the proliferation of growth hormones in these foods is playing havoc with human hormonal systems. Ninety percent of cattle raised for meat in the United States receive hormones to increase their growth and weight. Residues of those drugs are present in the animal products offered in the grocery stores.

When these hormones enter the human body, they can create endocrine imbalances. Scientists are studying the connection between abnormally high rates of circulating estrogen in women, increased rates of androgen in men, and the terrifying increase in hormone dependent cancers like breast, testicular, prostate, ovarian, and uterine. It is interesting to note that in countries where women rarely get breast cancer, men also rarely develop prostate cancer.

Many scientists are alarmed at the 30 percent drop in the sperm count of men in western cultures; a phenomenon researchers are certain is partially due to the regular consumption of female hormones in their food supply. As one scientist put it, "All people are now being exposed to an additional cancer risk due to milk from cows treated with bovine growth hormone."

Women who eat diets high in animal fat and cholesterol consistently show higher levels of estrogen and prolactin in their systems. These substances stimulate breast tissue, the lining of the uterus, and the ovaries by activating the DNA that is responsible for cell division. Whenever cells are stimulated to divide more frequently, the possibility of cancer increases.

There are two kinds of estrogen—hydroxylated-16, and hydroxylated-2. Type 16 appears to stimulate dependent tissues, while type 2 is far less dangerous. Type 16 was 50 percent higher in the blood of meat eating women. Type 2 was primarily found in women who exercise regularly, eat very little or no meat, and who eat a lot of vegetables.

Many plant-based foods are rich in type 2 estrogens. Receptor sites in vulnerable tissues become filled with them and are then protected from being influenced by the dangerous type 16 estrogens.

Soy products contain isoflavonoids, which appear to interfere with the action of strong estrogens. They are also rich in phytoestrogens—natural estrogens also produced by approximately 300 different plant-based foods such as bean sprouts, sesame seeds, carrots, corn, apples, oats, etc. They seem to mimic the body's estrogen without its detrimental effects. Researchers believe that during and after menopause, a woman's low levels of estrogen may boost the risk of heart disease and osteoporosis. However, phytoestrogens can provide the hormone without increasing the risk of cancer. In countries with high soy foods consumption, the symptoms of menopause are virtually unknown.

Should you eat dairy products? Most of us learned that milk is a perfect food. It is—if you're a calf with four stomachs that will need to double its weight in 50 days and grow to weigh hundreds of pounds within a year. Milk is ideal for growing calves; it is high in fat, protein, and cholesterol, low in carbohydrates and has no fiber. From a biochemical standpoint, milk should be considered liquid meat. Because it is high on the food chain, milk contains concentrations of pesticides, herbicides, hormones, and antibiotics.

The majority of the world's people do not consume milk after infancy. After the age of four, most people naturally lose their ability to digest the lactose found in milk. Consuming dairy products can result in diarrhea, gas, and stomach cramps, stuffed-up noses, and postnasal drip. About 20 percent of Caucasians seem to be born without the enzyme necessary to digest milk. Almost 90 percent of African Americans lack the enzyme—about the same number as Asians. In fact, about three quarters of the world's population is lactose intolerant. When the fat is removed from milk, the lactose content increases and can cause even greater difficulty.

Dairy is a tremendous mucus producer and a burden on the respiratory, digestive and immune systems.

Christiane Northrup, MD

One cause of allergies in America may be a protein called casein which is found in milk. People who react to casein can suffer from an enormous variety of symptoms including: canker sores, vomiting, colic, stomach cramps, abdominal distention, colitis, diarrhea, constipation, nasal stuffiness, runny nose, inner ear infections, sinusitis, asthma, skin, rashes, eczema, hives, irritability, headaches, and fatigue.

And the potential effects of drinking milk can be even more frightening.

Ovarian cancer rates parallel dairy eating patterns around the world. Researchers believe this is due at least in part to the presence of galactose in milk products — something which about 10 percent of American women cannot break down in their body. A Harvard study showed that when the consumption of dairy products exceeded the body's ability to break down galactose, it builds up in the bloodstream, and affects the ovaries. The risk for ovarian cancer tripled.

It may be true that "milk has something for everybody"—but is it something you want?

Should you eat chicken and eggs? Chicken can be a major source of dangerous bacterial contamination in the kitchen. And, it is filled with hormones, antibiotics, and oily yellow globules of fat. Inspection practices for the poultry industry are no better than the inspection practices for the beef industry.

Eggs are fiberless masses of saturated fat and foreign animal protein.

Michael Klaper, MD

Eggs are high in concentrated protein and fat—perfect food for a growing embryo, but not for a human being. Research shows that salmonella bacteria can enter the shell of an egg before it is even laid by the chicken. Egg protein is a leading cause of food allergies. Studies have indicated that the risk of fatal ovarian cancer for women who eat eggs is three to five times higher than for women who do not.

Finally, should you consume fish? Tragically, the chemical by-products of farming, industry, and households are poured into our rivers and oceans. Pesticides, herbicides, and heavy metals concentrate in the tissues of fish that eat at the top of the food chain. Although many types of fish are low in fat when compared with other sources of meat, they are still high in comparison to plant foods.

Chapter Nine

He who sees that the Lord of all is ever the same in all that is—immortal in the field of mortality—he sees the truth. And when a man sees that the God in himself is the same God in all that is, he hurts not himself by hurting others. Then he goes, indeed, to the highest path.

The Bhagavad Gita

What you place on your dinner table has enormous implications for all of life on Earth. As energy flows from the sun and through the food chain, about 85 percent is degraded into useless heat at each step of the chain. The shorter the number of steps between plants and man, the less energy is lost, and the greater the amount of food energy that is available.

Much of the world eats low on the food chain, avoiding meat products, and eating plants directly. The process of running plants through animals, and then eating the animals is profoundly inefficient and desperately energy expensive. Consider the fact that 90 percent of the protein that is fed to livestock is lost. The cattle of the world, taken all together, consume a quantity of food equal to the caloric needs of 8.7 billion people—which is nearly double the current population of the planet. The grain and soybeans that are given to livestock could be used to feed the people of the world. The practice of consuming meat effectively puts human beings in competition with farm animals for the Earth's food supply.

In "Diet for a Small Planet," Frances Moore Lappe states, "To imagine what eating meat means in practical every day terms, simply set yourself at a restaurant in front of an 8 oz steak and then imagine the room filled with 40-50 people with empty bowls in front of them. For the 'feed cost' of your steak, each of their bowls could be filled with a full cup of cereal grains."

Lappe's work has inspired countless other authors, perhaps the most notable of which is John Robbins. His work, "Diet for a New America" was published in 1995. Robbins created EarthSave, an organization that continues to track environmental information. I am indebted to EarthSave for the information contained in this chapter.

It takes nearly four acres to supply a human being with meat, but only .16 of an acre to supply the needs of a complete vegetarian. One acre of land can be used to produce 20,000 pounds of potatoes, or 165 pounds of beef. Twenty vegetarians could be fed on the amount of land that is needed to feed one person eating a meat-based diet. Growing grains, vegetables, and fruits for human consumption uses less than five percent of the raw materials that it takes to produce meat, eggs, and dairy foods.

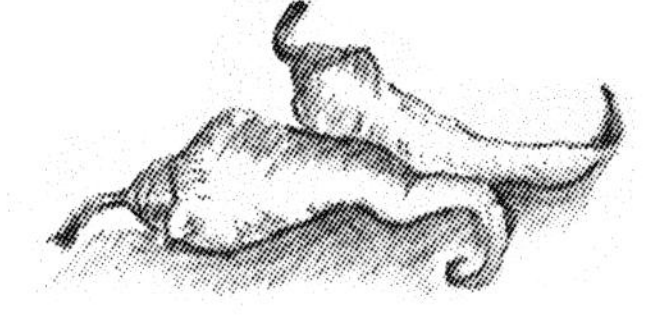

Never doubt that a small group of thoughtful, committed citizens can change the world; indeed, that is the only thing that ever does.

Margaret Mead

Let's look at costs a different way. Animal waste accounts for more than ten times as much water pollution as the total amount attributable to the entire human population. The livestock of the United States produces 20 times as much fecal matter as the entire human population—over one billion tons per year. Cattle herds produce astronomical amounts of manure, which finds its way into our rivers and streams. The pesticides and herbicides that are prolific in the production of animal products contaminate the water supply.

Over 50 percent of the water consumed in the United States goes to irrigate land to grow feed and fodder for livestock. To produce the food a meat-eater consumes in a day would take over 4,000 gallons of water; for a vegetarian diet, it takes only 300 gallons.

The tropical rainforests of the world are being erased at a horrifying rate. Indigenous people are turning the rainforest into pastureland in order to raise cattle to meet the demand for meat. Over 200 million pounds of meat are exported to the U.S. each year. This has a devastating impact on the natural balance of our planet's oxygen supply, and climate regulation. The transformation of Earth into a hot, carbon-dioxide rich planet no longer suitable for life is just over the horizon.

If products were priced according to their ecological costs, including fossil fuel depletion, environmental destruction, resource use and pollution, the price for a hamburger should be about $200.

The Center for Science and Development, India

Grazing lifestock contributes to a loss of the bio-diversity of our planet. Scientists say that more plant species in the United States have been eliminated or threatened by livestock grazing than by any other cause. Wild animals are disappearing from the ranges where cattle are present.

A plant-based diet not only creates better health for ourselves, but also contributes to the protection of our environment, and helps people, animal and plant life around the world.

A reduction in beef and other meat consumption is the most potent single act you can take to halt the destruction of our environment and preserve our natural resources. What's healthiest for each of us personally, is also healthiest for the life support system of our precious, but wounded planet.

John Robbins, Diet for a New America.

The impact of countless hooves and mouths over the years has done more to alter the type of vegetation and landforms of the West than all the water projects, strip mines, power plants, freeways, and subdivision developments combined.

Philip Fradkin, National Audubon Society

Chapter Ten

Habit is simply the easiest way to be wrong again.
Laurence Peter

Often the first concern people have when they think about eliminat ing animal products from their diet is whether or not they will become protein or calcium deficient.

Thanks in large part to the marketing campaigns of the meat and dairy industries, protein has become the dominant feature on American dinner tables. Many people believe that the more protein they consume, the better off they will be. To be sure, protein is an important substance. It supports many critical functions; it supplies the amino acids and nitrogen needed for building and repairing our bone and muscle tissues. Protein helps to regulate hormones and enzymes, helps to fight infections, and affects our genes. But, it does not make you feel energized, carbohydrates do that. It does not build muscle, exercise does that.

In the United States, the recommended daily protein allowance set by the Food and Nutrition Board is 47 grams for non-pregnant women, and 56 grams for men.Yet, the average American diet contains two to three times that amount. The World Health Organization, using careful studies from around the world suggests that 29 grams for non-pregnant women, and 37 grams for men, is plenty of protein to meet normal human requirements.

Most people believe that quality protein can only come from animal products. However, careful research shows that a person who eats sufficient calories each day, gets plenty of protein. All foods except fruit, fat, and sugar contain protein. For example: a slice of bread contains about two grams, a banana, one gram, a baked potato has four grams, and a bowl of cereal about three grams. A cup of beans delivers about 15 grams of protein—half of the total daily requirement. A 3,000 calorie intake of rice alone would offer 60 grams of protein. Eating 3,000 calories of potatoes would give you almost 80 grams. It is not difficult to come up with the protein required by the body.

Is the excess protein consumed by most Americans harmful? Very. Excess protein has been linked with osteoporosis, kidney disease, kidney stones, and some forms of cancer. When protein is eaten, your body produces an amino acid byproduct called homocysteine. Excess homocysteine is believed to contribute greatly to heart and blood vessel damage.

Many people believe that protein somehow just becomes muscle. But in fact, the body cannot store it. The liver and kidneys must break down any protein that is not used. Protein wastes like ammonia and amino acid fragments must be cleansed from the blood. This can create a burden for kidney tissue, and may result in the production of kidney stones. In fact, a Harvard study showed that the men who ate the most protein boosted their rates of kidney stones by 33 percent.

Urea is a protein waste product that acts as a powerful diuretic. It facilitates the excretion of large amounts of minerals, including calcium from the body. Researchers say that for every molecule of a protein component that is cleansed from the blood, the body looses an even larger amount of calcium. This results in a negative calcium balance—in other words, more calcium is being lost from the body than is being taken in. Our plague of osteoporosis has much more to do with calcium being leached out of the bones, than it does with inadequate calcium intake. High rates of osteoporosis are found in the very countries where dairy products are consumed in the largest amounts—the United States, Sweden, Finland, and the UK. Osteoporosis is rare in countries that consume much lower levels of protein, like those in Asia and Africa.

The more proteins, especially those from animal sources that are consumed by a group of people, the greater is the incidence of osteoporosis in that population.

John McDougall, MD

In 1930, the first study was published that showed a diet with high animal product content caused the loss of large amounts of calcium and set up a negative calcium balance. Studies show that the average measurable bone loss in male vegetarians was three percent. In male meat eaters, it was seven percent. In female vegetarians, it was 18 percent. In female meat eaters, it measured at 35 percent.

Ask yourself a question. How did humanity survive all of this time if we absolutely had to have a large amount of animal protein every day? How do the people in many parts of the world live on extremely low amounts of animal protein, or none at all, and remain healthy?

Is animal protein of higher quality than plant protein? Proteins contain strings of amino acids. Animal products have complete chains, and plant foods have incomplete chains. This has given rise to the idea that plant proteins are inadequate. But nature is wise. As long as different kinds of plant proteins are consumed each day, the amino acids will find each other and make complete proteins of excellent quality. Different kinds of plant proteins do not have to be consumed at the same meal, as was once thought. For example, a daily diet that included some beans or peas as well as some grain products, corn or seeds, would result in complete proteins. Soybeans and the products made from soybeans like tofu, textured vegetable protein, and soymilk come very close to being complete proteins on their own.

Plant protein offers all the materials your body needs without the saturated fat, contaminants, and cholesterol that animal proteins contain. Vegetable protein has the added benefit of offering dietary fiber, a host of vitamins and minerals, along with important phytochemicals. From the body's point of view, there isn't any difference in the quality of protein found in half a cup of soybeans or five ounces of steak, except that steak has five times the calories and close to 16 grams of fat! Furthermore, vegetable protein does not stimulate an increase in white blood cells that indicate an immune response.

What about iron? This mineral is essential to the function of the body; it is important to have an adequate supply of iron in our blood. We cannot manufacture it and we must replace the iron we lose. This is especially important to women who regularly lose iron stores through menstruation. Although iron is abundant in the Earth, obtaining enough is still a nutritional problem for some people. Paradoxically, this problem can be partially traced to increased hygiene in food preparation. Tiny particles of soil that contained iron were once regularly consumed along with the vegetables, fruits, grains and legumes. Now they are washed away. Still, iron deficiency is not a wide-spread problem in the vegetarian population, and it is not necessary to consume red meat in order to obtain iron. Prunes, dried fruits, nutritional yeast, molasses, beans, soy products, whole grains, potatoes, and fortified cereals all contain iron.

A considerable body of scientific data suggests positive relationships between a vegetarian lifestyle and risk reduction for several chronic degenerative diseases and conditions, such as obesity, coronary artery disease, hypertension, diabetes, colon cancer and others.

The American Dietetic Association

The only nutrient that may be inadequately supplied in a vegetarian diet is vitamin B-12. Although it can be found in sea vegetables, most Americans do not consume those products. The amount needed is very small. Studies of vegetarians around the world show a very low incidence of vitamin B-12 deficiency. B-12 can be easily found in a good quality supplement.

What about calcium? Calcium is an important mineral that promotes the normal development of teeth and bones, helps to maintain a regular heartbeat, and regulates hormonal activity. In fact, it is so important that the body will take the mineral from its own bone stores if it is inadequately supplied in the diet. However, the research shows that countries with the highest consumption of dairy have the highest rates of osteoporosis.

Every time dairy products are consumed, a whopping dose of protein is taken in. Maintaining a clean bloodstream is first in the body's priorities. It will take calcium from the bones in order to eliminate the byproducts of protein. So the real culprit in the development of osteoporosis is excess protein.

Calcium is plentiful in plant sources, and does not have the drawback of excess protein. Green leafy vegetables like spinach, whole grain bread, oats, soybeans, tofu, flax seed, carrots, cabbage, garlic, chives, and a wide variety of fortified products all contain calcium. If you still have concern, it makes more sense to take a calcium supplement than it does to flood your blood stream with the fat, animal protein, allergy-provoking substances, and excess calories found in dairy products.

The American National Research Council, which set the RDA values, acknowledges that people are able to maintain a healthy calcium balance on intakes of 200-400 grams per day. But 800-1200 mg. per day is recommended because of the excessively high protein diet of most Americans.

An interesting study showed that when young adults were placed on a diet high in protein—the 112 grams typical of many Americans—they lost substantial amounts of calcium in their urine even when their calcium intake was as high as 1400 mg. day. Additional research has shown that protein derived from plant sources, even at high levels, does not increase calcium excretion the same way that protein from animal sources does.

The more I have studied the medical literature, the harder it has gotten for me to listen to the dairy industry's promotion of milk for strong bones. In spite of its high calcium content, milk, because of its high protein content, appears actually to contribute to the accelerating development of osteoporosis. The occurrence of this condition has reached truly epidemic proportions in the us, and the promotion of dairy products as an answer to the suffering of millions seems to me to be not only self serving, but even criminal.

John Robbins

Examples of protein, iron and calcium in common plant foods

	PROTEIN	CALCIUM	IRON
whole grain bread	2 g.	50 mg.	1 mg.
whole grain pasta	8 g.	16 mg.	1 mg.
broccoli cup	5 g.	180 mg.	2 mg.
spinach	5.6 g.	160 mg.	4 mg.
kidney beans 1 cup	13 g.	64 mg.	5 mg.
garbanzo beans 1 cup	41 g.	300 mg.	14 mg.
wheat germ 3 T.	8 g.	20 mg.	3 mg.
bowl of whole grain with oat milk	10 g.	250 mg.	2 mg.
spaghetti with tomato sauce 2 cups	13 g.	38 mg.	2 mg.

Chapter Eleven

Re-examine all you have been told. Dismiss what insults your soul.

Anita Roddick

While agribusiness was busy convincing us that we would be come seriously deficient in calcium, protein and iron if we didn't eat animal products, they never mentioned the fact that their "health foods," contained a killer—fat.

Most people obtain about 40 percent of their calories from fat. Researchers believe that we should consume less than 20 percent. The World Health Organization has called for an intake of less than 15 percent. Fat is necessary to build cell membranes, brain and nerve tissues, produce hormones, and allow the healthy functioning of many systems in the body. But there is no need to add excess fat to your diet. A diet consisting of legumes, fruits, grains, and vegetables will naturally contain about 10 percent fat.

Excess dietary fat is transported in the blood stream in large molecules of fat and protein. Has your doctor ever ordered tests for you? It is necessary to do such tests first thing in the morning after fasting for many hours, because of the typical American diet. Blood drawn from a person who has just consumed a typical meal will show globules of yellow, sticky fat floating on the surface.

Unnecessary fat places an enormous burden on your system. It causes blood cells to actually stick together in clumps. Sticky cells block blood vessels and tissues; the essential nutrients and oxygen that your organs receive are greatly reduced. Plaque builds in arterial walls, causing spasms that can lead to heart damage. When blood vessels constrict, higher blood pressure results.

Dietary fat contains many cancer-promoting agents, including free radicals and environmental toxins. Numerous researchers have reported that fats promote the growth of certain kinds of cancer in animals. The higher the intake of dietary fat, the higher the rates of breast and colon cancer, kidney tissue damage, ovarian and uterine cancer, testicular and prostate cancers.

Research shows that eating animal fat sets off massive reactions from the immune system. The result can be inflammation, and chronic immune hyper-reactivity.

Thousands of studies have shown that societies around the world that eat diets high in animal fat have high rates of heart disease, cancer, diabetes, stroke, obesity, impaired circulation and impaired immune function.

Until we extend our circle of compassion to all living things, humanity will never find peace.

Albert Schweitzer

If animal fat isn't bad enough, consider the effect of eating processed and packaged foods. Rancid fat has become an unseen staple in the typical American diet. Prepared and processed foods like crackers, cookies, cakes, donuts, muffins, commercial peanut butter, and other packaged products are filled with oxidized oils, dried eggs, and animal proteins. Any food that lists hydrogenated or partially hydrogenated fat on the label contains a dangerous, technologically created substance called transfatty acids. Margarine, proclaimed as being healthier than butter, is filled with transfatty acids.

Since transfatty acids don't occur in nature, our bodies don't know how to deal with them safely. They end up in our cells, and act as poisons to crucial cellular reactions. They weaken the membranes' protective structure. This allows disease microbes and toxic chemicals to get into the cell more easily.

Transfatty acids appear to block the normal conversion of cholesterol in the liver and contribute to elevated cholesterol levels in the blood. They also cause an increase in low density lipoproteins (LDL's) highly associated with arterial disease. Transfatty acids have now been shown to create worse problems in our bodies than saturated animal fats.

The health risks associated with transfatty acids have been suspected for two decades. Yet, marketing campaigns continue to convince us that margarine and vegetable oils are better than animal fats. Many scientists believe that these substances are directly responsible for skyrocketing rates of heart disease. A Harvard study analyzed the diets of patients admitted to hospitals for a first heart attack. They compared them with a control group that did not have heart disease. After adjusting for lifestyle variables, they found that margarine intake was significantly associated with the risk of myocardial infarction.

Eating transfatty acids, particularly margarine, kills from 30.000 to 150,000 Americans every year from heart disease.

Walter Willett, MD
Harvard School of Public Health

I'm sorry to admit that I once put a donut containing hydrogenated fat outside for the squirrels to eat. They didn't touch it. Neither did the insects. After a week, the donut was dirty and wet, but even bacteria hadn't shown any interest in it. Yet, my family had consumed the rest of the donuts with gusto! It appears that only human beings are ignorant enough to eat things that so profoundly damage our health.

What about polyunsaturated vegetable oils? Commercial refining processes use toxic solvents, caustic agents, preservatives, and deformers, which results in the formation of transfatty acids and free radicals. Corn oil and safflower oil have been shown to alter body chemistry in a way that encourages the development of blood clots, and inflammatory diseases. Damage done to the cells by free radicals contribute to cancer and heart disease.

However, there is one group of fats that need special consideration. Essential fatty acids (EFA's) are vital to our health; without them, our bodies are unable to produce a type of fundamental regulating hormone called eicosanoids. Absolutely necessary for life, eicosanoids do not travel in the blood stream like the other hormones in the body; they are created in the cells themselves. They serve as catalysts for a large number of essential cellular processes like the movement of substances into and out of cells, inhibition and promotion of blood clotting, production of digestive acids, reproductive hormones, fluid balance, and cell division.

There are two types of EFA's—Omega-6 and Omega-3. Both types must be obtained from certain foods in our diet. In addition, they must be present in a balanced ratio in order to sustain health. The western world's diet is sorely lacking in Omega-3 EFA's, while our intake of Omega-6 is too high. Furthermore, most of our Omega-6 comes from refined and hydrogenated oils, which present many dangers to the body.

The dietary choices made by most people in the west allow for only about a third of the essential fatty acids needed for optimum human health. A plant-based diet rich in beans, fruits, grains, and vegetables is much more likely to provide what is needed. The two main sources of essential fatty acids are organic flax seeds, and cold water fish oil. As we have already discussed, most fish are flooded with environmental toxins caused by industrial and farming pollution. Furthermore, fish oil is taken from the liver—the organ that is likely to have the very highest concentration of contaminants. Luckily, organic flax seed oil provides a high natural vegetable source of Omega-3 and Omega-6.

Flax seeds provide another wonderful substance—lignans. These compounds have been found to have potent anticancer, antibacterial, antifungal, and antiviral properties. Lignans have been shown to shrink existing breast and colon tumors, and stop new ones from getting started. Many plants have some lignans, but flaxseeds have 75 times more than any other plant—¼ cup of flaxseed can yield as much as 60 cups of broccoli.

Flaxseed oil is very sensitive and must be processed under stringent conditions, and packaged in dark bottles to avoid oxidizing. But even the most careful human efforts to produce healthy oils always falls short of nature's accomplishments. Freshly ground organic flax seeds contain fresh oil protected by the husk.

Pulverizing three tablespoons of flax seeds in a blender will provide the approximate suggested daily amount of Omega-3, and an excellent supply of lignans. The ground seed can be mixed with cereal or blended into foods. However, flax seed oil cannot be mixed with hot foods because the essential fatty acids contained in them will be destroyed. Be sure to consume the seeds within 20 minutes of grinding to minimize air exposure and spoilage.

Every blade of grass has its Angel that bends over it and whispers, 'Grow, grow'.

The Talmud

Chapter Twelve

Let the mind be enlarged to the grandeur
of the mysteries, and not the mysteries contracted
to the narrowness of the mind

Sir Frances Bacon

There is one more kingdom of healing plants in Mother Nature's hands—herbs. From the highest mountain peaks, to the thick, humid swamps, in the stark beauty of the desert, and the lush complexity of the rain forest, herbs hold fast to their healing powers. Even in the cities, they find their way through cracks in the pavement, surviving the footfall of a thousand people, offering themselves up to unseeing eyes.

Armed with pesticides, we drive them from our lawns, not realizing that what kills them also kills us, not understanding that they are here to help us heal ourselves.

Some are tall, robust, even stately, and others must be discovered on hands and knees. Their capacity to support the body is complex and endless. An herb cannot fix a broken bone, but it can help to prevent the bone's vulnerability to being broken, and help to mend it more quickly. An herb cannot cure a raging infection, but it can act to build a strong immune system that will fight infection before it gets out of hand. An herb cannot prevent breast cancer, but it can help to stabilize the hormonal system, blocking those factors highly associated with the development of the disease. Even the lowly dandelion contains blood cleansing properties, improves digestive function, stimulates the liver, gallbladder, kidneys and bladder. It contains calcium, potassium, and vitamin C.

Herbs can act as effective partners to the other members of the plant kingdom we use in our food supply. For example, in a double blind study conducted by Cornell University, menopausal women were given either estrogen replacement therapy, or a combination of isoflavones derived from soy beans, and the herb known as black cohosh. Those on ERT reported about 10% fewer hot flashes. Those on the isoflavone and herb combination reported nearly 75% fewer hot flashes. While hormone replacement therapy has been highly associated with the development of breast and endometrial cancer, isoflavones have been equally associated with the prevention of those cancers. The addition of the herb seems to enhance the ability of the isoflavones to regulate destructive forms of estrogen, while enhancing positive forms of the hormone.

The roots, leaves, seeds and flowers, and even the bark of herbs have been used as the mainstay of healing for thousands of years. It is only in this century that they have been judged as elements of folklore and old wives' tales. Pharmaceutical companies have produced "scientific medicines" that are only high-priced versions of what herbalists gathered from the land. Foxglove has become the heart medicine digitalis, white willow bark is now aspirin, and moldy bread penicillin. Only in the last few years have consumers demanded free access to healing herbs. Business has responded by flooding the market with an enormous variety of products. While healers in the past trained their daughters in the use of medicinal herbs, today's consumers are caught in the medical model, believing that an herb should be taken in the same way any pill would be taken. In other words, a problem should have a specific, fast-acting solution in the herbal world.

But herbs are plants of enormous complexity. Most of them are slow and gentle. They act to support the body's natural abilities. Scientists have begun to apply western research practices to herbs. They have analyzed the constituents in herbs, determined what is effective, and business has produced "standardized extracts" which contain those specific constituents. But just as taking a capsule of vitamin C cannot substitute for eating a fresh orange, an isolated compound from an herb distorts its wholeness. Mother Nature has placed all of the elements within the herb—they are all there for a reason. By consuming the whole herb, you obtain all of the supporting constituents that allow the main constituent to be effective in the human body.

Naturally grown, organic herbs contain the life force, the vitality of nature. By consuming them, we regain our balance, we allow our bodies to do what they know how to do if only given support, and time to heal.

Throughout history, herbs have been recognized as a gift from spirit. In different cultures, they have been used as a sacred part of ceremony. Even today, the Catholic church still uses herbs to clear the way as the priest goes down the aisle. Herbs were used before battles to ensure survival, and used afterwards to heal the wounds. Herbs have been used in countless love charms, spells, and rites. They have been employed to create wealth and restore fertility. Their presence on the Earth has been ascribed to a hundred different goddesses. They have been gathered with respect and even reverence. They have been prepared with care and gratitude. Knowledge of their powers has been handed down from generation to generation in every culture. The properties of whole herbs have been well-researched by healers across time.

Common Herbal Actions:

Adaptogens assist the body to repair itself from the effects of stress
nettle leaf, licorice root, Siberian ginseng, ashwagndha

Alteratives assist the body to eliminate toxins. They boost the immune system and improve lymphatic function.
burdock root, echinacea, calendula, alfalfa

Analgesics lessen the excitability of the nerves which relieves pain
feverfew, passionflower, alerian root, lavender lower, chamomile, kava kava

Anticatarrhals used to clear excess mucus in the upper respirator tract — the sinuses, ears, nose and throat.
goldenrod, lemon balm, ginger, garlic

Anti-emetics reduce nausea and help stop vomiting
ginger, lemon balm, cinnamon, peppermint

Anti-inflammatories reduce inflammation, allowing the body to repair itself
calendula flowers, licorice root, skullcap

Antimicrobials strengthen the body's natural defenses against infection. Some can even or even killing off certain microorganisms.
bearberry, yarrow, garlic, echinacea, goldenseal

Antiseptics act to kill microorganisms directly
tea tree oil (used externally only), thyme, chamomile, echinacea, plantain

Antispasmodics slow or stop cramps and muscle spasms cramp bark, valerian root

Astringents slow the loss of body fluids, some help to stop bleeding, others help with diarrhea or heavy menstrual cycles
arrow, rose, witch hazel bark

Carminatives clear up gas and bloating and reduce spasms
peppermint, lemon balm, ginger root, parsley, spearmint

Demulcents soothe inflamed surfaces
plantain, marshmallow root, slippery elm bark, aloe vera

Diuretics	increase the volume of urine marshmallow, parsley, uva-ursi, milk thistle, dandelion
Emmenagogues	stimulate menstrual flow chasteberry, pennyroyal, mugwort
Hepatics	promote liver and gallbladder function dandelion, hops, milk thistle, goldenseal
Hypnotics	help with relaxation and sleep chamomile, passionflower, hops, valerian
Nervines	help regulate the nervous system
Soothing:	lemon balm, lavender flower, kava kava, St. Johnswort, hysop, lavender, skullcap, hops.
Stimulating:	peppermint, gotu kola
Vulneraries	help heal inflammation by disinfecting and helping cells to regenerate plantain, calendula, yarrow, comfrey

Herbs cannot help you if they have lost their power. Many herbal preparations are essentially devoid of healing properties. Plants are grown in poor soil, doused with pesticides, or imported from countries without quality controls in place. The result is that many herbs are sold as one thing when they are really another plant entirely. High-tech manufacturing processes often use excessive heat which destroys the healing constituents of the plant. Dried herbs are placed in geletin capsules (an animal product) and are excreted from the body without ever being dissolved.

An effective way to gain the healing effects of herbs is to make your own tea. First, you must either grow the herb yourself, or obtain it from a reputable organic farmer (see list in Appendix). Teas are classified as either infusions or decoctions. To make an infusion, use one ounce of dried herb to two cups of water. Boil the water and pour over the herb. Cover and steep for about twenty minutes, then strain. Drink one cup at a time, up to four cups a day.

A decoction is a tea that is simmered rather than steeped. Use this method when using herbs that have harder parts like twigs, bark, stems, seeds and roots. Again, use one ounce of dried herb to two cups of water. Place in a saucepan, cover, and simmer on medium low heat for fifteen to twenty minutes. Strain and drink one cup at a time, two to four times a day.

An easy way to take herbs is to buy tinctures or extracts. A tincture is an alcohol or glycerin solution that contains the concentrated extract of the whole plant. The solution should be made without using any heat, thereby protecting the valuable healing properties of the plant. An extract is similar to a tincture, but much more concentrated. Again, be sure you buy an organic product. (see list in Appendix)

The most common error people make with these is to take too little. A few drops of echinecea dropped into your tea is not going to make any difference at all in your system. Most tinctures should be taken at a rate of one teaspoon dissolved in a small amount of water three times a day. Most extracts can be taken at a rate of one half teaspoon dissolved in water three times a day.

For external use, a compress or poultice is needed. A compress is made with the liquid from an herb, a poultice is made with the herb still mixed in with the liquid. To make either of these, start with an infusion or a decoction.Then using a soft cotton cloth (cheesecloth works well), either dip into the liquid for a compress, or pour the entire contents of the saucepan into the cloth for a poultice. These preparations can be used to ease a sprain, sore muscle, incision wound, or bug bite. Place the compress or poultice over the affected area, cover with a dry cloth and allow to penetrate the tissues for at least twenty minutes. Repeat six times a day for an acute condition, and three times a day for a chronic or partially healed condition.

If you are lucky, you have a talented herbal healer in your community—perhaps even one with her own herb garden. If you can, go somewhere where you can see herb plants growing in all their glory. Perhaps you have room in your garden to plant some herbs for yourself. As a traditional herbal healer would do, spend a few minutes with each whole plant—see if it will offer you some of its secrets.

Chapter Thirteen

The person who is afraid to alter his living habits and especially his eating and drinking habits because he is afraid that others may regard him as eccentric or fanatic forgets that the ownership of his body, the responsibility for its well-being belongs to him, not them.

Paul Brunton

What can you say to people who become concerned about your new way of eating? It is amazing to listen to someone who has just consumed a large amount of fat, a ton of salt, countless contaminants, and an enormous dose of sugar, question how a plant-based diet can possibly be healthy! That just shows the power of the legacy of the four food groups and agribusiness marketing campaigns.

I've written this section to provide you with easy information to offer to the people around you who might be concerned about your new dietary plan. However, your very best argument to them will be your own glowing health.

Within a few weeks of eating a plant-based diet, people will begin to ask you what you've been doing for yourself. People will think you've had a long vacation, a face lift, or found a miracle cure. Your doctor may start using words like "spontaneous remission," to explain the disappearance of long term symptoms. As your weight drops to normal, and your energy levels rise, friends will want to know about "your new diet." The need to convince anyone will disappear—just recommend they do some reading and start the miracles in their own lives.

Why aren't you eating meat, chicken, dairy, fish, or eggs?

Numerous investigations by anthropologists, nutritionists, historians, and physicians have shown that human beings are meant to consume plant-based foods and not animal products. Our intestines, jaws, teeth, hands, and natural preferences all point to a diet based around grains, vegetables, fruits, legumes, nuts, and seeds.

These foods have successfully sustained human beings for thousands of years. Many studies, including those from Harvard, Yale, Cornell, and the Centers for Disease Control have shown that the incidence of heart disease, stroke, cancers of the breast, colon, prostate, uterus, and ovaries is dramatically lower in those who don't consume animal products.

Plant carbohydrates are accompanied by liberal amounts of dietary fiber, which has been shown to be important in the prevention and treatment of diabetes, heart disease, cancers, and colon problems.

Today's animals are raised on factory farms and given hormones and antibiotics, which end up in the food supply. These substances impair our hormonal balance and limit the effectiveness of antibiotics when we become ill. Many researchers are worried that antibiotics will soon become completely useless in the fight against disease.

- How can you be healthy without eating animal products?

As Dr. David Ryde has pointed out, "Some of nature's most powerful competitors, racehorses, depend solely on plant foods for their breath-taking speed and agility. Other powerful plant-eating animals include the elephant, gorilla, bull, hippopotamus and rhinoceros."

Plant-based foods contain all of the protein, complex carbohydrates, vitamins, minerals, and phytochemicals needed to be healthy. They do not flood the body with contaminants, cholesterol, fat, salt, and excess protein.

The typical American diet has far too much protein. Eating too much protein is hard on the liver and kidneys. Scientists have shown that it is the excess of protein that is the primary cause of osteoporosis, not the lack of calcium.

Vegetarian diets usually meet or exceed requirements for protein, although they typically provide less protein than non-vegetarin diets. This lower protein intake may be beneficial, may be associated with a lower risk of osteoporosis, and improved kidney function. A lower protein diet intake generally translates into a lower fat diet with all of its inherent advantages.

American Dietetic Association

Many prominent athletes, well known for their strength and endurance are vegetarians: Hank Aaron, Bill Walton, Martina Navratilova, and Jack LaLanne to name a few.

Energy comes from complex carbohydrates, not from protein. In fact, studies have shown that athletes on a high carbohydrate diet have three times the endurance of athletes on a diet high in fat.

- What about Calcium?

Calcium does not have to come from animal products. It is available in many vegetables, grains, soybeans and fortified products. The excess protein in the American diet leaches calcium from the bones; the kidneys must use the calcium in order to break down and eliminate the protein. Keeping strong bones depends more on preventing calcium loss than on increasing calcium intake.

- Why don't you eat any fat?

It is impossible to not eat fat. A plant-based diet naturally contains about 10 percent fat. The World Health Association, American Dietetic Association, and countless other agencies have called for a dramatic decrease in fat consumption. Dietary fat has been proven to contribute to heart disease and many different types of cancer. Excess fat plays havoc with the hormonal system, making people vulnerable to breast, uterine, ovarian, and prostate cancer.

- Aren't you miserable? What's left to eat?

  Most of the world eats a wonderful variety of delicious foods that do not include animal products. Because we were raised with the four food groups, we've learned to shop and to cook in a certain way. That doesn't mean it is the only way; it is just familiar. There is a whole world of wonderful food out there waiting to be discovered.

The best way to answer these concerns is to invite your friends to dinner. Cook up something from Part Two of this book and enjoy their reactions.

There are two ways of spreading light:
To be the candle or the mirror that reflects it.

Edith Wharton

Chapter Fourteen

The ceaseless rhythm of the oceans, a delicate drop of dew, a child's tears, a heavy raindrop, the mists in the forest, the trickle of a stream.—in these things beat the heart of the universe.

There is one more element that Mother Earth gives us in abundance—one that we cannot do without.

Just as we have forgotten that the plant kingdom holds the key to our health, so we have difficulty remembering how essential water is to life.

Water is our most important requirement, yet it is the one that is most ignored. The Earth's surface is largely covered with water. The plants, animals, birds, and insects are filled with water. Our own body is made mostly of water.

Our blood contains about 82 percent water, the muscle about 75 percent, our bones contain approximately 22 percent, and our brain about 74 percent.

Every one of the body's cells requires water in order to perform the tasks that keep it healthy. Water works as a shock absorber for joints, bones, and muscles, and keeps soft tissues from sticking together. It hydrates the skin and other organs, and regulates the body temperature. Water flushes waste products and toxins from your system, and transports nutrients. It facilitates electrical and chemical communication within the body, allowing the brain to function and the cells to obey the commands of their DNA.

If your body gets enough water, it works at its peak. Fluid and sodium remain in balance; glands and hormones function as they should. With adequate water, the liver is able to break down and eliminate fats. With a loss of only five percent of the body's water, your skin shrinks and your muscles become weak. A loss of about 20 percent is fatal—within two or three days without any water at all, death will be imminent.

Most people drink very little water. Many rely on coffee, and soft drinks for their fluid intake. But caffeine actually acts as a diuretic in the body. Water is lost, not gained. Caffeinated beverages leach out B vitamins, and calcium, constrict arterial blood flow, and provoke the adrenal glands to exhaustion, which can precipitate hormonal imbalances.

Others wait until they feel thirsty. But thirst is not a reliable signal that your body needs water. Because the American diet is so filled with artificial substances, the sensation of thirst is often confused with hunger. Excess pounds and chronic dehydration are the result.

Chronic dehydration creates higher levels of histamine in the blood. Histamine is associated with a host of painful problems like arthritis, muscle cramps, migraine headaches, and low back pain. When the body is dehydrated, opposing bone surfaces can rub together during the movement of a joint. Chronic pain and joint degeneration can result. The disks in the spine are highly dependent on water. This water supports the compression weight of the upper body. When water is inadequate, the disks begin to collapse, bringing back pain and eventual degenerative problems.

Because the brain is so high in water content, it is one of the most vulnerable organs to dehydration. Without enough water, electrical and chemical reactions become impaired and mental symptoms result. As a result, many people feel chronically "foggy", have difficulty remembering information, and are physically clumsy.

In fact, chronic dehydration can produce a variety of symptoms that appear to be disease related. If the symptoms of dehydration are not recognized, a misdiagnosis is entirely possible. Unnecessary tests, medication or even surgery can result, when all that was needed was a consistent, plentiful supply of water.

Symptoms of dehydration can include:

Chronic fatigue
Headaches
Irritability
Rapid heart beat and cardiac stress
Dizziness
Back pain
Nausea
General sense of not feeling well
Stomach or digestive problems
Bladder infections
Heart palpitations
Difficulty in sleeping
Difficulty in concentrating, confusion, feeling foggy
Poor skin quality—wrinkles, impaired elasticity
Evidence of toxic buildup—skin eruptions, dandruff, pallor
Constipation
Muscle weakness
Impaired vision
Gallstones, kidney stones
Joint pain

Eight glasses of water daily is barely adequate. Ten or more glasses of water will help your body to perform as it should. People who consume a typical American diet need even more water than those who eat a plant-based diet. The additional water allows the body to do the enormous amount of work required to eliminate the avalanche of toxins from the system.

Before you run to your faucet and start drinking up, consider the fact that over 500 disease causing bacteria, protozoa, viruses, and parasites have been identified in tap water. It is chlorinated, fluoridated, treated with toxic chemicals, and polluted with the heavy metals, nitrates, pesticides, and herbicides used by industry and agribusiness. It is estimated that over 10,000 people a year become ill from substances ingested in tap water.

The Centers for Disease Control and the United States Environmental Protection Agency had advised anyone with a compromised immune system to consult their physician before drinking ordinary tap water. The American Water Works Association, a trade group representing water utilities, took this warning one step further, advising all individuals with the HIV virus to boil tap water to eliminate possible bacteria and parasitic organisms before drinking it.

An Environmental Protection Agency report on the status of America's lakes and rivers stated that over 30 percent of all waterways are unsuitable for fishing or swimming because of pollution. The most common contaminants are sewage and bacteria, fertilizer, toxic metals, oil, and grease. Typical sources of the pollution include runoff from farms, industrial waste, and city sewer discharge. Many city water systems receive their supply from nearby lakes and rivers.

ABC network news reported that United States industry generates some 88 million pounds of toxic waste a year. The Environmental Protection Agency admits that about 90 percent of it is not properly disposed of. Americans throw away four million tons of hazardous waste each year. The problem goes beyond finding room in our landfills to accommodate this surplus of unsafe garbage. Hazardous household waste in local landfills slowly leaches into the ground, eventually contaminating groundwater supply. What you throw away today may come out of your kitchen faucet tomorrow.

More than one in five Americans unknowingly drink tap water polluted with feces, radiation, or other contaminants. Nearly 1,000 deaths each year and at least 400,000 cases of waterborne illness may be attributed to contaminated water.

The New York Times

Tap water contamination is increasing at an alarming rate. U.S. drinking water potentially contains more than 70,000 different chemicals. At least 2,000 of these have been implicated as suspicious in causing cancer, cell mutation, and nervous disorders. Most existing treatment plants were not designed to remove the new toxic chemicals, and the government is slow to regulate the high rate of contamination.

Investigate your options carefully. Bottled water has become popular in recent years, but the industry is inadequately regulated. Some investigations have revealed that some companies have simply taken tap water and bottled it to sell to unaware consumers. Others are using spring water that contains environmental contaminants.

There are a variety of water filtration systems on the market. Some are installed on individual taps. Others provide whole house water filtration. Considering the amount of water you need to remain healthy, the cost of an excellent water filtration system may be one of the best investments you can make for your health.

May all I say and all I think
be in harmony with Thee,
God within me,
God beyond me,
Maker of the trees.

The Chinook People

Chapter Fifteen

The adventure of the sun is the great natural drama by which we live, and not to have joy in it and awe of it, not to share in it, is to close a dull door on nature's sustaining and poetic spirits.

Henry Beston

As I write today, the cold morning air snaps outside, warning me that summer is truly over. It is time to start stacking firewood, and bring out the winter clothes. Invariably, I find colorful surprises stored away—forgotten sweaters and gloves, worn jeans and jackets that are like comfortable friends.

The sun seems pale today. The leaves seem to have taken its color and translated it into crimsons and golds that can be held in the hands. The diminishing light reminds me that it is time to direct my attention inward. Crops have been gathered. The roses lie in their beds, comfortable under the mulch offered from other parts of the garden. Here and there, a late flower still blooms, but it is like the last child to go to bed—a little too loud, out of place, on its way somewhere else.

Although we try hard to ignore it, nature still rules over our bodies and our hearts. Its rhythms speak to the deepest parts of us, even while our minds ignore the conversation. Everything is in motion, from the smallest molecular vibration, to the swirling of entire galaxies. The sun, the moon, the ceaseless cadence of the tides, the seasons' cycles of birth and death, the burst, bloom and deaths in the garden—all exists in a dance of many parts—a dance that has been the same since the beginning of time.

When we allow ourselves to move into the deeper parts of ourselves, we find a richness of awesome complexity. And, it becomes impossible to ever truly be alone. In the birds, the trees, the animals, the plants, and in human beings the song of Mother Earth is as powerful as ever. We belong to that multi-voiced chorus whose purpose is to sing its praise to the cosmos.

As our heart carefully maintains its rhythm, and our bodies respond to the travels of the moon, as our brain waves react to the bursts of power on the sun, we can pretend that we are only intellect, but our body will never agree.

The body is meant to move in correspondence to the natural rhythms, which constantly surround it. The body can hear the drums in the forest, the flute on the plains. It knows the chants the people offer in praise, it feels its own heart contribute its voice to the music of the one cosmic dance. It is only the mind that is deaf. When we ignore the voice of nature, we confine ourselves to a space that is so unnaturally small, our bodies cannot function as they should.

The wild goose comes north with the voice of freedom and adventure. He is more than a big, far ranging bird; he is the epitome of wanderlust, limitless horizons, and distant travel. He is the yearning and the dream, the search and the wonder, the unfettered foot and the wind's wild wing.

Hal Borland

They grow slow and rigid. Our energy system becomes so imprisoned, our spiritual abilities become impaired as well.

Take the time to move your body each day. Simple physical movement should be the most natural of all human events. It does not matter what movement you do—listen for the rhythms around you and allow your body to do what it longs to do. If you want to add your own music to this celebration, then sing, drum, play music that has been inspired by nature and the Earth.

Join others in types of movement that recall our connections to the unbroken web of life. Ancient forms of dance, traditional martial arts, drumming, Sufi whirling, running along a shore or deep in a forest, and yoga can draw energy up and send it through the body. Movement is prayer—a joining in with the great cosmic dance of energy—a dance that has gone on uninterrupted since the first breath of time.

Free yourself from the spell of lack, of limitation, of unworthiness. Do not lose yourself in the illusion of illness or impediment. Your essence is much larger than any injury or limitation. There is not a single flower, insect, bird, animal, or human being that was not born of the divine. Therefore, take that which you have been given and hold it up as a shining example that the universe is alive, wondrous, and loving.

Never look at what you do not have, but only what you can offer. Unfold your beauty, allow your wings to extend and catch the first breeze— to soar above the beliefs that would have you bowed into the ground. Remember to listen for the voice of the infinite singing all around you. When you are lost, do not run frantically to find your way. Instead, sit still and be silent. Open your heart, unbend your proud will, and allow spirit to guide you.

Take care of your body as best you can. Eat in accordance with deepest ecological and spiritual principles. Do not force your body to disobey nature—this it cannot do without harm. Do not contribute to the sickening of the planet, or of your own body, by supporting or consuming chemicals that were never meant to be. Create the best internal environment that you can, eating as you were meant to eat, turning away from all that is devoid of life, knowing that as you perform this sacrament, you help to heal the Earth.

And remember,

Past the wounds of childhood, past the fallen dreams and the broken promises, past the illnesses and the injury, the apparent limitations, and the aching heart there is a waiting soul. Patient, permanent, abundant, it opens its infinite heart and reminds you that all imperfection is only illusion. There can be no true injury to that which is divine.

With all your strength, lift your sight to the greater ground of your being. Know that you can step outside what you have always called "you." Unfasten your joy, release your passion, push away all that holds you back, And surrender into the embrace of spirit—it is there that you will find all healing.

To the heavens be peace, to the sky and the Earth;
To the waters be peace, to plants and all trees;
to the Gods be peace, to all men be peace,
again and again. Peace also to me.

Shukla Yajur Veda Samhita

Recipes

Over 200 Easy, All Natural, Low Fat, Family-Friendly Recipes

For each of us food is the source of sustenance, the basis of life;
and when we offer this gift to one another,
we are not only nourishing each other's bodies,
we are feeding one another's spirits.
So receive and give the food of your life
as the powerful gift that it is.

Daphne Rose Kingma

Easy Breakfasts

The word breakfast comes from the old English expression, "to break your fast." By morning most people have gone eight to ten hours without food. Your body is in desperate need of refueling. If you skip breakfast, you will be battling low energy levels all morning. This will likely result in overeating and unhealthy choices later in the day. Consider the following delicious choices!

Simple Good Morning Grains

Take advantage of seasonal fruit, and hearty, whole grains. Simply cook up the grain of your choice, and top with oat, soy, or rice milk and fresh fruit. This is a great opportunity to add ground flax seeds, or oat bran and get a good start on getting your fiber in for the day.

Whole Grains:

Amaranth	Barley	Brown Rice
Millet	Couscous	Oats (Bran, Rolled)
Polenta	Quinoa	Wheat Bran

Fresh or Dried Fruits:

Apples *or* Applesauce	Apricots	Bananas
Blueberries	Cranberries	Currants
Peaches	Pears	Raisins
Raspberries	Strawberries	

Delicious Extras:

Apple Juice	Soy Milk	Ground Flax Seeds
Orange Juice	Rice Milk	Maple Syrup

Great Combinations:

- Amaranth with dried apricots and maple syrup
- Brown rice cooked in apple juice and water, with shredded apples, maple syrup, vanilla, and cinnamon
- Couscous cooked in orange juice and water, with orange slices, honey and cinnamon
- Millet topped with chunky applesauce or apricot jam
- Oatmeal with fresh grated apple, berries or raisins and maple syrup
- Polenta cooked in orange juice and water with maple syrup and blueberries
- Quinoa with peaches and maple syrup

Winter Morning Cereal

A cold morning comfort food. Be sure to use organic raisins. Unfortunately, grapes are one of the most contaminated crops.

2/3 cup steel cut oats
1/3 cup pearl barley
1/2 cup organic raisins
1/3 cup date pieces or other dried fruit
1/8 tsp. cinnamon
3 cups water
1 cup oat, soy or rice milk
maple syrup (optional)

Combine all of the ingredients except maple syrup in a saucepan. Bring to a brief boil, reduce heat and simmer for 10 minutes. Cover, and remove from the heat. Let stand for 5 minutes. Stir in maple syrup if desired.

Baked Oatmeal

A delicious treat with a surprising cake-like texture! Ener-G egg replacer can be used in any recipe where eggs are called for. It contains no preservatives, artificial flavorings or added sugar.

3 cups oatmeal
1 cup Sucanat
2 tsp. baking powder
1/2 tsp. cinnamon
1/2 tsp. salt
1/2 cup applesauce
1 tsp. vanilla
1 T. Ener-G egg replacer + 4 T. water
1 cup oat milk
1/2 to 1 cup organic raisins or blueberries

Preheat the oven to 350°.

In a large bowl, mix together the oatmeal, Sucanat, baking powder, cinnamon, and salt. In another bowl, mix together the applesauce, vanilla, egg replacer, water, and oat milk. Combine the dry and the wet ingredients. Stir in the fruit. Pour into a 9 inch square pan that has been lightly coated with cooking spray. Bake for 25-30 minutes.

Sweet and Toasty Granola

Use your imagination to create different kinds of granola.
Just be sure to choose ingredients that are whole, natural, and low in fat.
Read the labels carefully on commercial granolas—
they are usually full of fat.

4 cups old-fashioned rolled oats (not quick cooking)
1 cup toasted wheat germ
1/2 cup organic raisins, currants or other chopped dried fruit (apricots, prunes, pineapple)
1/2 cup warmed honey

Preheat the oven to 300°.

Place the oats and wheat germ in a nonstick baking pan. Bake until they are fragrant and barely beginning to turn golden. Stir them often. The cooking time will depend on how thick your oats are. When the oats and wheat germ are toasted, stir in the other ingredients. This can be stored in the refrigerator in an airtight container. Make sure you allow it to cool completely first, or you'll end up with soggy granola.

Apricot Granola

This choice is high in natural sugars—use as a special treat.
Look for rolled oats in the cereal section of your market.

10 cups rolled oats
1 tsp. salt
1 tsp. vanilla
1/4 cup honey
1 10 oz. jar apricot jam

Preheat the oven to 350°.

Mix the ingredients together in a bowl. Then, spread the mixture out on a baking sheet that has been lightly coated with cooking spray.

Bake for 30 minutes, or until the oats begin to turn brown. Stir frequently throughout cooking.

Multi-Grain Pancakes

This makes a large amount of pancake mix to store in the refrigerator or freezer. Each time you are ready to make pancakes, just measure out the wet ingredients and add to a little more than 1 cup of the dry mix for delicious pancakes.

Dry Ingredients:

4 cups whole wheat pastry flour
1/3 cup wheat germ
1/4 cup each buckwheat flour, cornmeal, millet flour, oat flour
2 T. Sucanat (optional)
1 T. flax seeds
4 tsp. baking powder
2 tsp. baking soda
1 tsp. salt

Wet Ingredients:

1½ tsp. Ener-G egg replacer and 2 T. water
1 cup soy, rice or oat milk

Mix together all the dry ingredients in a large bowl and store in refrigerator or freezer to be used as needed.

To make pancakes, mix the egg replacer and water in a small bowl. Add the soy, oat or rice milk. Measure out a little over 1 cup of the pancake mix, and allow to warm to room temperature. Add the dry mix to the wet ingredients and stir just until moist. Do not let the batter stand for longer than 15 minutes unless refrigerated.

Heat a nonstick griddle over medium heat. Pour batter to make pancakes and cook until the bottoms are golden brown and the tops begin to bubble. Flip them over, and cook them until the undersides are golden brown. Serve immediately with fruit or maple syrup.

Variations: You can add a variety of fruits (or vegetables) to these pancakes—try grated apple, bananas, blueberries, grated carrot, cranberries, currants, raisins, pears, or puréed pumpkin. If you use bananas, pour slightly less than the usual amount of batter on the heated griddle, spread a single layer of banana slices on top of the batter, and dribble some batter over each slice to keep the fruit from sticking to the pan when you flip the pancakes. For apple and pear pancakes, add sprinkle of Sucanat and cinnamon on the top before the pancake cooks. For carrot or pumpkin pancakes, add a dash of pumpkin pie spice to the batter.

Blueberry Pancakes

A traditional favorite made without the eggs. Be sure you use pastry flour in this recipe for a light textured pancake.

1 cup whole wheat pastry flour
1 tsp. baking powder
1/4 tsp. salt
1/4 tsp. baking soda
1 T. Sucanat
1/2 cup oat milk
1/2 cup blueberries, fresh or frozen and thawed

In a large bowl, mix together the whole wheat flour, baking powder, salt, baking soda and Sucanat. Stir in the oat milk and the fruit. If the batter seems too thick, stir in small amounts of oat milk until the desired consistency is achieved.

Heat a nonstick griddle over medium heat. Pour batter to make pancakes, and cook until the bottoms are golden brown and the tops begin to bubble. Flip them over, and cook them until the undersides are golden brown. Serve immediately.

Apple Oatmeal Pancakes

A great example of healthy pancakes with wonderful taste. Oat bran is an excellent source of fiber. It has been extensively studied in connection with the prevention of heart disease.

3/4 cup whole wheat pastry flour
1/8 cup oats
2 T. oat bran
1/2 tsp. cinnamon
2 tsp. baking powder
1/4 tsp. salt
1/4 cup organic raisins
1/2 cup chopped apple
1 cup apple juice

In a large bowl, combine the whole wheat flour, oats, oat bran, cinnamon, baking powder and salt. Add the raisins and apple. Stir in the apple juice, making sure all of the dry ingredients are moistened.

Pour the batter by 1/4 cup-fulls onto a preheated, nonstick skillet. Cook until the bottom is brown and a spatula slips easily under the pancake. Then turn and brown the other side.

Homemade Applesauce 1

We enjoy fresh, homemade applesauce every fall. Try different varieties of apples to create a myriad of magical flavors. You'll never want to eat commercial applesauce again. Remember never use apples that have been gathered from the ground.

3 lbs. coarsely chopped red cooking apples
1 cup apple cider
1/3 cup Sucanat (optional)

Combine all ingredients in a large saucepan. Bring to a boil. Reduce heat and simmer 1 hour or until apples are tender, stirring occasionally. Serve hot or cold.

Homemade Applesauce 2

6 Granny Smith apples, peeled, cored and sliced
1/2 tsp. ground ginger
1/4 tsp. ground cloves
1/3 cup Sucanat (optional)
dash of vanilla extract
1 tsp. cinnamon
juice of 1/2 lemon

In a small saucepan over medium heat, add the apples with the other ingredients and cook until apples are soft. Serve either chunky style, or purée in a blender.

Crock-pot method: Put ingredients into a crock-pot. Cover; cook on low eight hours or high three to four hours. Serve warm.

Scrambles

Tofu makes a great, healthy substitute for eggs. These recipes can be enjoyed any time, but their protein content makes them particularly good for breakfast. Use the recipes to help get you started, but begin to experiment by adding any ingredient you would have used in an omelet or scrambled eggs. Many companies are beginning to make flavored tofu available—especially delicious when used in a scramble.

Tofu will take on the texture of scrambled eggs if frozen and defrosted. Or, you can place tofu on some paper towels with more towels on top of it. Put a heavy plate over it and leave for 15 minutes at an angle. This allows the tofu to drain; a lower water content creates a better texture when scrambled.

Simple Scramble

Use this basic recipe as a starting place. Add the vegetables that you like, and additional spices to compliment the flavors. Sautéed onions, bell peppers and mushrooms are especially good.

2 tsp. onion powder
1 tsp. garlic powder
1/2 tsp. turmeric
1/4 tsp. pepper
1/4 tsp. salt
1 tsp. parsley flakes
1 lb. firm, low fat tofu

Combine the onion powder, garlic powder, turmeric, pepper, salt and parsley flakes in a small bowl.

Crumble the tofu into a nonstick skillet that has been lightly coated with cooking spray. Sprinkle the combined seasonings over the tofu and cook over medium heat until heated through.

Scrambled Tofu

Nutritional yeast flakes are rich in B vitamins.
They lend a bit of a cheese flavor to the tofu.

1/2 cup chopped onions
2 cups low fat, firm tofu
2 T. chopped chives
1 T. Spike
1 tsp. nutritional yeast flakes
1/4 tsp. garlic powder
1/2 tsp. onion powder
1/4 tsp. turmeric
1/2 tsp. salt

Sauté the chopped onions in a small amount of water over medium high heat until they are just softened. Add the tofu and mash with a fork until it has the texture of scrambled eggs. Mix in the chives, spike, yeast flakes, garlic powder, onion powder, turmeric and salt. Heat through.

Spanish Scramble

A spicy alternative for Huevos Rancheros. Find cilantro next
to the parsley in the produce section of your market.

2 lbs. low fat, firm tofu, mashed with a fork
1/4 tsp. red pepper flakes
3 green onions, sliced
4 large cloves garlic, minced
1/4 tsp. turmeric
1 green bell pepper, seeded and chopped
1 T. soy sauce
3/4 cup chunky salsa—mild, medium or hot depending on preference
1 T. lime juice
1/4 cup chopped fresh cilantro

Heat a little water in a nonstick skillet over medium high heat and add the red pepper flakes. Add the green bell pepper and sauté for 2 minutes. Add the onions, garlic and turmeric and sauté for 3 minutes. Add the tofu and cook for 5 minutes, stirring frequently. Add the soy sauce, salsa, lime juice and cilantro, reduce the heat and simmer for 5 minutes. Serve with warmed tortillas.

Chicken-Flavored Scramble

A healthy dish with a familiar flavor.

1 lb. low fat, firm tofu
1/8 tsp. turmeric
1 tsp. vegetarian, chicken-flavored seasoning
1/2 lb. mushrooms, chopped
1 green onion, chopped
1/2 tsp. garlic powder
1 tomato, chopped
1 bell pepper, seeded and chopped

Heat a nonstick skillet over medium high heat. Add all of the ingredients except the tofu. Cook until the bell pepper has just softened. Put the tofu into the skillet, break it up with a fork, and cook until heated through.

Tofu Rancheros

Better than the original! Add more chili powder if you want a spicier dish.

12 oz. silken, extra firm tofu
1/2 lb. mushrooms, chopped
1 cup corn kernels, fresh or frozen and thawed
1 onion, chopped
2 cloves garlic, minced
2 tomatoes, chopped
4 oz. can diced green chilies
1 tsp. chili powder
1 T. nutritional yeast flakes

Place the tofu in a small bowl and crumble with a fork. Add the nutritional yeast flakes and chili powder. Toss until the tofu is coated. Heat a skillet that has been lightly coated with cooking spray over medium heat. Add the tofu and 1 T. of water. Stir until it has the appearance of scrambled eggs. Set aside.

In another skillet, heat a small amount of water over medium high heat. Add the onion, and garlic and cook for 2 minutes. Add the corn, mushrooms, green chilies, and tomatoes. Sauté until any water has evaporated. Stir in the tofu and sauté until heated through—about 1 minute. Serve with warm tortillas.

Breads, Muffins

Breads and Muffins provide a hearty accompaniment to any meal. Many companies are now producing whole grain breads made without oil or eggs. Just make sure you read the labels!

Corn Bread

This recipe makes a wonderful corn bread without any of the oil. Baby food provides a substitute for the fat. Excellent served with Perfect Pea Soup, Black Bean Soup, or just about anything else.

1/2 cup whole wheat flour
3/4 cup whole wheat pastry flour
3/4 cup of cornmeal
4 T. Sucanat
5 tsp. baking powder
1/2 tsp. salt
1/3 cup + 2 T. baby food applesauce
1/2 cup of low fat soy milk
1/2 cup water

Preheat the oven to 375°.

Mix the flour, pastry flour, cornmeal, Sucanat, baking powder and salt together in a medium bowl. In another bowl, mix the applesauce, soy milk and water together. Combine the wet and dry ingredients and mix well. Pour into an 8x11 baking dish that has been lightly coated with cooking spray. Bake for 30 minutes, or until the sides just pull away from the pan.

Corn Muffins

A surprising way to obtain the healthy benefits of tofu— no one will ever know it's there.

2 cups cornmeal
1 cup whole wheat pastry flour
6 oz. soft silken tofu
3 cups water
1/2 tsp. salt

Preheat the oven to 400°.

In a medium bowl, mix together the cornmeal and whole wheat pastry flour. Set aside. Crumble the tofu into a blender. Add the water and the salt. Blend until smooth.

Add the tofu to the flour and mix well. Spoon the mixture into muffin tins that have been lightly coated with cooking spray. Bake for 30 minutes, or until just golden brown.

Applesauce-Raisin Oat Bread

This low fat, moist creation is our favorite holiday bread. It's especially delicious when made with homemade applesauce.

1/3 cup organic raisins
1/4 tsp. baking soda
hot water to cover
1/4 tsp. salt
2 cups whole wheat pastry flour
1½ tsp. Ener-G egg replacer + 2 T. water
1 cup quick rolled oats
4 tsp. baking powder
1/2 cup Sucanat
1 tsp. cinnamon
1 cup applesauce
1/2 tsp. nutmeg
1/2 cup water
1/2 tsp. ground cloves
1/4 tsp. ground ginger

Preheat the oven to 350°.

Place the raisins in a small bowl and add hot water to cover. Let the raisins soak while you combine the remaining ingredients, then drain.

In a medium bowl, combine the whole wheat pastry flour, oats, baking powder, cinnamon, nutmeg, cloves, ginger, baking soda, and salt.

In a small bowl, beat egg replacer and water. Add the Sucanat, applesauce, drained raisins and water until they are well blended. Add this mixture to the flour mixture, stirring the ingredients just to moisten them. Pour the batter into a nonstick 9 x 5 x 3-inch loaf pan.

Bake the bread for 50 to 60 minutes or until a toothpick inserted in the center of the loaf comes out clean. Let the bread cool in the pan for 10 minutes and then turn it out onto a rack to cool completely.

Berry Muffins

A delicious muffin recipe with a sweet surprise inside. Raspberries or blueberries are especially good. The oat bran provides texture and fiber. Rice milk is a wonderful substitute for dairy products. Use it in coffee or tea, on breakfast cereal, or in recipes, it has a light, sweet taste and is low in fat.

1½ cups oat bran
1½ tsp. Ener-G egg replacer + 2 T. water
1/2 cup wheat germ
1/2 cup quick oats
2 large overripe bananas, mashed
2 T. flax seed meal
1¼ cups rice milk
1/4 - 1/2 cup Sucanat
2 tsp. pumpkin pie spice
3/4 cup ripe whole berries
1/2 tsp. baking soda

Preheat oven to 400°.

Lightly coat muffin tins with cooking spray. Combine the oat bran, wheat germ, quick oats, flax seed meal, Sucanat, and pumpkin pie spice in a large mixing bowl. In a medium bowl, whisk the egg replacer and water together. Add the bananas and rice milk. Combine wet ingredients with dry ingredients, just until moist.

Place half of the muffin batter in the bottom of each muffin tin. Add equal amounts of berries to each tin, then cover with remaining muffin batter. Bake for 15 to 20 minutes.

Zucchini-Carrot Bread

To enjoy this flavorful bread any time of the year, grate fresh zucchini and carrots in the summer and freeze in the quantities listed below.

1½ cups whole wheat pastry flour
1/2 cup Sucanat
1½ tsp. cinnamon
1 tsp. baking powder
1/2 tsp. baking soda
1/2 tsp. nutmeg
1/4 tsp. sea salt (optional)
1/4 tsp. ground cloves
1½ tsp. Ener-G egg replacer and 2 T. water
1/2 cup applesauce *or* 1-1/2 cups flaxseed meal
1 cup packed, finely grated unpeeled zucchini (about 1 medium zucchini)
1/4 cup packed, finely grated, scrubbed carrot (about 1 small carrot)
1 tsp. vanilla

Preheat the oven to 350°.

In a large bowl, combine the whole wheat flours, Sucanat, cinnamon, baking powder, baking soda, nutmeg, salt, and cloves. In a medium bowl, whisk together the egg replacer and water; add the applesauce or flaxseed meal, zucchini, carrot and vanilla. Add this mixture to the flour mixture, stirring the ingredients to combine them well. Pour batter into a 9 x 5 x 3-inch loaf pan that has been lightly coated with cooking spray. Bake the bread for 50 to 60 minutes or until a toothpick inserted in the center of the bread comes out clean.

Fruit, Flax & Bran Muffins

Once prized by the ancient Egyptians, flaxseeds are one of the healthiest sources of Omega-3 oils. Buy seeds whole, store them in the refrigerator and grind in your blender to make fresh flaxseed meal.

1½ cups whole wheat pastry flour
2 apples, peeled and shredded
3/4 cup flaxseed meal
1/2 cup organic raisins (optional)
3/4 cup oat bran
1 cup Sucanat
3 tsp. Ener-G egg replacer plus 4 T. water
2 tsp. baking soda
1 tsp. baking powder
3/4 cup vanilla rice or soy milk
1/2 tsp. salt
3 T. applesauce
2 tsp. cinnamon
1 tsp. vanilla
1½ large carrots, finely shredded

Preheat oven to 350°.

In a large bowl, combine flour, flaxseed meal, oat bran, Sucanat, baking soda, baking powder, salt, and cinnamon. Stir in carrots, apples, and raisins. In a medium bowl, whisk together egg replacer and water. Add rice or soy milk, applesauce and vanilla. Combine wet ingredients with dry ingredients, just until moist. Do not over mix batter. Fill muffin cups 3/4 full and bake for 15-20 minutes.

Oat Bran Muffins

This recipe will yield 12 muffins—they make a wonderful, healthy snack so you might want to make a double batch. Visit the farmer's market for the best in fresh organic berries.

2¼ cups oat bran
1¼ cups soy or rice milk
1 T. baking powder
1½ tsp. Ener-G egg replacer + 2 T. water
1/2 tsp. cinnamon
1/4 cup shredded coconut

2 large overripe bananas
1/4 cup maple syrup
2/3 cup fresh *or* frozen blueberries

Preheat the oven to 450°.

Lightly coat muffin tins with cooking spray. Combine all dry ingredients in a mixing bowl. Blend all other ingredients (if you use blueberries, it's easier if you add them by hand to the filled muffin tin) into a puree and mix thoroughly with the dry ingredients. Fill muffin tins, allowing some room for mix to rise. Bake until top of muffins are brown (about 15 minutes). As soon as they're cool, bag them and put them in the freezer.

Pumpkin-Spice Muffins

Pumpkin can be used for more than jack-o-lanterns and pumpkin pies. These muffins are an unusual way to obtain beta-carotene, a powerful antioxidant.

Muffin:

1¾ cups whole wheat pastry flour
2/3 cup low fat vanilla soy milk
1 tsp. baking powder
3 T. applesauce
1/2 tsp. baking soda
1/2 cup honey
1/4 tsp. salt
1½ tsp. Ener-G egg replacer + 2 T. water
1 tsp. ground cinnamon
3/4 cup fresh, cooked pumpkin *or* canned pumpkin
1/3 cup organic raisins (optional)

Topping:

1 T. Sucanat
1 T. wheat germ

Preheat the oven to 400°.

Lightly coat a 12-cup muffin tin with cooking spray or line with muffin papers. In a large bowl, sift together flour, baking powder, baking soda, salt and cinnamon. In another bowl, stir together remaining ingredients. Combine contents of two bowls, stirring until just blended. Add raisins. Divide batter equally among 12 muffin cups. Add an equal amount of topping to each muffin. Bake 20 minutes, or until muffins are springy to the touch and lightly browned.

Cinnamon Raisin Apple Muffins

This recipe uses baby food prunes instead of oil. You can replace oils or animal fats with prune puree, apple sauce, or ripe mashed banana. In baking, substitute these ingredients one for one.

2 cups whole wheat pastry flour
1 tsp. cinnamon
1 tsp. baking powder
1/2 tsp. baking soda
1/4 tsp. salt
1/2 cup organic raisins
1 cup apple juice
1/2 cup applesauce
2 T. baby food prunes

Preheat the oven to 350°.

In a large bowl, mix together the pastry flour, cinnamon, baking powder, baking soda, and salt. Stir in the raisins. In a separate bowl, mix together the apple juice, applesauce and baby food prunes. Combine the wet and the dry ingredients. Spoon the mixture into muffin tins that have been lightly coated with cooking spray.

Bake 20-25 minutes, or until lightly browned.

Blueberry Muffins

A perennial favorite, fresh blueberries make the difference.

1 cup fresh blueberries
1 cup whole wheat pastry flour
1/2 tsp. salt
1/2 tsp. cinnamon
1/2 cup wheat germ
3 T. applesauce
1/4 cup Sucanat
1½ tsp. Ener-G egg replacer + 2 T. of water
3/4 cup low fat soy milk
1¾ tsp. baking powder

Preheat the oven to 375°.

Lightly coat a twelve cup muffin tin with cooking spray. Wash and drain the berries. In a large bowl, mix together all the ingredients except for the blueberries and baking powder. When well mixed, add the remaining ingredients and mix again.

Spoon into the muffin tins and bake for 15-20 minutes, or until lightly browned.

Sandwich Spreads, Dips

Sandwiches can be made with hearty whole wheat or multi-grain breads, pita pockets or tortillas. Add a healthy spread, fresh tomatoes, onions, lettuce and other veggies for a delicious treat. Use dips with oven baked tortilla chips, fresh cut up vegetables or fat free whole grain crackers.

Healthy Dip Base

You can still enjoy all of the dips you usually make with mayonnaise or sour cream. Just add the flavoring ingredients to one of the following recipes.

1 package firm silken tofu, drained and crumbled
2 T. fresh lemon juice
1 T. rice vinegar
1-2 tsp. Sucanat
1 tsp. salt
1 tsp. prepared yellow mustard

Place all ingredients in a blender and process until smooth. Add flavorings as desired. Onion soup mix, dill weed and onion, curry powder are delicious alternatives.

Dip Base - 2

1 lb. low fat, silken tofu
1 T. cider vinegar
1 T. lemon juice
1 tsp. soy sauce
1 T. maple syrup

Place all ingredients in a blender and process until smooth. Add any dip flavoring ingredients that you like.

Artichoke Dip

Good enough to take to a party, serve this dip with multi-grain crackers.

2 cans of artichoke hearts packed in water, drained and chopped
1 package low fat, firm, silken tofu
1½ T. lemon juice
2 tsp. garlic powder
1 tsp. parsley
1 tsp. sage powder

1 T. rice vinegar
2 T. nutritional yeast flakes
paprika to garnish (optional)

Preheat the oven to 300°.

Place the tofu, lemon juice, garlic, parsley, sage, rice vinegar and nutritional yeast flakes in a blender. Process until smooth, adding a little water if needed.

Fold in the artichoke hearts. Pour the mixture into a baking dish that has been lightly coated with cooking spray. Sprinkle a little additional nutritional yeast on top.

Bake for about 50 minutes, or until very lightly browned. Dust with paprika if desired.

Hummus - 1

Hummus is a wonderful sandwich stuffing with origins in the Middle East. It usually contains tahini, which is high in fat. This recipe provides great taste without the fat. Use it to stuff pita pockets, add cucumber, tomatoes and onion for a delightful, healthy lunch.

1½ cups cooked garbanzo beans (if canned, rinse and drain)
4 cloves garlic, chopped
1 tsp. ground cumin
2 T. lemon juice
4 dashes Tabasco sauce
1 pinch cayenne pepper
2 T. dried parsley
2 T. vegetable broth

Combine all of the ingredients except the parsley in a blender and process until smooth. Add the parsley and process briefly.

Hummus - 2

1 can garbanzo beans, rinsed and drained
1/2 medium onion, finely chopped
4 cloves garlic, chopped
2 tsp. cumin
2 tsp. coriander
1 tsp. chili powder
1 T. lemon juice
1 tsp. vinegar

Place all of the ingredients in a blender. Process until smooth, adding a small amount of water if needed to achieve desired consistency.

Lentil Spread

A good way to use leftover lentils to make a tasty spread. If you don't have leftovers, add ½ cup of lentils to 1¼ cups of water. Bring to a boil in a saucepan, reduce heat and simmer for about 20 minutes, or until tender. Check midway to make sure the water hasn't been completely absorbed. Allow to cool, then use for recipes.

1 cup cooked lentils
1 T. + 1 tsp. tomato paste
1 large onion, chopped
2 tsp. chili powder (or more to taste)
3 cloves garlic, crushed

Place all of the ingredients in a blender and process until smooth. Chill for at least 1 hour, then use to make sandwiches.

Black Bean Spread

This makes a great dip for baked tortilla chips, or a spread for a good sandwich. Dill is very easy to grow in your garden.

2 cans black beans, rinsed and drained
3 cloves garlic, minced
1 small onion, chopped fine
1 bunch fresh dill

Place all ingredients in a blender and process until smooth. Chill for at least an hour.

Pinto Bean Dip

Excellent with corn tortillas, lettuce and fresh tomatoes.
Or, serve with oil-free tortilla chips.

4 cups cooked pinto beans (if canned, rinse and drain)
1 medium onion, chopped fine
2 T. rice vinegar
1 tsp. salt
1 tsp. cumin
1 tsp. oregano
4 cloves garlic, crushed
1 tsp. chili powder
2 dashes of Tabasco sauce
1/8 tsp. liquid smoke

Place all ingredients in a blender and process until smooth.

Spicy Black Bean Dip

This recipe can be made as hot as you like! Look for
jalapeño peppers in the fresh produce section.

2 cups cooked black beans (if canned, rinse and drain)
2 jalapeño peppers, seeded and chopped
3 cloves garlic, chopped
1 cup tomatoes, chopped
1/2 small red onion, chopped
2 T. fresh cilantro, minced
3 T. lemon juice
salt and pepper to taste

Place the beans, jalapeños, garlic, salt and pepper in a blender. Process until smooth, adding a small amount of water if needed. Place in a bowl.

Combine the tomato, red onion, cilantro and lemon juice. Stir well and spoon over the bean mixture. Serve with oil free tortilla chips.

White Bean Spread

A flavorful treat! Excellent with sliced tomato, cucumber, lettuce, sprouts and shredded carrot in a whole wheat pita pocket.

1 cup cooked small white beans (if canned, rinse and drain)
4 cloves garlic, chopped
1 T. stone ground mustard
3 T. lemon juice
1 tsp. tarragon
3 green onions, chopped

Place all of the ingredients in a blender. Process until smooth, adding a little water if needed.

Veggie Dip

Serve with fresh, cut up vegetables.
Be sure you read the labels when choosing an onion soup mix.
Many of them contain oils, or animal products.

1 lb. low fat, soft silken tofu
1 package vegetarian onion soup mix
dash garlic powder
dash onion powder
1 tsp. horseradish

Place all of the ingredients in a blender. Process until smooth, adding a small amount of water if needed.

Chili Bean Spread

Try this spread on a jalapeño pepper flavored bread for a little extra pizzazz. This is also great as an appetizer, or served with corn chips and fresh vegetables.

1 can no-fat refried beans with green chilies
dash cayenne pepper
4 pita bread, rolls, or tortillas
1 clove garlic, pressed
1 large tomato, sliced
1 tomato, chopped (optional)
1 small cucumber, sliced
2 T. chopped onion
Romaine lettuce, shredded
2 T. fresh parsley, chopped
1 tsp. Dijon mustard
1/4 tsp. each chili powder and cumin
sprouts, rinsed
carrot, shredded

Combine beans, garlic, tomato, onion, parsley, mustard, chili powder, cumin and cayenne pepper in a blender or food processor. Process until smooth. Refrigerate for two hours.

Cut pita pockets or rolls in half, or warm tortillas, and spread bean mixture on one half. Top with sliced tomato, cucumber, lettuce, sprouts and shredded carrot, and the other half of pita, roll or tortilla.

Soups, Stews and Chilies

Soups, stew and chilies provide an easy way to incorporate whole foods into your diet. If you double the recipe when you cook, you can have another meal ready in the freezer when you need it. Beans have replaced the meat in the following recipes.

Many people have had trouble digesting beans. However, the more regularly you eat them, the less difficulty you will have. Often, gas is simply caused by increasing the fiber in your diet. Once you make the adjustment to a healthy fiber intake, the problem will resolve itself. However, some people have problems digesting a certain sugar contained in the skins of beans. Rinsing canned beans, and soaking dry beans helps to neutralize it. If you still have problems after eating beans for a few weeks, try the product, "Bean-O." Found in markets, natural food stores and pharmacies, it contains an enzyme that helps your system process beans. Don't give up! Beans have an incredible wealth of nutrients, fiber and protein to offer—and they are very economical.

- *For a quick soup*: take one cup of cooked grain or beans, one cup of fresh cut vegetables, and three cups of vegetable broth together and you have a homemade soup in minutes.
- *Try using your own favorite recipes* for soup, stew and chili. Simply remove all oils and animal products and replace with beans and whole grains.
- *For creamy soups minus the milk*: throw a handful of oats (about 1/2 cup) into a vegetable soup (4 to 5 cups), then purée it for a creamy effect.
- *Add finely chopped greens* to your soups to enhance the flavor and increase the nutritional value.
- *For a wonderful soup broth*: save organic vegetable peelings and tops (onion skins, carrot tops, etc) in the freezer and then boil and strain for a soup broth. In your slow cooker, add the frozen veggies (about 4 cups), cover with water, add a few cloves and black peppercorns, and cook on low for 8 to 10 hours. Strain out the veggies and freeze the broth in 1-cup or 2-cup portions.
- *For a ready to use vegetable broth*: try Pacific Foods of Oregon fat-free Organic Vegetable Broth. It contains no preservatives or artificial ingredients and is made only with organically grown vegetables.

Minestrone Soup

In Italy, minestrone soups come in countless variations which can be eaten cool in the summer and hot in the winter. Vary the recipe using fresh vegetables, pasta, barley or rice.

1 cup dry kidney beans, soaked overnight in water to cover
2-3 cloves garlic, crushed
1 large onion, chopped
2 quarts water
2 stalks celery with leaves, sliced
2 carrots, scrubbed and sliced
1 white potato, scrubbed and chopped
1 cup fresh or frozen green beans (sliced into 1-inch pieces)
8 oz. can tomato sauce
2 T. parsley flakes, or 1/4 cup chopped fresh parsley
1½ tsp. dried basil
1½ tsp. dried oregano
1/2 tsp. dried marjoram
1/2 tsp. rosemary
1/4 tsp. ground black pepper
1/4 tsp. celery seed
1 zucchini *or* yellow squash, chopped
1 cup shredded cabbage
1/2 cup uncooked whole wheat elbow macaroni
15-ounce can garbanzo *or* pinto beans (rinsed and drained)
15 oz. can chopped tomatoes
2 cups tightly packed washed and dried fresh spinach

Drain the soaked beans, then place with the garlic, onion and water in a soup pot and cook for one hour to make a rich broth.

Add the celery, carrot, potato, green beans, tomato sauce, and seasonings. After 30 minutes, add the zucchini. Cook another 30 minutes and add the cabbage, elbow macaroni, garbanzo beans, and chopped tomatoes. Cook another 20 minutes. Add the spinach, cook until tender, 2 to 5 minutes.

Tomato-Rice Soup

A mild and tasty soup that kids really enjoy. Sun-dried tomatoes can be found in the produce section of your market. You can make your own if you live somewhere with abundant sunshine.

2 cups sliced mushrooms
1 medium onion, chopped
3 cups vegetable broth
6 T. oil free sun-dried tomatoes, chopped
1 tsp. Sucanat
1/4 tsp. salt
1 T. Tabasco sauce
1/8 tsp. allspice
1/8 tsp. black pepper
1 can stewed tomatoes
1 cup brown rice

Sauté the mushrooms and onion in a little water for about 5 minutes. Add 3 cups of vegetable broth, and the sun-dried tomatoes, Sucanat, salt, Tabasco sauce, allspice, black pepper and stewed tomatoes. Bring to a boil. Add the brown rice, cover, reduce the heat and simmer hard until the rice is cooked—from 25-45 minutes, depending on the type of rice you use.

Asian Hot and Sour Soup

This soup is traditionally prepared using chicken broth and eggs. I think you'll be pleased with this healthier choice.

4 green onions, chopped
1 clove garlic, chopped
1 T. fresh ginger, chopped
1 T. Sucanat
2 T. rice vinegar
2 T. soy sauce
1 tsp. Tabasco sauce
8 cups water
1 can bamboo shoots drained and chopped
1/2 cup mushrooms, chopped
1 package low fat, firm tofu cut into small cubes
1 T. cornstarch

In a saucepan, sauté the green onions, ginger, and garlic in a little water for 2 minutes. Add the Tabasco sauce, rice vinegar, Sucanat and soy sauce. Add 8 cups of water, bamboo shoots, mushrooms, and tofu. When the soup boils, lower the heat to a simmer.

Mix the cornstarch with a small amount of cold water in a separate bowl, then add to the soup, stirring constantly. Let the soup simmer for 10 minutes. Taste. You may wish to add additional soy sauce. Sprinkle some chopped green onions on top and serve.

Smoky Black Bean Soup

This soup is full of flavor. Many markets now carry a variety of dried chili peppers in the Mexican foods section. Habañero's impart a smoky, spicy flavor. You can substitute a 4 oz. can of diced green chilies if you prefer.

2 cups dried black beans
8 cups vegetable broth
1 green pepper, seeded and chopped
1 medium onion, chopped
2 stalks celery, chopped
3 medium carrots, chopped
1 bay leaf
1/4 tsp. cumin
1/2 tsp. liquid smoke
2 cloves garlic, crushed
2 dried habañero peppers, whole
1/4 cup sherry

In a soup pot cover the beans with water and soak overnight, then drain. Or, use the quick method to prepare the beans. Place the beans in a soup pot, and cover with water. Bring to a boil, and cook for 3 minutes. Remove from the heat, cover and let stand, undisturbed for one hour. Drain.

Put the prepared beans into a soup pot with 8 cups of vegetable broth. Bring to a boil, cover, reduce heat, and simmer for 1½ hrs. Add the remaining ingredients except the sherry and simmer until beans and veggies are tender—about 30 minutes. Add sherry and cook for 10 minutes more. Remove the habañero peppers and serve.

Cream of Tomato Soup

You don't need to include dairy products to enjoy an old favorite. You can use rice milk, soy milk or oat milk in this recipe.

1 large onion, finely diced
2 T. soy sauce
2 cups tomato sauce
4 cups unflavored oat milk
4 T. cornstarch
1/2 tsp. salt
1/2 tsp. black pepper
1 tsp. Italian spice blend

Over medium high heat, sauté the onion in the soy sauce until onion is tender. Add 3 cups of oat milk, and the tomato sauce to the onions and bring to a boil.

In a separate bowl, mix the cornstarch with the remaining oat milk. Add to the soup, and stir constantly until soup is thickened. Add the spices and cook over low heat for 15 minutes.

Superb Split-Pea Soup

Children love this soup. Serve with a whole-grain bread roll and a green salad for a delicious supper.

1 yellow onion, chopped
1 tsp. celery seed
2 bay leaves
1 cup green *or* yellow split peas (if canned, rinse and drain)
1/2 cup white beans
1/2 cup hulled barley
10 cups water
2 carrots, scrubbed and chopped
2 stalks celery plus leaves, chopped
1 leek (white part only), chopped
1 white potato, scrubbed and chopped
1 bunch chopped greens such as spinach, kale, or collard (optional)
1/4 cup chopped fresh parsley *or* 1 T. parsley flakes
1-2 tsp. salt

1 tsp. dried basil
1/2 tsp. paprika
1/4 tsp. ground black pepper
dash ground white pepper

In a large soup pot, sauté the onion, bay leaves, and celery seed in water or broth until soft. Rinse the split peas, barley, and beans in a colander. Add the split peas, barley, beans, and water to the soup pot. Bring to a boil, reduce the heat, cover, and simmer for 1½ hours.

Add the carrots, celery, leek, potato, greens, paprika, parsley, salt, basil, black pepper, and white pepper. Simmer the soup for another half hour. If it is thicker than you like, add more water.

Perfect Pea Soup

A delectable combination of herbs, peas and vegetables. Especially great when it's cold outside. Serve this soup to someone who's convinced, "a meal without meat will leave me hungry," and watch what happens.

1 large onion, coarsely chopped
8 Knorr's vegetable cubes + 8 cups of water (or 8 cups of seasoned vegetable broth)
16 oz. dried peas
1 tsp. basil
1 bay leaf
1/2 tsp. marjoram
1/4 tsp. thyme
2 tsp. garlic powder
1 tsp. liquid smoke
1 tsp. paprika
1 tsp. red pepper flakes
2 carrots, peeled and sliced
1 large potato, peeled and diced

In a soup pot, sauté the onion in a little water until just tender, about 5 minutes. Add peas, broth, bay leaf, liquid smoke and spices. Heat to boiling, reduce heat to simmer, cover and simmer, stirring occasionally about 30 minutes. Add carrots and potato to soup, cover and simmer until tender, about 15 minutes.

Gentle Vegetable Soup

A soup that is filled with nutrition and very mild.
Increase the seasonings if you prefer a stronger taste.

8 cups of vegetable broth
4 fresh tomatoes, chopped or 1-16 oz. can of diced tomatoes with juice
1 large onion, chopped
4 stalks of celery, sliced thin
5 carrots, sliced thin
4 potatoes, cut into 1" chunks
1 cup corn, fresh or frozen
1 cup peas, fresh or frozen
2 tsp. basil
2 tsp. rosemary
2 tsp. salt
2 tsp. pepper
1/2 cup uncooked barley

Place all ingredients in a soup pot. Bring to a brief boil. Reduce heat and simmer hard for about 1 hour, or until the barley is tender.

Two Bean Soup

Filled with spices and beans traditionally found in Mexican cuisine, this soup can be made mild, medium or hot.

2 cups dried pinto beans
1-2 tsp. salt
2 cups dried black beans
several dashes Tabasco sauce
8-12 cups water
4 cups vegetable broth
1 onion, chopped
30-ounce can chopped tomatoes
1 cup celery, chopped
1 green pepper, chopped
1 cup corn
1 red pepper, chopped
green onion, sliced
3 cloves garlic, minced

fresh tomatoes, chopped
2 tsp. chili powder
1-2 tsp. cumin
fresh cilantro, chopped
1 tsp. paprika
oil free corn chips, crushed
1/2-1 tsp. red pepper flakes

Rinse the beans in a colander. Place them in a large soup pot and add water (make sure the beans are covered with at least 3 inches of water). Soak the beans overnight, or bring to a boil for 2 minutes, turn off the burner and cover. Allow the beans to sit for at least 2 hours. Cook the beans over medium-low heat for 2 to 2½ hours. Drain. Mash half of the beans with a potato masher.

In a large soup pot, sauté onion, celery and peppers in a small amount of water or vegetable broth until tender. Add the garlic, chili powder, cumin, paprika, red pepper flakes, salt, and Tabasco sauce. Stir thoroughly over medium heat. Stir in the vegetable broth and chopped tomatoes (with their liquid). Add the mashed and whole beans, and more vegetable broth if needed and mix well. Bring to a boil, reduce heat, cover and simmer for 30 minutes. Add the corn and cook another 30 minutes.

Top each serving with green onion, fresh tomatoes, cilantro and crushed corn chips. Serve with brown rice or polenta and a fresh green salad.

Variation: Cook the pinto beans and black beans separately. Mash the pinto beans and add the black beans whole, for a more colorful effect.

Spinach Soup

The health benefits of spinach are legendary. It is rich in iron and its chlorophyll content helps to detoxify the digestive tract. It is famous in folklore for its power to restore vitality and energy. Here's a tasty way to include the leafy dynamo in your diet.

4 cups sliced mushrooms
1 large onion, chopped
6 cups vegetable broth
6 oz. oil free sun-dried tomatoes, diced
2 tsp. Sucanat
1/2 tsp. salt
2 T. Tabasco sauce (or more to taste)
1/4 tsp. allspice
1/4 tsp. black pepper
4 cups chopped tomatoes
2 packages of fresh spinach, chopped
2 cups quick cooking brown rice

In a soup pot over medium high heat, sauté the mushrooms and onions in a small amount of water until tender. Add the remaining ingredients, except spinach and brown rice. Bring to a boil. Cover, reduce heat and simmer hard for 10 minutes. Add the brown rice and spinach. Cover and cook until the rice is tender—about 10 minutes.

Luscious Lentil Soup

The combination of rice and lentils produces a hearty, high-protein meal. Lentils are one of the most nutritious and delicious of all the legumes. They are eaten in many diverse cultures and a low-cost source of protein.

5 cups vegetable broth
3 cups water
1½ cups lentils
1 cup long-grain brown rice
28-ounce can chopped tomatoes (save the juice)
3 carrots, chopped
1 large onion, chopped
1 large celery stalk plus leaves, chopped
1 leek (white part only), chopped
3 large cloves garlic, minced

1 tsp. crumbled dried basil
1/2 tsp. crumbled oregano
1/2 tsp. crumbled thyme
1/2 tsp. paprika
2 bay leaves
1/2 cup minced fresh parsley
salt to taste
freshly ground black pepper, to taste

Place the vegetable broth and water in a large soup pot with the lentils, rice, tomatoes, reserved tomato juice, carrots, onion, celery and leaves, leek, garlic, basil, oregano, thyme, paprika, and bay leaves. Bring the soup to a boil, reduce the heat, cover the pan, and simmer the soup, stirring it occasionally, for 45-55 minutes, or until the lentils and rice are both tender. Remove and discard the bay leaves.

Stir in the parsley, salt and pepper. If necessary, thin the soup with additional hot broth or water. Serve with a green salad and whole-grain bread.

Quick and Easy Lentil Soup

Lentils are easy to digest, quick cooking, and provide valuable minerals for almost every organ in the body. Serve with whole grain rolls and a green salad.

4 cups vegetable broth
2 garlic cloves, minced
1 cup water
16-oz. can chopped tomatoes
1/4 cup dry red wine
1 bay leaf
1 cup lentils
1/2 - 1 tsp. basil
1 carrot, sliced
1/2 - 1 tsp. thyme
1 onion, chopped
1/4 tsp. fennel seed
1 celery stalk, sliced

Combine all the ingredients in a large saucepan and bring to a boil. Reduce heat and cook covered for 20-25 minutes.

Ribollito

Enjoy this delicious soup the fall. We experiment with different varieties of summer squash that are available at the farmer's market.

1 large onion, chopped
4 cloves garlic, minced
2 T. minced fresh parsley
1 tsp. dried thyme
1 tsp. dried rosemary
2 celery ribs, chopped
2 carrots, chopped
2 cups tomato puree or sauce
2 20-oz. cans white beans (rinsed and drained)
4 cups water
1 large yellow squash, chunked
salt and freshly ground pepper to taste

Heat a small amount of water in a soup pot over medium-high heat. Add the onion and sauté until soft, about 5 to 7 minutes. Stir in garlic, parsley, thyme, and rosemary and cook for an additional minute. Stir in the celery, carrots and tomato puree or sauce.

In a food processor or in a bowl, mash one cup of the beans. Add mashed beans and water to the saucepan. Bring to a boil, reduce heat and simmer, covered, 15 minutes.

Add squash and remaining 3 cups beans. Simmer 10 minutes. Remove from heat and season with salt and pepper.

Southwestern Black Bean Soup

Delicious served with a green salad and cornbread muffins

1 pound dried black beans
1½ tsp. chili powder
2 quarts water
1 tsp. fresh lemon juice
1 large onion, chopped
1/2 tsp. crushed red pepper flakes
3 cloves garlic, minced
1/4 cup chopped fresh cilantro
16-oz. can tomato sauce
16-oz. can chopped tomatoes with liquid
4-oz. can chopped green chilies
1½ tsp. ground cumin
cooked brown rice
green onions, chopped
black olives, sliced
fresh tomato, chopped
oil free corn chips (optional)

Soak the beans overnight in enough water to cover. Drain, then add 2 quarts of water. Bring to a brief boil, reduce the heat and simmer for 1 hour, then add the remaining ingredients, except the cilantro. Cook until the beans are tender, about 2 hours. Add the cilantro just before serving. Mix it in well and let the soup rest, covered, for about 15 minutes. Serve hot over cooked rice, top with green onions, black olives, and fresh tomato.

Note: This can be made in a slow cooker. Put everything into the pot, except the cilantro, rice, green onions, olives and fresh tomato, early in the morning. (No need to soak the beans first.) Set the cooker on high, cover, and let it cook all day. Add the cilantro just before serving. Serve the soup over cooked rice and top with green onions, olives and fresh tomato. Crunch up baked corn chips to use as a topping if you like.

Black Bean and Sweet Potato Stew

A surprising combination that you're sure to enjoy! Sweet potatoes contain beta-caroteve and phytochelatins—substances that bind with toxic metals like mercury, lead and cadmium. Once bound, this metal can find a pathway out of the body.

3 medium onions, finely sliced
1 cup vegetable broth
2 cloves garlic, minced
1/2 tsp. red pepper flakes
1/2 tsp. allspice
16 oz. diced tomatoes
1 small hard-skinned squash such as butternut—peeled, seeded and cut into small pieces
1 lb. sweet potatoes, peeled and cut into small pieces
16 oz. cooked black beans (if canned, rinse and drain)

Sauté the onions in a small amount of water until soft. Add the remaining ingredients, except the black beans. Cover and cook on medium low until the squash and potatoes are tender, about 25 minutes.

Add the black beans, and cook for 10 minutes more.

Country Stew

This stew is highly adaptable to your vegetable preferences. I suggest you first try it as described, and then use your own creativity. You could add eggplant, zucchini, green beans-almost any vegetable tastes good.

1½ cups vegetable broth (you may not use all of this)
2 cups mushrooms, cut into quarters (use portobello mushrooms for an especially great taste)
2 carrots, sliced
3 large potatoes, cut into small chunks
1 can pearl onions, rinsed and drained
4 cloves garlic, minced fine
4 cups cooked small white beans (if canned, rinse and drain)
6 oz. tomato paste
3 oz. tomato sauce
1/2 cup port or other red wine

1 tsp. rosemary crumbled very fine
1 tsp. thyme
1 tsp. salt
1 tsp. pepper
pinch allspice
1 bay leaf

Heat a small amount of vegetable broth in a soup pot over medium high heat Add garlic, mushrooms, onions, and carrots. Cook 5 minutes, stirring frequently. Add 1/2 cup of vegetable broth, add spices and cover and cook for 10 minutes.

Add remaining ingredients and as much vegetable broth as needed to produce a stew consistency. Do not add too much broth. Bring to a boil, then reduce heat and simmer, covered for 40 minutes, or until vegetables are tender. Check frequently, and add more broth as needed. Remove bay leaf. Serve.

Red Wine and Pinto Bean Stew

This is a mild combination that is easy to adapt.
Add other vegetables as you like.

1 large onion, chopped
1 large carrot, sliced
1 large potato, peeled and cubed
1½ cups vegetable broth
3 T. tomato paste
1 tsp. thyme
2 bay leaves
1½ cups dry red wine
4 cups cooked pinto beans (if canned, rinse and drain)
2 cloves garlic, crushed
8 oz. mushrooms, sliced

In a soup pot, sauté the onion in a little water until it is tender. Add the carrot and potato, and stir in one cup of the broth, tomato paste, thyme and bay leaves. Bring to a brief boil, then reduce heat and simmer until the potato and carrot are cooked—about 20 minutes. If needed, add more broth to keep the vegetables covered.

Add the wine, beans, and garlic. Return to a boil, then lower the heat and simmer uncovered for 10 minutes. Remove and discard the bay leaves.

Meanwhile, sauté the mushrooms over low heat in a little broth. When they have wilted, add them to the stew. Cook for 5 minutes and serve.

Zucchini, Tomato and White Bean Stew

This is a very mild dish. Add more spices if you wish.

1 large onion, chopped
1/4 cup water
4 small zucchini, sliced
16 oz. can peeled tomatoes with juice, or 2 medium fresh tomatoes, chopped
2 cups cooked white beans (if canned, rinse and drain)
1 green bell pepper, seeded and chopped
3 cloves garlic, minced
2 T. minced fresh basil or 1 T. dried basil

In a large skillet over medium high heat, sauté the onion in a small amount of water until soft. Add the zucchini, tomatoes, beans, bell pepper, garlic, and basil. Reduce heat to medium, and cover. Simmer 20 minutes, stirring occasionally. Add water if needed.

Buttercup Squash, Parsnip and Garbanzo Bean Stew

This is a wonderful soup to make in the fall. It's worth the effort to find the chipotle pepper—it adds a unique flavor that you'll really enjoy. Look for it in the Mexican foods section of your market.

2 stalks celery, sliced
4 cloves garlic, minced
1 chipotle pepper (available dried or canned)
4 large tomatoes, diced
1½ T. paprika

1 T. oregano
salt and pepper to taste
2 cups peeled and diced buttercup or butternut squash
2 large parsnips, peeled and diced
8 oz. can pearl onions, rinsed and drained
2 carrots, diced
2½ cups water
1½ cup garbanzo beans (if canned, rinse and drain)
8 oz. fresh or frozen corn kernels (thawed)
10 broccoli florets

In a soup pot, heat a little water. Add the celery, garlic and chipotle. Sauté for 3-4 minutes. Add the tomatoes, paprika, oregano, salt and pepper. Cook about 10 minutes more over medium low heat, stirring frequently until mixture resembles a thick pulp.

Add the squash, parsnips, onions, carrots, and water. Cook, stirring occasionally, until squash and parsnips are tender—about 30 minutes.

Stir in the beans, corn and broccoli. Cover and cook 5-10 minutes.

Aztec Stew

This is a favorite in my house!
Serve it with corn bread, and a fresh green salad.

1/4 cup cooking sherry
2 onions, chopped
2 stalks celery, chopped
1 carrot, chopped
1 red bell pepper, seeded and chopped
4 cups cooked black beans (if canned, rinse and drain)
16 oz. corn kernels
2 cups vegetable broth
2 T. minced garlic
1 large tomato, chopped
2 tsp. cumin
4 tsp. chili powder or to taste
1/2 tsp. oregano
1 T. Sucanat
2 T. tomato paste

Combine the sherry and 3 T. of water in a soup pot.

Heat the mixture over medium high heat, then add the onions. Sauté until tender. Add the celery, carrot and bell pepper. Sauté for 5 minutes.

Add the remaining ingredients, bring to a boil, then lower the heat. Simmer for 30 minutes.

Barley Bourguignon

You won't miss the beef in this variation on a traditional favorite! Leeks are a cousin to the onion, and are very mild. Use only the white part, and wash well to remove sand particles.

1/2 cup pearl barley
2 leeks, chopped fine
2 lbs. mushrooms, quartered
3 parsnips, peeled and chopped
1 tsp. thyme
1 tsp. sage
1 bay leaf
2/3 cup red wine
3 tomatoes, chopped
2 T. tomato paste
1½ cups broccoli florets

Dry roast the barley for 2-3 minutes in a heavy pan. Then, add enough boiling water to cover by one inch, and cook for 45 minutes. Drain, reserving the liquid.

Heat a little water in a large pot and gently sauté the leeks for 5 minutes or until soft. Add the mushrooms, parsnips, herbs and cooked barley. Stir well, and cook for 3 minutes.

Add the wine, tomatoes, the tomato paste and 2/3 cup reserved broth. Bring to a boil, cover and cook gently for 35 minutes, adding reserved broth if the mixture begins to become dry.

Add the broccoli, and cook for 10 minutes, or until tender.

Taos Stew

This stew is quite mild. Adjust the seasonings to your liking. Cumin has been known for thousands of years—its origins are in the upper region of the Nile. It has an aromatic, spicy taste frequently found in Mexican foods.

2 cups cooked red kidney beans (if canned, rinse and drain)
1 large onion, diced
1 green pepper, seeded and diced
1 red pepper, seeded and diced
4 cloves of garlic, minced
4 fresh tomatoes, chopped, or 28 oz. can diced tomatoes
15 oz. can stewed tomatoes
2 T. chili powder
1 T. oregano
2 tsp. ground cumin
2 tsp. paprika
1 T. liquid smoke
2 tsp. Tabasco sauce
1 tsp. black pepper

Heat a little water in a soup pot. Add onion, bell peppers, and garlic. Sauté until vegetables are tender, about 7 minutes. Stir in the tomatoes, beans, stewed tomatoes and seasonings. Bring to a simmer. Cook uncovered over low heat, stirring occasionally for 45 minutes.

Sprinkle with additional chopped onion if desired. Serve with cornbread and a fruit salad (pineapple is especially good).

Curried Lentil Stew

Lentils and curry pair together very well. Remember, curry powder comes in hot, medium or mild—this recipe is written using medium—adjust according to your taste.

1 medium onion, chopped
2 stalks celery, chopped
2 cloves garlic, minced
1 T. curry powder
1 tsp. cumin
1/8 tsp. red pepper flakes
2 cups vegetable broth

3/4 cup lentils
28 oz. crushed tomatoes
1/2 lb. fresh spinach
1/2 cup diced carrot
2 T. fresh cilantro

In a large skillet over medium high heat, sauté the onion, celery and garlic in a small amount of water until soft. Stir in the curry powder, cumin, and pepper,

Add the vegetable broth, lentils, and tomatoes. Bring to a brief boil. Reduce the heat and simmer, uncovered for 25 minutes. Add the spinach and carrot, and simmer for 15 minutes. Stir in the cilantro and serve.

Sweet Kidney Bean Stew

This is a delicious dish, filled with subtle flavors. Serve with rice, egg-free noodles, or crusty French bread, and a simple green salad.

4 cups cooked kidney beans (if canned, rinse and drain)
15 oz. can pearl onions, rinsed and drained
1 tsp. allspice
1 tsp. cinnamon
1 tsp. thyme
8 oz. mushrooms, quartered
1 cup organic raisins
2 fresh tomatoes, diced
8 oz. tomato sauce
1/4 cup water
1 T. plus 1 tsp. orange zest
1 T. red wine vinegar

Heat a little water in a soup pot, and sauté the onions until just tender. Add the spices and cook for 3 minutes.

Stir in the remaining ingredients, bring to a very brief boil, then reduce heat and simmer for 40 minutes.

Fifteen Bean Stew

Look for fifteen bean mixture in the dried beans section of your market. Orange zest is the grated peel of an orange. You can buy it in the spice section, or make your own.

1 cup dried 15 bean mixture
4 cups vegetable broth
1 large onion, chopped
2 large green peppers, seeded and chopped
4 cloves garlic, minced
2 cups peeled and diced butternut squash
15 oz. corn kernels
15 oz. can stewed tomatoes
6 oz. tomato paste
1 T. dried oregano
1 T. chili powder
1½ tsp. cumin
1 T. pepper
1 T. lemon juice
2 tsp. allspice
2 T. orange zest
1 tsp. liquid smoke

In a large soup pot, combine beans with 6 cups of water. Bring to a boil. Boil for 3 minutes, remove from the heat, cover and allow to stand for 1 hour. Drain and discard the water. (Or, you can cover the beans with water and let stand overnight. Drain).

In a large skillet, heat a little water, add onion, bell pepper and garlic. Sauté until onion is just tender. Pour into the soup pot with the beans, 4 cups of vegetable broth, squash, stewed tomatoes, tomato paste, lemon juice, liquid smoke, and seasonings. Bring to a brief boil, reduce heat and simmer 50 minutes over low heat. The longer you simmer the stew, the better it tastes.

Old Fashioned Barley Stew

This dish offers a gentle mixture of tastes and is definitely a "comfort food". It contains pearled barley, a wonderful grain that was once very common on dinner tables. Barley adds nutrition and fiber, while thickening this stew. Serve with crusty bread and a green salad.

1/2 cup medium pearled barley
1 onion, chopped
1½ lbs. mushrooms, quartered
3 parsnips, peeled and coarsely chopped
2 tsp. thyme
2 tsp. sage
2 bay leaf
2/3 cup red wine
3 tomatoes, chopped or 15 oz. can chopped tomatoes
8 oz. tomato paste
2 cups green beans

In a skillet over medium high heat, dry-roast the barley for 3 minutes, stirring frequently. Then, add 2 cups boiling water, cover and simmer hard for 35 minutes. Add more water if necessary. Drain.

Heat a little water in a soup pot, and gently sauté the onions and mushrooms for 5 minutes. Add the parsnips, herbs, and cooked barley. Stir well, and cook for 3 minutes.

Add the wine, tomatoes, tomato paste, and 2/3 cup of water. Bring to a boil, cover and cook gently for 45 minutes, adding water if mixture begins to become dry.

Add the green beans, and cook for 10 minutes, or until tender.

Ratatouille

It seems there are just as many recipes for ratatouille as there are cooks! Try the following recipes and adjust them to your liking. Avoid eggplant if you suffer from joint pain. It contains sotanine which can cause inflammation in people with sensitivity to it.

1 eggplant, peeled and diced
1 onion, chopped
3 cups zucchini, sliced
1 green pepper, seeded and diced
2 cups fresh or canned chopped tomatoes
1/2 cup tomato puree or tomato paste
1 clove garlic, crushed
1 cup red wine
1 tsp. Sucanat
1 tsp. dried basil leaves

Place all of the ingredients in a soup pot and mix well. Bring to a brief boil, then reduce heat, cover and simmer for 40 minutes, or until the vegetables are tender.

Ratatouille - 2

1 large red onion, chopped
4 cloves garlic, minced
1 eggplant, peeled and cubed
3 medium zucchini, cut into 1/2 inch pieces
1 green pepper, seeded and cut into 1/2 inch pieces
2 large tomatoes, chopped
2 T. tomato paste
2 T. capers, rinsed and drained
2 tsp. basil
1/2 tsp. rosemary
1/2 tsp. oregano

Heat a small amount of water in a large skillet over medium heat. Add the onions and garlic. Sauté for 3 minutes. Add the eggplant, zucchini and peppers. Cook, stirring frequently for 5 minutes.

Add the tomatoes, tomato paste, capers, basil, rosemary and oregano. Reduce heat to low. Simmer for 15 minutes, stirring occasionally until vegetables are tender and liquid thickens.

Barley Ratatouille

Enjoy this recipe in late summer when eggplant, peppers and zucchini are ripe and flavorful—fresh from the Farmer's Market.

1 large eggplant, peeled and chopped
1/2 cup green onions, chopped
1 green bell pepper, seeded and chopped
3 small zucchini, chopped
1½ cups water
16-oz. can stewed tomatoes
1/2 cup uncooked barley
1/2 tsp. salt
1/2 tsp. oregano
1/2 tsp. basil

Heat a small amount of water in a skillet over medium heat. Add the eggplant, green onions, green pepper, and zucchini. Mix well and cook until vegetables are tender crisp. Stir in water, tomatoes, barley, salt, oregano, and basil. Bring to a boil, reduce heat, cover, and simmer 50 minutes, or until barley is tender and sauce is thickened.

Three Bean Stew

This is really a cassoulet—a kind of stew, but with a drier consistency. Its subtle flavors are very pleasing.

16 oz. can stewed tomatoes, undrained
8 oz. cooked butter beans
8 oz. cooked great northern beans
8 oz. cooked garbanzo beans
2 carrots, finely chopped
1 onion, chopped
2 cloves garlic, minced
2 tsp. dried basil
2 tsp. dried parsley
1/2 tsp. thyme
1/2 tsp. salt
1/8 tsp. pepper
1 bay leaf

Place all the ingredients in a soup pot. Mix well. Bring to a brief boil, then reduce heat, cover, and simmer hard for 1½ hours. Be sure to stir occasionally to prevent sticking to the bottom of the pot. Add a little water only if necessary to prevent sticking.

Remove bay leaf, and serve.

Traditional Bean Chili

Meatless bean-based chili dates back thousands of years. It wasn't until the arrival of the Spanish in Mexico that the dish contained meat. Serve this chili over brown rice or polenta.

2 cups dried beans (mixed beans are best)
1 handful barley
1 handful lentils
8 cups water
1 onion
2-3 cloves garlic, crushed
1 green pepper, diced
1 red pepper, diced
2 tsp. chili powder
2 tsp. cumin
1 tsp. paprika
1/2 tsp. crushed red pepper flakes
15-oz. can diced tomatoes
15-oz. can tomato sauce
1-2 tsp. sea salt
1 cup fresh or frozen corn
1/4 cup cilantro, chopped
dash of Tabasco sauce (optional)
cooked brown rice or polenta
scallions or red onion, chopped
tomato, chopped

Rinse the beans, barley, and lentils in a colander. Place in large saucepan and add water. Bring the beans to a boil for a few minutes, turn them off, cover, and let stand for 2 hours.

Sauté the onion in water or broth until tender. Add the garlic and red or green pepper. Sprinkle in chili powder, cumin and red pepper flakes. Stir over low heat for a few more minutes. Add the presoaked beans (with liquid) and the tomatoes. Bring to a boil, reduce heat, cover and simmer for an hour or so, until the beans are tender; add water as needed. Add the salt, corn and cilantro the last 15 minutes.

Ladle chili over brown rice or polenta. Top with fresh scallions, black olives, and tomato.

Arizona Corn and White Bean Chili

This is very pretty to look at and excellent to eat. It contains oregano which is helpful to the body's efforts to expel toxins.

1 large onion, diced
1 red bell pepper, seeded and diced
1 medium zucchini, diced
2 cloves garlic, minced
2 cups corn kernels
15 oz. cooked white beans (if canned, rinse and drain)
15 oz. can stewed tomatoes
15 oz. can crushed tomatoes
2 T. dried parsley
2 tsp. dried oregano
2 tsp. ground cumin
1 tsp. chili powder
1/2 tsp. salt
1/2 tsp. pepper

Heat a little water in a soup pot. Add the onion, bell pepper, zucchini, and garlic. Sauté over medium high heat until the vegetables are just tender. Stir in the corn, beans, stewed and crushed tomatoes, and dried seasonings. Bring to a brief boil, then reduce heat and simmer hard uncovered for 25 minutes. Be sure to stir frequently to prevent sticking to the bottom of the pan.

Eggplant Chili

An interesting alternative to more familiar types of chili. Remember to avoid eggplant if you suffer from joint pain.

1 onion, diced
1 green bell pepper, seeded and diced
2 cups peeled, diced eggplant
2 cloves garlic, minced
30 oz. cooked kidney beans (if canned, rinse and drain)
15 oz. can stewed tomatoes
15 oz. can crushed tomatoes
2 T. dried parsley
2 tsp. chili powder
1 T. oregano
1 tsp. thyme
1/2 tsp. salt
1/2 tsp. pepper
4 large green onions, chopped

Heat a little water in a soup pot over medium high heat. Add the onion, bell pepper, eggplant, and garlic. Cook until vegetables are tender—about 10 minutes.

Stir in the beans, stewed tomatoes, crushed tomatoes, parsley, chili powder, oregano, thyme, salt, and pepper. Cook over low heat, stirring frequently, about 30 minutes. Remove from the heat and let stand 5 minutes. Top with green onions and serve.

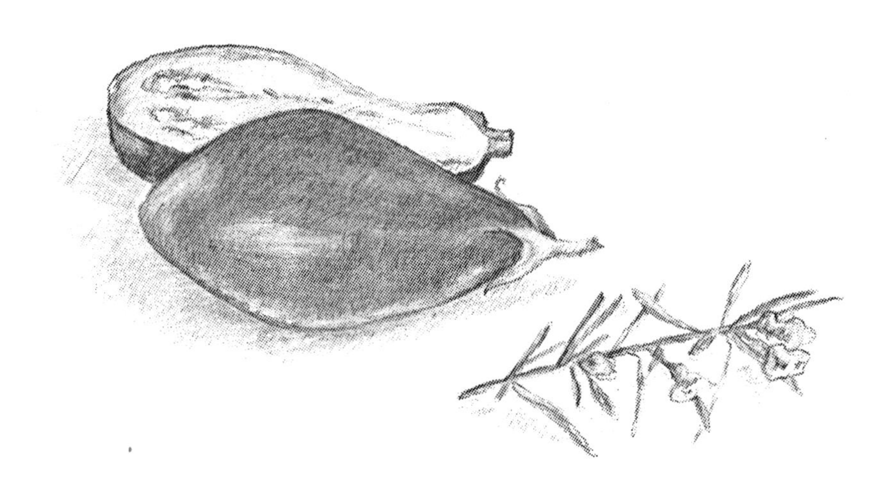

Loafs, Casseroles and Dinner Pies

Loafs and casseroles form the mainstays of the American diet. This section contains delicious recipes that can provide the centerpiece for the holiday table, or your contribution to an informal potluck. They also provide a comfortable transition to healthy eating.

Vegetarians are often asked what they have for holidays like Thanksgiving or Christmas. Here are a trio of recipes which make wonderful main dishes for special occasions. Serve these along with traditional side dishes, like stuffing and sweet potatoes, made the healthy way.

Holiday Lentil Loaf

This recipe provides a special treat. Because it contains walnuts which are higher in fat, use it for holidays and other celebrations.

1 small onion, chopped fine
1 clove garlic, crushed
2 stalks celery, chopped fine
2 tsp. sage
3 cups cooked lentils (see Appendix for instructions)
3 cups cooked wild rice
1/2 cup chopped walnuts
1/4 cup whole wheat breadcrumbs
2 T. vinegar
1 T. Ener-G egg replacer + 4 T. water
2 T. whole wheat flour

Preheat the oven to 350°.

Heat a little water in a skillet over medium high heat. Sauté the onion, garlic, and celery until the onion is just tender. Add the sage.

In a large bowl, combine the skillet mixture, lentils, wild rice, walnuts, breadcrumbs, vinegar, and whole wheat flour. Mix very well. In a separate bowl, beat together the Ener-G egg replacer and the water. Add to the mixture in the large bowl.

Lightly coat a loaf pan with cooking spray, and fill it with the mixture. Press down. Bake 30 minutes covered, uncover and bake 10 minutes more. Let stand for 10 minutes before serving.

Pilgrim's Lentil Loaf

With the flavors of Thanksgiving, this dish is excellent warm or cold at any time during the year. Serve with Sweet Potatoes and Apples.

2 cups dry lentils
6 cups water
2 onion, diced
2 green peppers, seeded and diced fine
1 cup whole wheat crumbs
4 T. whole wheat flour
1 tsp. sage
1 tsp. thyme
3 T. Ener-G egg replacer + 8 T. of water
1 cup vegetable broth
2 T. red wine vinegar
1/2 tsp. pepper
2 tsp. soy sauce

Preheat the oven to 350°.

Place the lentils and water in a saucepan. Bring to a boil, reduce heat and simmer for 30 minutes. Check at 20 minutes to make sure all of the water has not been absorbed.

Meanwhile, heat a small amount of water in a large skillet. Sauté the onions and pepper until just tender. Remove from the heat. Add lentils, bread crumbs, flour, sage and thyme to the onion and pepper mixture. In a separate bowl, whisk together the Ener-G egg replacer and water, then add the broth, soy sauce and vinegar. Combine the Ener-G mixture with the lentil mixture. Stir well.

Pour into a casserole dish that has been lightly coated with cooking spray. Bake uncovered for 45 minutes.

Lentil-Oat Loaf

Serve this with garlic mashed potatoes, gravy, bread stuffing and steamed vegetables. It also makes great sandwiches for lunch.

4 cups water
1 cup lentils
3/4 cup rolled oats
1 small onion, finely chopped
2 stalks celery, finely chopped
5 slices whole-grain bread, crumbled
1 tsp. garlic powder
1 tsp. ground sage
1 tsp. parsley
salt and black pepper to taste
1½ tsp. Ener-G egg replacer and 2 T. water
8-oz. can tomato sauce

Preheat oven to 400°.

Place the 4 cups of water in a medium saucepan and bring to a boil. Rinse the lentils in a colander. Add lentils to the boiling water, reduce the heat, cover, and simmer for 45 minutes.

Meanwhile, combine the onion, celery, oats, crumbled bread, garlic, sage, salt and pepper, parsley, and celery salt in a large bowl.

Drain the lentils. Add the egg replacer, lentils, and tomato sauce to the bread and vegetable mixture. Mix well.

Lightly coat two small loaf pans with cooking spray. Place the mixture in the prepared loaf pans and press down firmly with the back of a spoon. Bake, uncovered, for 45 minutes. Let stand 10 minutes, then invert onto a serving plate. Cut into slices to serve.

Millet-Lentil Loaf

Millet is a grain that sustained humanity for hundreds of years until it was forgotten in the 20th century. Try this delicious recipe with a healthy gravy and mashed potatoes.

1/2 cup millet
1 cup lentils
2 green onions, thinly sliced
2 cups fresh, coarsely chopped spinach
1 T. Ener-G egg replacer + 4 T. of water
2 apples, grated

1 T. coriander
1 T. lemon juice

Preheat the oven to 350°.

Place the millet and two cups of water in a saucepan. Bring to a boil, and cook for 30 minutes. Meanwhile, place the lentils in 4 cups of water. Bring to a boil and cook for 30 minutes, then drain.

In a large skillet over medium high heat, sauté the green onions in a little water for one minute. Then stir in the spinach and cook for 2 minutes. Add the cooked millet, lentils, apples, coriander and lemon juice. In a very small bowl, whisk together the egg replacer and water, then mix into the other ingredients.

Place in a loaf pan that has been lightly coated with cooking spray. Bake for 30-40 minutes or until firm and golden brown on top.

Southwestern Hash

Leftovers make an excellent breakfast when reheated on a griddle.

4 medium potatoes, diced
2 onions, diced
5 cloves garlic, minced
1 red bell pepper, seeded and diced
1 green bell pepper, seeded and diced
2 tsp. chili powder (more to taste)
1/4 tsp. ground cumin
1/2 tsp. oregano
3 tomatoes, diced
2 cups cooked black beans (if canned, rinse and drain)

Preheat the oven to 375°.

Heat a little water in a large skillet over medium high heat. Sauté the potatoes and onions until the onions are just tender.

Add the garlic and peppers. Continue to cook until the peppers have softened, adding more water as needed.

Stir in the spices. Add the tomatoes and black beans.

Place in a casserole dish that has been lightly coated with cooking spray. Bake for 40 minutes. Garnish with green onions and fresh cilantro.

Spiced Vegetable Couscous

Whole wheat couscous can be found in green supermarkets and health food stores. Not only is it more nutritious than common couscous, but it's more flavorful.

1 small yellow summer squash, diced
1 small zucchini, diced
1 medium red onion, diced
2 cloves garlic, minced
1 cup cooked garbanzo beans (if canned, rinse and drain)
1 tsp. cumin
1 tsp. curry powder
1 tsp. red pepper flakes
1/2 tsp. sea salt
pepper to taste
3 cups cooked whole wheat couscous

Preheat the oven to 350°.

Heat a little water in a large skillet, and sauté the squash, zucchini, red onion, and garlic for 5 minutes.

Stir in the garbanzo beans and spices, then gently stir in the cooked couscous. Spoon into a large casserole dish, and bake about 20 minutes. Garnish with parsley.

Roasted Vegetables and Quinoa

Quinoa is an ancient grain that is high in protein. Each grain contains a perfect spiral—a timeless symbol of infinity.

2 cups vegetable broth
2 cups quinoa
6 cloves garlic, minced
1 medium red onion, diced
2 medium carrots, diced
2 stalks celery, diced
1 fennel bulb, or 1/2 tsp. dry fennel seeds
2 medium eggplants, peeled and diced
1/4 tsp. marjoram
4 roasted red bell peppers, chopped (available in jars in most produce sections)
2 large tomatoes, chopped
3 T. lemon juice

Preheat the oven to 400°.

Heat the vegetable broth to a simmer. Combine the broth with the quinoa in a casserole dish. Mix well, cover, and bake for 20 minutes or until the broth is absorbed.

Heat a small amount of water in a soup pot over medium high heat. Sauté the garlic, onion, carrots, celery, and fennel for 2 minutes. Add the zucchini, eggplant, and marjoram. Cook until the vegetables are tender, but still crisp—about 2 minutes.

Add the cooked vegetables, roasted peppers, tomatoes, and lemon juice to the quinoa and mix well.

Bake for 20 minutes.

French Vegetable Casserole

Take advantage of fresh summer vegetables in this great casserole.

2 large onions coarsely chopped
3 cloves garlic, minced
2 green peppers, seeded and chopped
3 small zucchini, sliced
2 medium eggplants, peeled and diced
2 large potatoes, peeled and diced
1/2 lb. mushrooms, sliced
3 ripe tomatoes, peeled and chopped
6 oz. tomato paste
2 bay leaves
1 T. chopped parsley
1/2 tsp. oregano
1/2 tsp. thyme

Preheat the oven to 350°.

Heat a small amount of water in a large skillet. Sauté the chopped onions and minced garlic until just softened. Add the green peppers, zucchini, eggplants, potatoes and mushrooms and cook over medium heat, stirring frequently, 3-5 minutes. Add the tomatoes, tomato paste, and herbs to a brief boil, stirring until blended.

Transfer the vegetables to a casserole dish. Bake for 1 hour and 15 minutes.

Baked Beans Creole

1 large onion, chopped
2 cloves garlic, minced
2 green bell peppers, seeded and diced
3 celery stalks, sliced
2 T. whole wheat flour
1 large tomato, diced
8 oz. tomato paste
1/4 tsp. basil
1/4 tsp. rosemary
2 cups cooked small white beans (if canned, rinse and drain)
1/2 cup whole wheat breadcrumbs

Preheat the oven to 350°.

Heat a small amount of water in a skillet, and sauté the onions and garlic until tender. Add the green pepper and celery. Sauté until tender. Stir in the flour and tomatoes. Add the tomato paste, herbs, and beans. Mix in the breadcrumbs. Add a little water if the mixture appears too dry. Spoon into a casserole dish that has been lightly coated with cooking spray. Sprinkle more breadcrumbs on top.

Bake for 30 minutes.

Stuffed Cabbage Casserole

This is a variation on old-fashioned stuffed cabbage rolls.
It's equally good and easier to prepare.

Preheat the oven to 350°.

Prepare 3 cups of brown rice

Peel and dice 2 large potatoes. Cover with boiling water and cook for about 15 minutes, or until potato is tender.

While the potato and rice are cooking prepare, the filling ingredients:

1 head of cabbage, shredded, steamed for 5 minutes
3 carrots, shredded
1/2 cup organic raisins
1 apple, unpeeled, finely diced
1 tsp. allspice
1/8 tsp. black pepper

Prepare the sauce:

Mix in a saucepan,

- **30 oz. tomato sauce**
- **3 T. lemon juice**
- **1/4 cup firmly packed Sucanat**
- **1 onion, chopped**

Simmer for 10 minutes. Note: as an alternative, you could use Healthy Choice Spaghetti sauce.

Mix together the rice, cabbage, potato, carrot, raisins, apple, allspice and pepper.

Layer the cabbage mixture with the sauce in a large casserole dish. Bake covered for 45 minutes, or until sauce is bubbly.

Oven Baked Vegetables

A combination of tangy and sweet flavors, this dish is both pretty and delicious.

- **3 medium sweet potatoes, peeled and cut into medium sized chunks**
- **2 medium Idaho potatoes, peeled and cut into medium sized chunks**
- **2 medium tomatoes, coarsely chopped**
- **1 green pepper, seeded and cut into strips**
- **1 onion, sliced**
- **2 cloves garlic, minced**
- **1/2 cup soy sauce**
- **1/4 cup honey**
- **3 T. lemon juice**
- **1/2 tsp. marjoram**
- **3/4 tsp. pepper**

Preheat the oven to 375°.

Cook the sweet potatoes and Idaho potatoes in boiling water for 10 minutes. Drain, then place in a 3 quart casserole. Stir in the tomatoes.

Sauté the green pepper, onion, and garlic in a little water until onion is just tender. Add to the other vegetables in the casserole dish and mix.

In a small saucepan over low heat, mix together the soy sauce, honey, and lemon juice. Add the herbs and heat for one minute. Pour over the vegetables.

Cover and bake for 45 minutes.

Spiced Tofu Casserole

This recipe combines some unusual flavors. Serve with rice pilaf.

1 large onion, chopped fine
1 package low fat, firm silken tofu, cut into bite-sized cubes
1 tsp. allspice
1 tsp. cumin
1/2 tsp. ground ginger
1/2 tsp. turmeric
1 lb. tomatoes, chopped
1 red pepper, seeded and cut into strips
1 green pepper, seeded and cut into strips
1 large eggplant, peeled and chopped
2/3 cup organic raisins

Preheat the oven to 350°.

Heat a small amount of water or vegetable broth in a soup pot, and sauté the onion until soft. Add the tofu and spices and sauté for 5 minutes.

Stir in the remaining ingredients, cover and cook for 30 minutes. Spoon the mixture into a baking dish that has been lightly coated with cooking spray.

Bake for 30 minutes.

Roasted Spiced Vegetables with Garbanzo Beans

Sometimes garbanzo beans are called cici's or chick-peas. They have a nutty flavor.

1 cup cooked garbanzo beans (if canned, rinse and drain)
3 cups cooked brown rice
4 large carrots, chopped
2 onions, chopped
1 red bell pepper, seeded and thinly sliced
2/3 cup of vegetable broth
8 oz. tomato sauce
2 T. soy sauce
2 tsp. powdered ginger
2 tsp. chili powder
1½ tsp. coriander
1/2 tsp. allspice
1/2 tsp. cardamon
1 T. balsamic vinegar or 2 tsp. lemon juice

Preheat the oven to 400°.

Mix together the broth, soy sauce, ginger, chili powder, coriander, allspice, and cardamon. Add the onion, carrots, and pepper. Toss well and place in a large casserole dish.

Bake, stirring occasionally for 30 minutes. Remove from the oven and add the garbanzo beans and tomato sauce. Stir in the balsamic vinegar or lemon juice. Bake for 10 minutes more.

Serve over the rice.

Italian Veggie Casserole

Easy to prepare and filled with nutrition, this is a delicious, healthy alternative to old-fashioned meat loaf. Look for naturally sweetened catsup in your natural foods store.

1½ cans garbanzo beans, slightly mashed
(if canned, rinse and drain)
8 oz. mushrooms, chopped
1 large onion, chopped fine
1 large carrot, very finely diced
1/4 cup wheat germ
3 cloves garlic, minced
1 green pepper, chopped fine
4 T. catsup + catsup to spread on top of casserole
1 T. Spice Hunter Italian Seasoning, or other Italian seasoning mix.
1/4 tsp. black pepper

Preheat the oven to 350°.

Combine all ingredients in a large bowl, and mix well.

Pour into 2 quart casserole dish and flatten with a spoon. Cover with catsup as desired.

Bake for 45-50 minutes. Allow to stand for 5 minutes before serving.

Quinoa and Pumpkin

This dish is power-packed with nutrition. Quinoa provides excellent protein, and pumpkin offers beta-carotene. Spinach contains calcium, and garlic enhances your immune system.

1 medium onion, chopped
8 oz. mushrooms, sliced
1 large red bell pepper, seeded and diced
1 jalapeño pepper, seeded and minced
1 small zucchini, diced
3 cloves garlic, minced
3 cups water
1½ cups dry quinoa
2 cups peeled and diced pumpkin, other hard-skinned squash
1 cup chopped spinach
2 T. fresh minced parsley or 1 T. dried parsley
1/2 tsp. sea salt
1/2 tsp. pepper

Preheat the oven to 400°.

In a large saucepan, heat a little water over medium heat. Sauté the onion, mushrooms, peppers, zucchini, and garlic for about 8 minutes. Stir in the remaining ingredients.

Transfer mixture to a 9 by 13 casserole and cover. Bake until liquid is absorbed, about 40 minutes. Remove from the oven, and fluff with a fork. Let stand for 5 minutes and serve.

Winter Squash Casserole

This is an absolutely delicious recipe; even non-vegetarians will be pleased!

2 cups hard skinned squash, peeled and chopped
2 Granny Smith apples, cored and chopped
1 cup of sliced peaches, fresh or canned
1/2 cup Sucanat
1 cup apple juice
1 T. curry powder

Preheat the oven to 350°.

Place the squash, apples and peaches in a casserole dish. In a saucepan, blend together the Sucanat, curry powder and apple juice. Bring to a brief boil. Pour the sauce over the squash mixture.

Bake covered for 40 minutes. Uncover, stir and bake for another 15 minutes or until sauce is bubbly.

Many of us grew up with meat-filled pot pies and shepherd's pies. In this Those nostalgic favorites can be translated into healthy fare.

•

Sunshine Dinner Pie

A shepherd's pie using sweet potatoes, this dish is beautiful to look at, filled with the healing power of beta-carotene, and absolutely delicious.

4 large sweet potatoes
2 T. regular molasses
2 tsp. ground ginger
1/4 tsp. black pepper
2 cups butternut squash, peeled and cubed
8 oz. mushrooms, sliced
2 parsnips, peeled and sliced
1 turnip, peeled and diced
2 carrots, diced
1 large onion, chopped
3 cups vegetable broth

Preheat the oven to 375°.

Pierce the sweet potatoes with a knife and place them in the oven with foil on the rack below them. Bake until very tender—about 1 hour. Remove them and reduce the oven temperature to 350°.

Meanwhile, heat a small amount of water in a soup pot over medium high heat. Sauté the onions and mushrooms for 5 minutes. Add the squash, carrots, parsnips, and turnip, along with the broth. Bring to a boil, cover, reduce heat and simmer for 20 minutes.

Peel the baked sweet potatoes. Place them in a large bowl, and mash them thoroughly. Mix in the molasses, ginger and pepper.

Using a slotted spoon, place the squash mixture into a large casserole dish. Spoon the sweet potato mixture over the squash mixture. Cover and bake for 45 minutes. Remove the cover and bake for 10 minutes more.

Tamale Pie

High in fiber and wonderful in taste, don't be afraid to experiment with this one. As written, it is mildly spicy. Add or subtract the amount of chili powder and green chilies according to your preferences.

3 cups cooked pinto beans (if canned, rinse and drain)
1 medium onion, chopped
2 tsp. chili powder
1 cup tomato sauce
2 cups corn kernels
4 oz. can diced green chilies
1½ cups yellow cornmeal
2½ cups water
1/2 tsp. chili powder

Preheat the oven to 350°.

Heat a small amount of water in a soup pot over medium high heat. Sauté the onions until they are just tender. Add the corn, green chilies, tomato sauce, and 2 tsp. of chili powder. Cook 5 minutes. Add the beans, reduce the heat and cook for 5 minutes. Remove from heat and set aside.

Combine the cornmeal, water, and 1/2 tsp. chili powder in a saucepan. Cook over medium high heat until the mixture thickens, stirring constantly. Do not overcook. The cornmeal is ready when a spoon just stands up in the pan.

Coat a casserole dish with cooking spray. Pour the bean mixture into the casserole. Top with the cornmeal mixture.

Bake uncovered for 35-40 minutes.

Lentil, Barley and Potato Pie

Lentils and barley combine for a hearty pie. Don't be afraid to include the turnip. Look for smaller ones, and enjoy their sweet, mild flavor. Turnips contain dithiolthiones, compounds that act as antioxidants, and sulphur which is an antibiotic.

1/2 cup dry lentils
3 cups pearled barley
1 medium onion, chopped
3 tomatoes, chopped
2 cups cauliflower flowerets
2 celery stalks, sliced
1 small onion, thickly sliced
1 turnip, thinly sliced
2 carrots, diced
1 T. Italian spice blend
1½ lbs. Idaho potatoes, peeled and diced
3 T. oat milk

Preheat the oven to 400°.

Place the lentils, barley, onion, tomatoes, cauliflower, celery, turnip, carrots, and herbs in a soup pot. Add 1½ cups water. Bring to a boil, cover and simmer for 45 minutes or until the vegetables are just tender.

Meanwhile, cook the potatoes in just enough boiling water to cover for about 20 minutes, or until tender. Drain, and mash with the oat milk.

Place the lentil mixture in a casserole that has been lightly coated with cooking spray. Spoon the mashed potatoes on top. Bake for 35 minutes.

Italian Dinner Pie

This dish takes a little time to prepare, but it is scrumptious enough for company.

1½ cups yellow cornmeal
2½ cups water
2 medium onions, chopped

3 cloves garlic, minced
2 cloves garlic, crushed
2 red bell peppers, seeded and cut into strips
1 large eggplant, peeled and diced
3 small zucchini, diced
2 cups chopped tomato or 16 oz. can diced tomatoes with juice
1 6 oz. can tomato paste
1/4 cup chopped parsley
1 tsp. rice vinegar
1 tsp. rosemary, crumbled
1/2 tsp. thyme
1/2 tsp. marjoram
1 tsp. garlic powder
1/2 tsp. pepper

Preheat the oven to 350°.

In large skillet, heat a small amount of water over medium high heat. Sauté the onion, and garlic until the onion is just tender. Remove from the heat.

Combine the cornmeal and water in a saucepan. Cook over medium high heat until the mixture thickens, stirring constantly. Do not overcook. The cornmeal is ready when a spoon just stands up in the pan. Remove from the heat.

Add 1/2 cup of the onion and garlic mixture, plus two cloves crushed garlic to the cornmeal and mix well. Spread 2/3 of the cornmeal in the bottom of a large casserole dish that has been lightly coated with cooking spray to form a bottom crust.

Add the bell peppers to the onion and garlic remaining in the skillet. Cook over medium high heat, stirring until just tender. Add the eggplant, and zucchini and cook, stirring until slightly softened. Stir in the tomatoes with their juice, and the tomato paste. Stir in garlic powder, parsley, vinegar, salt, rosemary, thyme, marjoram and pepper. Cover and cook on low heat for 10 minutes, checking to make sure mixture does not stick to the pan. Spoon over the cornmeal.

Bake for 25 minutes. Crumble remaining cornmeal mixture over the top and return to the oven for 15 minutes more. Let stand for 5 minutes and serve.

No Shepherd's Necessary Pie

This is a delicious recipe that is excellent as is, or very easy to adapt to your own preferences. Change the vegetables or the type of beans as you wish.

2 cloves of garlic, minced
3 cloves of garlic, crushed
1 red bell pepper, seeded and chopped
1 green bell pepper, seeded and chopped
2 medium zucchini, thinly sliced
1 cup of crushed tomatoes with juice
1/2 tsp. sea salt
1/8 tsp. pepper
4 cups vegetarian, no fat refried beans
1/4 tsp. paprika
4 large Idaho potatoes, peeled and diced

Preheat the oven to 375°.

Place the potatoes in a soup pot with enough water to cover. Bring to a boil and cook until tender—about 15 minutes. Drain and place back in the soup pot. Mash, adding a small amount of water until desired consistency is achieved. Set aside.

Heat a small amount of water in a large skillet over medium high heat. Sauté the minced garlic for one minute. Add the red and green peppers and zucchini and sauté until just tender. Add 3/4 cup of the crushed tomatoes, salt, and black pepper and cook uncovered for 3 minutes.

In a medium bowl, mix the crushed garlic together with the refried beans, and the remaining 1/4 cup of tomatoes.

Spoon the bean mixture into a large casserole dish that has been lightly coated with cooking spray. Top with the skillet mixture. Spoon the mashed potatoes on top.

Bake uncovered for 25 minutes. Dust with paprika.

Burritos, Enchiladas, Fajitas

Burritos of various kinds make wonderful meals that everyone enjoys. I have given you some alternatives to begin with, but begin to create burritos loaded with your own healthy choices. There are a variety of tortillas on the market. Look for those made with whole wheat or multi-grains. Be sure you read the labels! Many corn tortillas are loaded with animal fat.

Pintos and Chilies Burrito Stuffing

Pinto beans are used extensively in Mexican cooking.
They are mild and earthy in flavor.

2 cups cooked pinto beans (if canned, rinse and drain)
1 onion, chopped
4 oz. diced green chilies
2 cups corn kernels
2 cups salsa
1/2 tsp. chili powder
3 cloves garlic, minced
corn or multi-grain tortillas

Place all of the ingredients except tortillas in a large saucepan. Cook over medium heat for 15 minutes. Serve over brown rice, or use to stuff burritos.

Black Beans and Rice Burrito Stuffing

1 cup cooked brown rice
2 cups cooked black beans (if canned, rinse and drain)
1 large onion, chopped
3/4 tsp. oregano
3/4 tsp. chili powder
1/2 tsp. paprika
1/2 tsp. Tabasco sauce
1/4 tsp. cumin
salsa
whole wheat tortillas
lettuce

In a large skillet over medium high heat, sauté the onion, oregano, chili powder, paprika, hot sauce, and cumin for 5 minutes. Add the beans, mix well and heat through. Assemble into burritos, including rice, salsa and lettuce if desired.

Incredible Burritos

whole wheat or multi-grain tortillas
1 cup uncooked brown rice
2 cups water
2 cups pinto beans, cooked and mashed
2 cloves garlic, minced
Mexican taco seasoning, to taste *or* **1½ tsp. cumin, 1 tsp. oregano and 1 tsp. chili powder**
2 cups black beans, cooked
1 medium zucchini, cut into rounds
1/2 green pepper, cut into long strips
1/2 red pepper, cut into long strips
1/4 onion, sliced
fresh veggies: **shredded lettuce, corn, ripe tomato, sliced black olives, avocado, sprouts, shredded red cabbage, cilantro, chopped scallions, a squeeze of lime**
salsa
oil free corn taco shells *or* **oil free corn chips (optional)**

Place the brown rice in the two cups of water. Bring to a boil and then simmer for 45 minutes.

Place the mashed pinto beans in a saucepan (it helps to reserve some of the cooking liquid when mashing the beans to get a creamy consistency), add the minced garlic and stir in taco seasoning. Add the black beans and mix well. Heat the bean mixture over low heat, stirring occasionally.

Sauté the zucchini, green and red pepper, and onion in a small amount of vegetable broth, until tender. Sprinkle some of the taco seasoning on the cooked brown rice, to taste.

Warm the tortillas in the oven. Spread the bean mixture on the tortilla, add a scoop of rice, sautéed vegetables and then top with fresh vegetables and salsa. Roll the tortilla and enjoy!

Tom's Variation: Spread the bean mixture on the tortilla and add a scoop of rice. In a crisp corn tortilla, spoon in sautéed vegetables and top with fresh vegetables. Place the filled corn tortilla inside the whole wheat tortilla and fold like a big taco shell.

Andi & Brent's Variation: Use a can of no-fat refried beans instead of the black and pinto beans, and season with cumin, chili powder, fresh garlic or garlic powder and celery salt. Crunch corn chips on top of the fresh and sautéed vegetables.

April & Rick's Variation: Add 1 cup corn and 1/2 cup sliced black olives to the seasoned bean mixture. Spoon equal amounts of the bean filling, brown rice and sautéed vegetables onto flour tortillas. Roll up from the bottom, pressing filling to distribute. Place seam side down on the baking sheet. Cover with foil and bake for 20 minutes. Top with mild salsa, scallions, and olives.

Lentil Burritos

This is a tasty alternative!

1 large onion, chopped fine
2 stalks celery, minced
2 cloves garlic, minced
1 cup cooked lentils
1 T. chili powder
2 tsp. ground cumin
1 tsp. dried oregano
2 cups vegetable broth
2 T. organic raisins
1 cup salsa (mild, medium or hot depending on taste)
whole wheat tortillas

In a large pan over medium heat, sauté the onions, celery, and garlic in a small amount of water for about 5 minutes. Stir in the lentils, chili powder, cumin, and oregano. Cook for one minute. Add the broth and raisins. Cover and cook for 20 minutes, or until the lentils are tender. Remove the lid and cook for another 10 minutes.

Stir in the salsa. Wrap in warmed tortillas.

Enchiladas

You can make exceptional enchiladas without cheese or beef.

8 low fat corn tortillas
1 medium onion, chopped
1 green pepper, seeded and chopped
4 oz. can diced green chilies
2 cloves garlic, minced

1/2 tsp. cumin
1 package low fat, firm silken tofu mashed
2 cups diced tomatoes, drained
2 cups chunky salsa

Preheat the oven to 350°.

Lightly coat a baking dish with cooking spray.

In a medium bowl, combine all the ingredients except the tortillas and salsa. Place about 1/2 cup of the mixture in the center of each tortilla, and roll up. Place in the baking dish, seam side down.

When all of the tortillas have been place in the dish, pour the salsa over them. Cover with foil, and bake for 30 minutes.

Variations: Instead of the salsa, you can use prepared enchilada sauce.

Instead of the tofu, you can use black beans or pinto beans, combined with corn.

Fajitas

Try this delicious alternative to the traditional, high-fat restaurant version. Serve with heated nonfat tortillas, nonfat refried beans, brown rice and salsa.

Sauce:

1/4 cup balsamic vinegar
1 T. liquid smoke
1/4 cup water
1 package Lawry's Fajita Seasoning

Vegetables:

1 lb. mushrooms, cut into quarters (use portobello mushrooms for an outstanding taste)
1 large onion, cut into rings
2 red bell peppers, seeded and cut into strips
1 green pepper, seeded and cut into strips
3 carrots, sliced very thin

Mix the sauce ingredients together in a large bowl. Marinate the vegetables in the fajita sauce for an hour or longer.

Spoon the vegetables into a skillet, with 1/4 cup of the marinade. Sauté the vegetables until tender, adding reserved marinade as necessary to keep the vegetables from sticking to the pan.

Three Bean Tostadas

The Mexican version of an open-faced sandwich.

1 large onion, diced
1 red bell pepper, seeded and diced
1 green bell pepper, seeded and diced
1 T. chili powder
2 tsp. oregano
1 tsp. cumin
2 cloves garlic, minced
1 cup cooked garbanzo beans (if canned, rinse and drain)
1/2 cup cooked black beans
1/2 cup cooked pinto beans
8 oz. tomato sauce
lettuce
tomato
salsa
whole wheat tortillas

Heat a small amount of water in a large skillet over medium high heat. Sauté the onion, peppers, chili powder, oregano, cumin, and garlic for four minutes. Add the beans and tomato sauce. Bring to a brief boil, then reduce heat, and simmer for 25 minutes.

Serve with tortillas, salsa, lettuce and tomatoes.

Skillet Dinners

Here are a selection of delicious recipes that require only a skillet an an occassional saucepan to make. Many of them are very quick—perfect for workday meals.

Cauliflower and Lentil Curry

An outstanding dish, this is a good way to obtain the healthy benefits of lentils and cauliflower. Good cauliflower is creamy white, heavy and compact. Its outer leaves should be fresh and green. Avoid those with spots or yellow leaves.

1 cup dry lentils
2 medium onions, chopped
1 T. + 1 tsp. curry powder (mild, medium or hot)
1 tsp. salt
1/2 tsp. turmeric
4 large tomatoes, chopped
6 cups cauliflower florets
2 jalapeño peppers, seeded and chopped
1/2 tsp. cumin
8 cloves garlic, minced
1 T. + 1 tsp. fresh ginger, minced
1 T. + 1 tsp. cayenne pepper
4 T. lemon juice
2 T. fresh cilantro, chopped
2 tsp. Sucanat

In a large saucepan, combine lentils, onions, curry powder, salt, turmeric and two cups water. Bring to a brief boil, reduce heat, and bring to a simmer. Cover and cook, stirring occasionally until the lentils are tender and the sauce has thickened, about 35 minutes. Add the tomatoes, cauliflower, and peppers and simmer, covered until the cauliflower is tender, about 10 minutes. Remove from the heat.

Heat a little water in a small skillet over medium high heat. Add the garlic, ginger, and cumin. Sauté until the garlic is soft, about 2 minutes. Stir in the cayenne and add this mixture to the lentil-cauliflower mixture in the other pan. Stir in the lemon juice, cilantro, and Sucanat and serve.

Mediterranean Vegetable Couscous

This is an adaptation of a vegetarian meal I was served on an airplane. Take the time to call ahead for vegetarian fare when you fly. The taste and quality are usually superior to what everyone else on the plane will be eating—and, you'll probably be served first.

3 cloves garlic, minced
1 onion, coarsely chopped
1½ cups boiling water
2 large celery stalks, cut into 1/2 inch slices
1/2 tsp. fennel seeds
1 large red bell pepper, seeded and thinly sliced
1 large carrot, cut to 1/2 inch slices
8 oz. mushrooms, halved
2 medium zucchini, cut to 1½ inch chunks
2 tomatoes, coarsely chopped
1½ tsp. basil
1½ tsp. oregano
1 tsp. salt
1/4 tsp. cinnamon
1/8 tsp. pepper
2 T. balsamic vinegar
1½ cups whole wheat couscous

Heat a little water in a skillet over medium high heat. Add the garlic, and cook, stirring constantly for one minute. Add the onions and cook, stirring frequently for 2 minutes. Add 1½ cups of boiling water, fennel seeds, celery, bell pepper, carrot, mushrooms, zucchini, tomatoes, basil, oregano, salt, cinnamon and pepper. Cover and cook until tender.

Stir in 1 T. of vinegar and the couscous. Replace the lid, and remove from the heat. Allow to steam for 5 minutes. Stir, taste, and add more vinegar if desired.

Split Pea and Potato Hash

A creative alternative for corned beef hash. Rosemary is very easy to grow. The fresh herb is dramatically different from the dried. For centuries, rosemary was used to ward off evil spirits and bring good luck.

6 potatoes, peeled, cut into chunks
2½ cups water
1 cup dry split peas
2 medium onions, finely chopped
2 cloves garlic, chopped
1 red pepper, seeded and finely chopped
1 tsp. thyme
1/2 tsp. rosemary, crumbled
1/4 tsp. black pepper
1/2 cup vegetable broth

In a saucepan, place the potatoes in enough water to cover, and boil for 10 minutes. Drain. Meanwhile, bring the peas and 2½ cups of water to a boil. Reduce heat to low, cover and simmer for 25-30 minutes, or until the peas are tender. Drain.

Heat some water in a skillet. Add the onions, red peppers, thyme, rosemary, and pepper. Cook until the onion is tender.

Add the potatoes to the skillet. Cook for 10 minutes, stirring frequently. Stir in the vegetable broth, and the split peas. Cook for 7 minutes.

Priscilla's Couscous with Garbanzos

Gourmet vegetarian fare, this dish is very beautiful to look at, and even better to eat!

1 onion, sliced thin
2 carrots, sliced thin
1 cup diced tomatoes with juice
1/2 tsp. ground turmeric
1/2 tsp. ground cumin
1/3 tsp. ground cinnamon
1 cup cooked garbanzo beans (if canned, rinse and drain)

4 green onions, sliced thin
2 cups uncooked whole wheat couscous
1 tsp. jalapeño chilies, diced small
3 cups vegetable broth
1/4 cup parsley, chopped

Heat a small amount of water in a soup pot over medium high heat. Sauté the onion, carrots, and tomatoes until tender. Add water as needed.

Add the spices and cook for about a minute. Add the garbanzo beans, green onions, jalapeño peppers, couscous and vegetable broth. Bring to a boil, cover the pot and remove from the heat. Let stand until all of the liquid has been absorbed—about 5 minutes. Fluff the couscous, and add the parsley. Top with green onions if desired and serve.

Peppers and Tofu

Spicy and unique! Turmeric contains a powerful cancer inhibiting compound called curcumin.

1 large onion, chopped
2 T. minced jalapeño or pepperocini pepper
4 cloves garlic, minced
3 T. minced fresh ginger
1/2 tsp. turmeric
6 red potatoes, quartered
1 package low fat, extra firm tofu cut into bite-sized pieces
3/4 cup fresh cilantro, chopped

Heat a small amount of water in a large skillet over medium high heat. Sauté the onion, chili pepper, garlic, ginger, and turmeric until the onion is tender.

Add the potatoes. Cook, stirring frequently, until the potatoes are tender—about 15 minutes. Add a little water if needed to prevent sticking.

Add the tofu and cook, stirring frequently for 5 minutes. Stir in the cilantro and serve.

Carrot Curry

Leftovers are great for breakfast! Most bananas come from outside the U.S. where heavy dousing with banned pesticides is common. Be sure to use only organic fruit.

8 medium carrots, sliced
1 banana, peeled and sliced
1/2 cup organic raisins
1 cup orange juice
1 T. curry powder
1 T. cornstarch, mixed together with 3 T. water

Place the carrots and orange juice in a skillet. Simmer for 10 minutes, or until carrots are just tender. Add the raisins and banana and simmer for 3 minutes. Add the curry powder and cornstarch, stir constantly until sauce is thickened.

Serve over rice.

Black Beans and Apples

The earthy taste of black beans combines well with the sweetness of apples.

3 cups cooked black beans (if canned, rinse and drain)
1 green bell pepper, seeded and chopped
1 large onion, chopped
2 apples, cored and chopped
1 cup chopped tomatoes
2 cloves garlic, chopped
1 T. chili powder
1/4 tsp. allspice
1/4 tsp. pepper
1/4 cup organic raisins

Heat a small amount of water in a large skillet over medium high heat. Sauté the onion, green pepper, garlic, and apple for 5 minutes or until tender. Add additional water if needed.

Stir in one cup of water, chili powder, allspice, tomatoes, and pepper. Cover and cook over low heat for 10 minutes.

Add the beans and raisins. Cook until warmed through—about 5 minutes.

Curried Vegetables

Garam masala is very similar to curry powder, but it adds a more complex taste. Substitute medium curry powder if you like.

1 onion, sliced
1 red pepper, seeded and sliced
1 green pepper, seeded and sliced
3 cups mushrooms, sliced
2 carrots, peeled and sliced
1 apple, cored and chopped
1 can bamboo shoots
3 cloves garlic, crushed
1 T. curry powder
1 tsp. garam masala
1½ T. whole wheat flour
1¾ cups vegetable broth
2 bay leaves

Heat a small amount of water in a large skillet over medium high heat. Sauté the onion, carrots, and green pepper until tender. Add the curry, garam masala and mushrooms and cook for 10 minutes. Remove from the heat and stir in the flour. Add the broth, garlic, bay leaves. Return to the heat, bring to a boil, stir constantly until thick and smooth.

Serve over rice.

Cuban Beans

A traditional dish made without meat.

2 cups cooked red kidney beans
1 onion, finely chopped
2 cloves garlic, crushed
1½ T. red pepper flakes
2 red bell peppers, seeded and chopped
2 cups mushrooms, chopped
1 medium potato, peeled and diced
3 tsp. paprika
1½ tsp. thyme
4 T. tomato paste
1/4 tsp. salt

Heat a small amount of water in a soup pot over medium high heat. Sauté the onion until just tender. Add the garlic and mushrooms, and cook for 5 minutes. Cover, reduce the heat to low, and cook for 15 minutes.

Add the beans, potato, red pepper flakes, paprika, thyme, tomato paste and salt to stew. Simmer gently for 30 minutes, adding liquid as necessary to prevent sticking to the bottom of the pot.

Garbanzo Beans, Raisins and Couscous

Always use fresh mushrooms. Simply remove the stems, wash and add to your recipe. Canned mushrooms are soaked in salt and preservatives, and have lost their flavor.

1 medium onion, thinly sliced
3 green bell peppers, seeded and thinly sliced
2 medium potatoes, sliced
3/4 cup cooked garbanzo beans (if canned, rinse and drain)
1/4 cup organic raisins
1 lb. mushrooms, sliced
2 cups sliced zucchini
2 T. tomato paste
1/4 tsp. red pepper flakes
1 tsp. coriander
1 tsp. cumin

pinch of pepper
2 cloves garlic, minced
1/2 tsp. paprika
1/4 cup white wine
1½ cups whole wheat couscous

Heat a small amount of water in a large skillet over medium high heat. Sauté the onion until tender. Add the bell peppers, and cook for 5 minutes, adding more liquid if necessary.

Add the potatoes, garbanzo beans, raisins, zucchini, tomato paste, coriander, cumin, pepper, garlic, paprika and wine. Cover and simmer for 35 minutes. Let stand for 10 minutes.

Bring 2¼ cups water to a boil in a medium saucepan. Add the couscous. Cover and remove from heat. Let stand for 5 minutes. Top with vegetables.

Lentils in Tomato Sauce

This is great served over whole wheat toast!

1 medium onion, chopped
3 cloves garlic, minced
1½ cups dry lentils
1/2 tsp. pepper
1/4 tsp. basil
1/4 tsp. oregano
16 oz. mushrooms, chopped
2 cups water
2 cups vegetable broth
2 cups stewed tomatoes
6 oz. tomato paste
1 T. balsamic vinegar

Heat a small amount of water in a large skillet over medium high heat. Sauté the onions and garlic until just tender.

Add the remaining ingredients, bring to brief boil, reduce heat, and simmer uncovered about an hour, stirring occasionally.

Quinoa, Black Beans & Corn

Perfect for a potluck or a light summer dinner.

1 cup green onion, chopped
2-3 cloves garlic, minced
1/2 tsp. red pepper flakes
1 tsp. cumin
1 cup quinoa, rinsed well, drained
2 cups canned diced tomatoes, drained, juice reserved
1½ cups vegetable broth
2 cups canned black beans, drained and rinsed
1 cup cooked corn (fresh or frozen and thawed)
1 T. lime juice
2 T. cilantro, chopped

In a soup pot, heat some water or vegetable broth and sauté onion, garlic, and pepper flakes, stirring occasionally, until onion is soft, 3 to 5 minutes. Stir in cumin.

Add quinoa, reserved tomato juice, and broth (there should be exactly 2 cups of liquid) to the sautéed onions and garlic. Bring to a boil, cover, and cook until the quinoa is tender and nearly all the liquid has been absorbed, about 10 minutes.

Add the diced tomatoes, black beans, corn, and lime juice. Stir together over medium-low heat until heated through. Transfer to a serving dish and sprinkle with cilantro. Serve with a basket full of soft, warm corn tortillas and a salad of avocado, romaine lettuce, and sliced oranges. Use a dressing of your choice.

Note: This mildly spicy dish can be prepared completely ahead and reheated at serving time, so it's a great choice for a buffet.

Spiced Couscous and Fruit

Add more curry powder for a spicier taste.

6 green onions, sliced
1 carrot, finely chopped
1/2 cup diced tomato
1/2 cup organic raisins or other dried fruit
2 cups uncooked whole wheat couscous

1½ cup vegetable broth
1 cup apple juice
2 tsp. curry powder (or to taste)

Heat a small amount of water in a large saucepan over medium heat. Sauté the green onions, carrot and tomato for 5 minutes, or until vegetables are tender. Add the fruit. Cook for a minute, stirring frequently.

Add the couscous, broth, apple juice, curry powder, and salt. Bring to a boil. Cover the saucepan, and remove from heat. Let stand until liquid is absorbed—about 5 minutes. Fluff with a fork.

Hot Vegetable Couscous

Garlic has many medicinal qualities. It acts as an antiseptic, antifungal and antibiotic agent in the body. Many studies have indicated its usefulness in improving heart health.

3/4 cup vegetable broth
1 medium onion, chopped
3 cloves garlic, minced
3/4 cup corn kernels, fresh or frozen and thawed
1 green bell pepper, seeded and chopped
8 oz. chopped mushrooms
3 cups tomato puree
1 tsp. chili powder
1 tsp. balsamic vinegar
1 cup whole wheat couscous

Heat 1/4 cup of the vegetable broth in a large skillet over medium high heat. Sauté the onion and garlic for 5 minutes. Add the corn, green pepper, and mushrooms. Cook for 5 minutes.

Add the tomato puree, chili powder, and balsamic vinegar. Cover and simmer for 15 minutes.

While the vegetables are simmering, bring 1½ cups of water to a rolling boil in a saucepan. Add the couscous. Cover the pan and remove from heat. Let stand for 5 minutes. Spoon the vegetables over the couscous and serve.

Fragrant Lentils

Your kitchen will smell delicious when you cook this dish.

1 large onion, sliced thin
2 whole cinnamon sticks
1 lb. dried lentils
1/2 tsp. fresh ginger
2 cups vegetable broth
2 cups hot water
1 tsp. chili powder
1 T. lemon juice
2 garlic cloves, minced
1/2 green chili, seeded and chopped
2 bay leaves
parsley to garnish

In a large saucepan, heat a small amount of water over medium high heat. Sauté the onions and garlic until soft. Add the cinnamon, chili pepper, and ginger and cook for 2 minutes.

Add the broth, hot water, lentils, chili powder, and bay leaves. Bring to a brief boil, reduce heat, add the lemon juice and simmer hard for about 30 minutes, or until lentils are tender. Check at about 20 minutes to be sure all of the water has not been absorbed.

Spiced Garbanzos and Couscous

Many Indian spices have a positive impact on lowering blood sugar levels in diabetics.

1 medium onion, thinly sliced
2 carrots, sliced diagonally
1 cup diced tomatoes
1/2 tsp. ground turmeric
1/2 tsp. ground cumin
1/2 tsp. cinnamon
1 cup cooked garbanzos (if canned, rinse and drain)
4 green onions, sliced
2 cups uncooked whole wheat couscous
1 tsp. jalapeño chilies, diced
3 cups vegetable broth
1/4 cup parsley

Heat a small amount of water in a large saucepan over medium high heat. Sauté the onion, carrots, and tomatoes until tender.

Add the spices, and cook one minute, stirring frequently. Add the garbanzos, green onions, chilies, couscous and broth. Bring to a boil. Cover the pan and remove from heat. Let stand until liquid is absorbed, about 5 minutes. Add parsley. Fluff couscous and serve garnished with additional green onion if desired.

Vegetable-Bean Ragout

This dish requires a few more steps, but it's well worth it!

Ragout

2 large green bell peppers, diced
1½ cups onion, chopped
1/4 tsp. crushed red pepper flakes
28 oz. can crushed tomatoes, with liquid
16 oz. can navy beans, rinsed and drained
15 oz. can garbanzo beans, rinsed and drained
3/4 cup water
1/2 cup fresh basil, chopped
1½ tsp. Italian seasoning blend
1/2 tsp. salt
1/4 tsp. black pepper
2 T. flat-leaf parsley, minced
1 clove garlic, minced
1 tsp. lemon zest

Soft Polenta:

2¼ cups water
1/4 tsp. salt
1/8 tsp. black pepper
1/2 T. chopped fresh basil
1/2 T. chopped flat-leaf parsley
1/2 cup yellow cornmeal

Coat a soup pot with cooking spray; place over medium high heat until hot. Add bell peppers, onion, and crushed red pepper; cook 8 minutes until tender. Stir in tomatoes, navy beans, garbanzo beans, water, basil, Italian seasoning, and salt and pepper. Cover and cook over medium heat for 15 minutes or until thoroughly heated.

Combine parsley, garlic, and lemon zest in a small bowl. Stir well and set aside.

Ladle ragout into bowls; top each with parsley mixture. Serve with soft polenta.

Soft polenta: Bring water to a boil in a medium saucepan. Stir in salt, black pepper, basil, and parsley. Slowly add yellow cornmeal in a stream, stirring constantly, about 15 minutes. Pour into a serving bowl and spoon ragout on top.

Pasta Dinners

Everyone knows that pasta comes in all shapes and sizes, but remember it can also be made from a variety of grains. Corn, quinoa, rice, spelt, and whole wheat all make delicious pasta.

Whole grain pasta retains the fiber from its bran, the outer coating of the grain, as well as the vitamins and minerals found in the germ. Both the bran and germ have been stripped away from conventional pasta. To attempt to regain what is lost nutritionally, United States law requires that the flour be fortified with iron, niacin, thiamin and riboflavin. Whole grain pasta offers fewer calories and more protein, and up to four times the calcium, iron, and magnesium.

Whole wheat pasta is the easiest of the whole foods pasta to find. Now, even many regular grocery stores are carrying it. Whole wheat pasta used to be a very chewy product. It's now being made with a form of wheat that is much lighter. It has about the same texture as conventional pasta, with a fuller flavor. Brown rice pasta substitutes well for wheat pasta. Made from brown rice flour, it's easily digested and offers vitamin E and almost all the B vitamins.

Corn pasta has a subtle corn flavor and comes in a variety of pasta shapes. It contains the amino acid lysine that is usually scarce in other grains. It also provides some calcium and vitamin A. Corn pasta blends well with fresh vegetables, beans, and tomato sauces.

Quinoa pasta contains high quality protein, generous amounts of B vitamins, calcium, and iron. Its nutty flavor blends well with a variety of sauces.

You can experiment with different types of pasta in any of the following recipes.

Artichoke Spirals

Once thought to be an aphrodisiac, artichokes may help to neutralize toxins in the digestive tract. Be sure you don't use artichokes that have been packed in oil.

16 oz. package dry spiral pasta
3 green onions, minced
4 cloves garlic, minced
1 9 oz. package frozen artichoke hearts, thawed
3½ cups diced tomatoes
1/3 cup white wine
1/2 tsp. salt
1/4 tsp. pepper
1 tsp. dried basil
1/2 tsp. dried oregano
1/4 tsp. dried thyme

Prepare the pasta according to package instructions.

Meanwhile, in a large skillet sauté green onions and garlic in a little wine over medium heat for about three minutes. Add artichokes and sauté two minutes more. Stir in tomatoes, white wine, salt, basil, oregano, and thyme. Cover skillet with a lid and reduce heat to medium low. Simmer for 20 minutes. Stir pepper and salt into the sauce, and cook for 5 minutes.

Drain pasta, cover with sauce, and serve.

Spaghetti and Lentils

An unusual pairing that results in great nutrition and excellent taste. Try to use fresh basil whenever possible. It has a pungent, sweet flavor that is quite different when dried.

1 onion, chopped
1 carrot, diced
1 celery stalk, sliced thin
1 green pepper, seeded and diced
8 oz. mushrooms, sliced
1 tsp. basil
1 tsp. oregano
4 oz. tomato paste
14 oz. can stewed tomatoes
1 cup cooked lentils
16 oz. dry whole wheat spaghetti

Heat a small amount of water in a large skillet and sauté the carrot, celery, and pepper for 5 minutes. Add the mushrooms, basil, and oregano and cook for 3 minutes. Add the tomato paste and tomatoes and stir well. Add the lentils. Add a little water if the mixture seems too thick, and simmer for 20 minutes.

Fettuccine with Mushroom Sauce

Portobello mushrooms are definitely worth the expense! They impart a meaty flavor and texture to your recipes. Sometimes as much as 5″ in diameter, they're located next to the common mushroom in the produce department.

16 oz. whole wheat fettuccine noodles
5 large portobello mushrooms (1½ lbs.)
1/2 lb. white mushrooms
6 green onions, minced
4 cloves of garlic, minced
2 tsp. minced fresh rosemary or 1 tsp. dried rosemary, crumbled
1/2 cup dry red wine
1 T. capers

Stem the portobellos and cut into 1/2 inch slices. Stem the white mushrooms and cut them into 1/2 inch slices. Combine the different mushrooms and set aside. Prepare the pasta according to package directions.

Meanwhile, heat a small amount of wine in a large skillet over medium heat. Sauté the green onions, and garlic until soft. Add the mushrooms and sauté, stirring occasionally, until they start to wilt—about 4 minutes. Raise the heat and cook until most of the mushroom liquid has evaporated—about 8 min.

When the mushrooms are barely moist, stir in the rosemary and cook for one minute. Add 1/2 cup of red wine and cook until the sauce thickens—about 3 minutes. Stir in the capers and remove the pan from the heat. Toss the cooked pasta with the sauce.

Wild Mushroom and Tofu Ragout

This would make a great dish for a dinner party. Serve it with an excellent Merlot, a fresh green salad and crusty bread.

1 package low fat, firm tofu cut into bite-sized pieces
1½ cups chopped green onions
6 cloves garlic, minced
16 oz. white mushrooms, stemmed and thinly sliced
2 lbs. cremini mushrooms stemmed and cut into 1 inch cubes
3 portobello mushrooms stemmed and cut into 1 inch cubes
1 cup dry red wine
2 tsp. finely chopped fresh rosemary or 1 tsp. dried rosemary
1 bay leaf
salt

In a soup pot, heat a little wine over medium high heat. Sauté the green onions and garlic until they soften, about 6 minutes.

Stir in the white mushrooms and cook until they release their liquid, 6-8 minutes. Stir in the cremini and portobello mushrooms. Cook until they release their liquid, about 10 minutes. Continue to cook the mushrooms, stirring often, until most of the liquid has been cooked away.

Add 1 cup of red wine and simmer vigorously until it has almost evaporated. Stir in the rosemary and one cup water. Add the tofu and bay leaf. Reduce the heat to medium and simmer mixture for 5 minutes, adding more water to keep the mixture moist. Remove bay leaf. Season to taste with salt and pepper.

Serve over pasta.

Mama's Mock Meatballs

This is a delicious mock meatball.
Don't limit yourself to "meatballs and spaghetti."
Try them in a hero sandwich for a hearty, satisfying lunch.

2 cups cooked millet
1/4 cup yellow onion, minced
1/2 cup mushrooms, minced
3 tsp. dried parsley
1/2 tsp. garlic powder
1/2 tsp. ground black pepper
1/2 tsp. sea salt
1/4 tsp. paprika
1/4 tsp. oregano
1/2 cup dry bread crumbs
1½ tsp. Ener-G egg replacer + 2 T. water
6 cups marinara sauce

Combine all ingredients, except bread crumbs, egg replacer and sauce, in mixing bowl. Stirring constantly, add bread crumbs and egg replacer until mixture is firm enough to form into balls (you may need to add more than the 1/2 cup of bread crumbs). Using wet hands, shape mixture into balls, using about 1½ tablespoons mixture per ball. Balls can be frozen at this point or simmered in sauce for 30 minutes. Alternatively, balls can be baked in the oven on baking sheet at 325° for 30 minutes and served with sauce. Makes about 20 to 22 meatless balls or about 7 servings of 3 balls each and 1/2 cup sauce.

Note: To cook millet, bring 1 cup millet and 2½ cups water to a boil. Cover with a tight-fitting lid and reduce heat to medium. Cook 15 minutes. Remove from heat and let sit uncovered for 20 minutes. Yields about 3 cups.

The meatless balls freeze well and reheat best if cooked in sauce (do not let the balls thaw before reheating in sauce). For best results, reheat the frozen meatless balls in marinara or mushroom sauce. As a time-saver, make a double batch.

Stir-Fry Recipes

Stir-frying is a fast, waterless method of cooking that seals in nutrients. It is a technique you will use often to cook up fast, healthy and delicious meals. Although most stir-fry recipes use oil, it is very easy to eliminate it and simply use vegetable broth. Keep your eyes open for a world of stir-fry recipes. They are quick, easy and fun to experiment with. There are many prepared sauces on the market. Explore Asian markets, grocery stores, and natural food stores for prepared sauces. You can find an amazing variety that do not contain animal products or fat. There's really no easier or faster meal to prepare than a stir-fry!

Tofu can be added to any stir-fry recipe for added protein and flavor. Be sure to use low fat, extra-firm varieties. You can find tofu in the produce section of your market. Mori-Nu now makes a product that does not need refrigeration.

The Basics of Stir-Frying:

- It really pays to invest in a nonstick, flat bottomed wok. It's a versatile pan that works well for a variety of dishes.
- Have everything ready before you start. Cut all your vegetables to a uniform size and thickness so that they will cook evenly.
- First heat the empty wok over medium high heat for a few minutes. Turn up the heat to high and begin to add ingredients in the following order:

  Add 2 T. vegetable broth, and any spices. Heat until fragrant—about 1-2 minutes. As you go along, continue to add just enough broth to keep the vegetables from sticking to the pan. If you add too much, you end up with stewed vegetables—nice, but not good for a stir-fry dish.

  Add ginger, garlic, and/or onions, if you're using them, and heat for about 2 minutes.

  Add vegetables that take longer to cook—cauliflower, broccoli, carrots, celery, and cook for about 2 minutes.

  Add lighter vegetables—mushrooms, summer squash, bell pepper, bok choy, eggplant, water chestnuts, bamboo shoots—and cook for 1-2 minutes.

  Add scallions or tofu, and cook—1-2 minutes.

  Finally, add sauce and stir until it bubbles.

- Be sure you don't crowd your wok with too much food. You need to be able to stir and toss your ingredients constantly throughout the cooking process.
- You can add tofu to any stir-fry recipe. In order to retain the appropriate texture and shape, prepare the tofu as follows before cooking: Cut tofu into 1 inch slices. Lay the slices on some paper towels and cover with more towels. Set a flat pan on the top. Put a one pound can on top of the pan. Let the tofu drain 10-15 minutes. Then cut the tofu into 1 inch cubes. Tofu is usually added toward the end of the stir-frying process, since it requires only a minute or two to be ready.
- Experiment! As you become familiar with stir-frying, you'll want to use your favorite vegetables and sauces in different combinations. Stir-frying is a wonderful way to use vegetables that are in season.

A Basic Stir-Fry Sauce

1 T. cornstarch
1/3 cup Sucanat
1/2 tsp. fresh ginger, minced
1 T. soy sauce
1/4 cup rice vinegar
1/4 cup vegetable broth

Mix the ingredients together in a small bowl with a whisk and set aside. After stir-frying all vegetables, stir in the sauce, and stir-fry for about 2 minutes, or until sauce is thickened and bubbly.

Thai Sauce

You can make this sauce as hot as you wish by adding Tabasco sauce.

2 cloves garlic, minced
4 green onions, sliced diagonally
3 T. fresh lime juice
1 tsp. Sucanat
4 T. soy sauce
1/4 tsp. Tabasco sauce (or more to taste)
2 tsp. cornstarch

Mix all ingredients together in a small bowl with a whisk and set aside. After stir-frying all vegetables, stir in the sauce and stir-fry for about 2 minutes, or until thickened and bubbly. Serve over brown rice.

Sweet Stir-Fry Sauce

Ginger root can be found in the produce section. It is a beautiful, gnarled product that will last quite a long time in your refrigerator. Simply cut off the amount you need, peel it and add to your recipes for a zingy flavor.

4 cloves garlic, minced
1½ tsp. fresh grated ginger root
1/2 tsp. salt
1/2 tsp. ground red pepper
1/4 tsp. ground black pepper
1/4 tsp. cinnamon
1/4 tsp. cardamom
1 T. catsup
1 T. red wine vinegar
1 tsp. water

Mix all ingredients together in a small bowl with a whisk and set aside. After stir-frying all vegetables, stir in the sauce and stir-fry for about 2 minutes, or until thickened and bubbly.

Hot Vegetable Stir-Fry

2 onions, chopped
1 carrot, sliced
1 small zucchini, sliced
1 green pepper, seeded and sliced
8 oz. chopped mushrooms
2 T. soy sauce
1 tsp. cornstarch
1/4 tsp. powdered ginger
3 cloves garlic, chopped
1 tsp. Tabasco sauce (or more according to taste)
1 T. sherry

In a small bowl, mix together the soy sauce, cornstarch, Tabasco sauce, ginger and sherry. Set aside. Lightly coat a nonstick wok with cooking spray. Heat the wok over medium high heat. Add the onions and sauté for 2 minutes. Add the green pepper and sauté for 1 minute. Add the mushrooms and sauté for 2 minutes. Add the sauce, cover and simmer for about a minute, or until bubbly.

Serve over rice.

Spiced Cauliflower and Carrot Stir-Fry

Look for "Lite" soy sauce. It contains much less salt.

1/4 cup vegetable broth
1 T. orange juice
1 T. soy sauce
1½ tsp. cornstarch
1½ tsp. grated fresh ginger root
4 cloves garlic, minced
1/8 tsp. red pepper flakes
2 cups chopped cauliflower
1 cup sliced carrots
1 small zucchini

In a small bowl, stir together the broth, orange juice, soy sauce and cornstarch. Set aside. Lightly spray an unheated wok with cooking spray. Heat the wok over medium high heat. Add the ginger, garlic and red pepper flakes. Stir-fry about a minute, or until fragrant. Add the cauliflower and carrots, and stir-fry for 2 minutes. Add the zucchini and stir-fry for 2 minutes. Stir in the sauce. Bring to a simmer. Cover and simmer about 1 minute or until sauce thickens.

Serve over brown rice.

Asian Vegetable Stir-Fry

Use savoy cabbage if you can't find bok choy. You can find hosin sauce in the Asian foods section of your market.

4 cloves garlic, minced
1 large onion, chopped
1 stalk celery, chopped fine
1 medium bok choy chopped
1 large carrot, chopped
1 cup mushrooms, chopped
4 green onions, sliced
1 can bamboo shoots
2 T. soy sauce
2 T. hosin sauce

Lightly coat a nonstick wok with cooking spray. Heat the wok over medium high heat. Sauté the garlic and onions for 2 minutes. Add the carrots and celery and cook for 2 minutes. Add the cabbage and bamboo shoots and sauté for 2 minutes. Add the green onions and cook for 1 minute. Lower the heat and stir in the soy sauce and hosin sauce. Cook for about 2 minutes, or until the sauce bubbles. Serve over brown rice.

Garlic Sauce Stir-Fry

Chinese garlic sauce is one example of the delicious prepared sauces that are fat free. Look for it in Asian markets or green supermarkets.

1 large onion, chopped
2 cups broccoli, cut into bite sized pieces
2 cups cauliflower, cut into bite sized pieces
1 large carrot, sliced
1 cup mushrooms, chopped
1 cup snow peas
6 cloves of garlic, minced
3 T. soy sauce
2 tsp. cornstarch
1/8 tsp. ground ginger
2 tsp. hot Chinese garlic sauce
2 T. sherry

In a small bowl, mix together the soy sauce, cornstarch, ground ginger, hot Chinese garlic sauce and sherry. Set aside.

Lightly coat a nonstick wok with cooking spray. Heat the empty wok over medium high heat. Add the garlic, and stir-fry for 2 minutes. Add the carrots, broccoli and cauliflower. Stir-fry for 2 minutes. Add the mushrooms and snow peas and stir-fry for 2 minutes.

Reduce heat, add the sauce and stir-fry for about 2 minutes, or until the sauce is bubbly. Serve over rice.

Sweet and Sour Stir-Fry

This is a very different dish from the Sweet and Sour Pork that many people order by habit. Try it and enjoy the difference.

2 cups unsweetened pineapple chunks
1 large onion, sliced
1 bunch of green onions, sliced
1 red bell pepper, seeded and chopped
2 large carrots, sliced
2 cups broccoli, cut into bite sized pieces
4 cloves garlic, crushed
1 tsp. grated fresh ginger
1 cup unsweetened pineapple juice
1/3 cup Sucanat
1/4 cup rice vinegar
3 T. soy sauce
2 T. cornstarch

In a small bowl, combine the pineapple juice, Sucanat, rice vinegar, soy sauce and cornstarch. Set aside.

Lightly coat a nonstick wok with cooking spray. Heat over medium high heat. Add the garlic, onions and ginger and sauté for 2 minutes. Add the carrots and broccoli and sauté for 2 minutes. Add the bell pepper and green onions and sauté for 2 minutes.

Add the pineapple chunks to the sauce mixture. Then, add the sauce to the wok. Cook and stir until the sauce has thickened and is bubbly. Serve over rice.

Chicken-Flavored Tofu Stir-Fry

Broccoli was known in pre-Roman times.
It contains almost as much calcium as whole milk.

1/2 cup water
1/4 cup dry sherry
2 T. soy sauce
1 T. cornstarch
1 tsp. Sucanat
1 tsp. vegetarian chicken-flavored seasoning
3/4 tsp. powdered ginger
1 cup thinly sliced carrots
2 cloves garlic, minced
3 cups broccoli flowerets
1 package, low fat, extra firm silken tofu cut into small cubes

Cut tofu into 1 inch slices. Lay the slices on some paper towels and cover with more towels. Set a flat pan on the top. Put a heavy plate on top of the pan. Let the tofu drain 10-15 minutes. Then cut the tofu into 1 inch cubes.

In a small bowl, mix together the water, sherry, soy sauce, cornstarch, Sucanat, chicken seasoning and ginger. Set aside.

Lightly coat a nonstick wok with cooking spray. Heat the empty wok over medium high heat. Add the garlic and stir-fry 2 minutes. Add the carrots and broccoli and stir-fry 2 minutes. Add the tofu and cook for 1 minute.

Stir in the sauce mixture. Cook until the sauce is thickened and bubbly—about 2 minutes. Serve over brown rice.

Chinese Five Spice Stir-Fry

Chinese Five Spice is a seasoning blend that provides the familiar taste found in many Chinese dishes. Look for one that does not contain MSG.

1/2 cup of pineapple chunks, drained, reserve juice
1 cup broccoli
1/2 cup green beans
1/2 cup snow peas
2 cloves garlic, minced
1/2 cup tofu

1/2 tsp. Chinese five spice mix
soy sauce

Cut tofu into 1 inch slices. Lay the slices on some paper towels and cover with more towels. Set a flat pan on the top. Put a heavy plate on top of the pan. Let the tofu drain 10-15 minutes. Then cut the tofu into 1 inch cubes.

Lightly coat a nonstick wok with cooking spray. Heat over medium high heat. Add the garlic and Chinese spice mix and cook for 2 minutes. Add the broccoli and stir-fry for 2 minutes. Add the green beans and cook for 2 minutes. Add the snow peas and cook for one minute. Add the tofu and cook for 1 minute. Add the pineapple and the soy sauce and cook for 1 minute. Serve over brown rice.

Broccoli and Cauliflower Stir-Fry

Broccoli is a member of the powerful cruciferous vegetable family. Renowned as cancer-fighters, these vegetables contain potent phytochemicals that help neutralize toxins.

1 onion, chopped
1 cup mushrooms, chopped
2 cups broccoli, cut into bite sized pieces
2 cups cauliflower, cut into bite sized pieces
1 cup snow peas
1 large carrot, cut into bite sized pieces
3/4 cup vegetable broth
6 cloves garlic, minced
3 T. soy sauce
2 tsp. cornstarch
pinch of powdered ginger
2 cloves garlic, chopped
2 tsp. Tabasco sauce
2 T. sherry

In a small bowl, mix together the soy sauce, cornstarch, ginger, 2 cloves or garlic, Tabasco sauce and sherry. Set aside.

Lightly coat a nonstick wok with cooking spray. Heat over medium high heat. Add the garlic and onions, stir-fry for 2 minutes. Add the broccoli, cauliflower and carrots, stir-fry for 2 minutes. Add the mushrooms and snow peas, stir-fry for 2 minutes. Stir in the sauce, and cook until thickened and bubbly—about 2 minutes. Serve over rice.

Cauliflower and Red Pepper Stir-Fry

Shallots taste like a blend of garlic and mild onions.
Find them next to garlic in the produce section.

4 carrots, sliced
1 cucumber cut into matchsticks
1 cauliflower cut into bite sized pieces
1 red bell pepper, cut into strips
4 cloves garlic, minced
1/3 cup chopped shallots
1 tsp. red pepper flakes
1/2 tsp. turmeric
1/2 cup rice vinegar
1/2 cup white wine
2 T. Sucanat
2 tsp. cornstarch

In a small bowl, mix together the turmeric, rice vinegar, white wine, cornstarch and Sucanat. Set aside.

Lightly coat a nonstick wok with cooking spray. Heat the empty wok over medium high heat. Add the garlic and shallots and sauté for 2 minutes. Add the carrots and cauliflower and cook for 2 minutes. Add the red bell pepper and cook for 2 minutes. Add the cucumber and cook for 1 minute. Reduce the heat and stir in the sauce. Cook until bubbly. Serve over brown rice.

Sugar Pea Stir-Fry

Sugar Peas are one of nature's great taste treats!

3/4 cup pineapple juice
1 T. Sucanat
1 T. lemon juice
1½ tsp. cornstarch
1 tsp. soy sauce
1 cup broccoli, cut into bite sized pieces
2 medium carrots, sliced
1 cup cauliflower, cut into bite sized pieces
3 stalks celery, sliced
1 red bell pepper, seeded and cut into strips
1 cup sugar peas

In a small bowl, combine the pineapple juice, Sucanat, lemon juice, cornstarch and soy sauce. Set aside.

Lightly coat a nonstick wok with cooking spray. Heat the empty wok over medium high heat. Add the broccoli, carrots, cauliflower and celery, cook for 2 minutes. Add the bell pepper and sugar peas, cook for 2 minutes. Reduce the heat and stir in the sauce. Cook until thickened and bubbly—about 2 minutes.

Serve over brown rice.

Sweet and Sour Tofu

Try to use fresh pineapple whenever possible.
The taste difference is amazing!

1 package low fat, extra firm tofu cut into small cubes
1 large onion, very coarsely chopped
2 cloves garlic, minced
1/2 lb. mushrooms, chopped
1 tsp. fresh ginger, minced
2 cups unsweetened pineapple chunks with juice
1 green bell pepper, seeded and chopped
1 red bell pepper, seeded and chopped
3 T. Sucanat
1/4 cup rice vinegar
1/4 cup catsup
1 T. soy sauce

Cut tofu into 1 inch slices. Lay the slices on some paper towels and cover with more towels. Set a flat pan on the top. Put a heavy plate on top of the pan. Let the tofu drain 10-15 minutes. Then cut the tofu into 1 inch cubes.

In a small bowl, mix together the pineapple, Sucanat, rice vinegar, catsup and soy sauce. Set aside.

Lightly coat a nonstick wok with cooking spray. Heat the empty wok over medium high heat. Add the onion, ginger and garlic—sauté for 2 minutes. Add the bell peppers and sauté for 2 minutes. Add the mushrooms and sauté for 2 minutes. Add the tofu and sauté for 1 minute.

Reduce the heat and stir in the sauce. Cook until bubbly—about 2 minutes. Serve over rice.

Singapore Vegetables

This is an adaptation from a favorite Chinese restaurant.

1 T. cornstarch
1/3 cup Sucanat
1/2 tsp. fresh ginger, minced
1 T. soy sauce
1/4 cup rice vinegar
1/4 cup vegetable broth
1/2 red onion
3 cloves garlic
1 cup carrots, chopped
1 red bell pepper, seeded and chopped
1 small zucchini, sliced
3 cups mushrooms, sliced

In a small bowl, mix together the soy sauce, rice vinegar and vegetable broth. In a separate small bowl, mix together the cornstarch and Sucanat. Add the two mixtures together. Add in the ginger. Set aside.

Lightly coat a nonstick wok with cooking spray. Add the garlic and onion—sauté for 2 minutes. Add the carrots and sauté for 2 minutes. Add the bell pepper and sauté for 2 minutes. Add the mushrooms and zucchini and sauté for 2 minutes.
Reduce heat and stir in the sauce. Cook until thickened and bubbly—about 2 minutes. Serve over rice.

Tahiti Stir-Fry

For a different taste, this recipe uses baked tofu.

6 T. soy sauce
2 tsp. balsamic vinegar
2 tsp. honey
1 T. rice wine
2 tsp. grated fresh ginger
1 package low fat, extra firm tofu, cut into cubes
2 cloves garlic, minced
6 green onions, sliced
2 medium carrots, sliced
3 stalks celery, sliced
1 red bell pepper, seeded and cut into strips
1 green bell pepper, seeded and cut into strips
8 oz. mushrooms, sliced

Preheat the oven to 400 degrees.

In a small bowl, mix together the soy sauce, balsamic vinegar, honey, ginger and garlic. Set aside.

Lightly coat a cookie sheet with cooking spray. Place the tofu cubes on the cookie sheet. Pour ½ of the sauce over the tofu, and bake for 25 minutes.

Lightly coat a nonstick wok with cooking spray. Heat over medium high. Add the carrots and celery—sauté for 2 minutes. Add the bell peppers and sauté for 2 minutes. Add the mushrooms and sauté for 2 minutes.

Reduce the heat, and stir in the remaining sauce. Heat until bubbly—about 2 minutes. Add the tofu.

Spicy Bok Choy with Tofu

1 package low fat, extra firm tofu
3/4 lb. bok choy, chopped
3 cloves garlic, minced
4 green onions, thinly sliced
1 large red bell pepper, seeded and cut into strips
2 T. water
3 T. soy sauce
2 tsp. Sucanat
1 tsp. Tabasco sauce
1 tsp. cornstarch, mixed with 1 T. water

Cut tofu into 1 inch slices. Lay the slices on some paper towels and cover with more towels. Set a flat pan on the top. Put a heavy plate on top of the pan. Let the tofu drain 10-15 minutes. Then cut the tofu into 1 inch cubes.

In a small bowl, mix together the soy sauce, Sucanat, Tabasco sauce, and cornstarch and water combination. Set aside.

Lightly coat a nonstick wok with cooking spray. Heat the empty wok over medium high heat. Add the onion and garlic—sauté for 2 minutes. Add the bell pepper and sauté for 2 minutes. Add the tofu and sauté for 1 minute.

Reduce the heat and stir in the sauce. Cook until bubbly—about 2 minutes. Serve over rice.

More Great Meals

Sloppy Joes

You'll never miss the meat in this traditional kids' favorite. Serve over whole wheat, or multi-grain buns.

1 cup textured vegetable protein
3/4 cup water
1 green pepper, seeded and chopped
1 onion, minced
2 carrots, chopped
1/2 lb. mushrooms, chopped
16 oz. tomato sauce
1½ T. red wine vinegar
1 T. regular molasses
2 T. chili powder
2 tsp. garlic powder

In a small saucepan, bring the water to a boil. Add the TVP, remove from the heat, cover, and set aside. Heat a little water in a skillet and sauté the green pepper, onion, mushrooms, and carrot until soft. Add the TVP, tomato sauce, vinegar, molasses, chili powder, and garlic powder to the skillet. Cook over medium heat for 10 minutes.

Vegetarian Chicken Burgers

Try these with whole wheat hamburger buns, cranberry sauce, and lettuce for a great treat!

1/2 cup bulgur
1 cup boiling water
1 medium onion, chopped very fine
1 tsp. vegetarian chicken flavored seasoning
1/2 tsp. garlic powder
1 cup cooked garbanzo beans, mashed
(if canned, rinse and drain.)

Preheat the oven to 350°.

Stir the bulgur into one cup of boiling water in a saucepan and reduce heat to simmer. Cover and cook for 30 minutes, or until the water has been absorbed. Meanwhile, sauté the onions in a small amount of water until tender.

When the bulgur is cooked, add the onion and the seasonings and mix well. Add the mashed garbanzo beans and mix well.

Make patties. Place on a baking sheet that has been lightly coated with cooking spray. Cook for 10 minutes, then turn over and cook for 15 minutes more.

Veggie Burgers

There are many prepared veggie burgers on the market. Use Garden Burgers, Nature Burgers, or Boca Burgers for convenience. But I think you'll like these even better.

1/2 cup bulgur
1/8 cup steel cut oats
boiling water
1 small onion, finely chopped
1 medium carrot, coarsely shredded
2 cups rolled oats *or* 1 cup quick oats and 1 cup rolled oats
1 cup bread crumbs
1 tsp. thyme
1 tsp. parsley
1 tsp. sage
1 tsp. savory
salt and black pepper to taste
water as needed

Preheat oven to 375°.

In a large bowl add the bulgur and steel cut oats. Cover the bulgur and steel cut oats with boiling water and set aside. Sauté the onion in vegetable broth or water until soft; add the carrot and sauté for another minute. Add the vegetables to the soaking bulgur and steel cut oats and mix well. Add the rolled oats, bread crumbs, thyme, parsley, sage, savory, salt and pepper. Stir well.

Scoop some burger mixture into your hand and squeeze. If the mixture does not hold together, continue adding water a little at a time, until the mixture holds together. Form about 6-8 balls and flatten them into burger shape.

Lightly coat a baking sheet with cooking spray, and arrange the burgers on the sheet. Bake for 10 minutes, then carefully turn each burger to bake the other side for 10 minutes.

Grilled Portobello Sandwiches

Portobello mushrooms are a major treat!
This sandwich is a delicious alternative to a burger.

1 T. balsamic vinegar
2 T. water
1/2 cup oil free Italian salad dressing
1 tsp. minced fresh rosemary
1/2 tsp. pepper
3 garlic cloves, minced
4 portobello mushroom caps
whole wheat buns
lettuce
red onion
tomato

Combine the balsamic vinegar, salad dressing, water, garlic and seasonings in a plastic bag, seal and marinate for at least 30 minutes.

Remove mushrooms from bag, and reserve marinade.

Place the mushrooms on a broiler pan coated with cooking spray. Broil about 6 minutes on each side or until browned, basting with marinade occasionally. Serve on whole wheat buns with lettuce, tomato, red onion, and additional salad dressing if desired.

Summer BBQ's are a tradition for many people. You don't have to be left out. "Kabobs" can be made with vegetarian ingredients and delicious sauces. Try the following recipes, then invent your own.

Spicy Tofu Kabobs

2 packages low fat, extra firm tofu
1/4 cup hosin sauce
1/4 cup white wine
2½ T. soy sauce
1½ T. Sucanat
1½ T. catsup
1 T. powdered ginger
2 red bell peppers, seeded and cut into 1 inch squares
12 small mushrooms
12 pearl onions

Cut the tofu into several slices, and place on paper towels. Top with more paper towels and lay a heavy plate on top. Leave for 15 minutes, then cut into 1½ inch chunks.

In a medium bowl, whisk together the hosin sauce, wine, soy sauce, Sucanat, catsup, garlic and ginger. Add the tofu and toss gently to coat. Cover and let stand at room temperature for an hour.

Add the peppers, mushrooms and onions to the marinade. Toss to coat.

Thread the tofu and vegetables onto 10 skewers. Place on a BBQ grill, or on a single layer on a broiler pan. Brush with marinade and grill for 10 minutes. Turn skewers over and brush with marinade. Grill 10 minutes longer or until vegetables are tender.

Ginger and Garlic Tofu Kabobs

10 pearl onions, peeled or canned
10 medium mushrooms
2 cups pineapple in chunks
2 green peppers, cut into one inch squares
1 lb. of small, whole potatoes
1 package low fat, extra firm, silken tofu
8 cherry tomatoes

Marinade:

1/4 cup soy sauce
1/4 cup dry red wine
1/4 cup water
1 tsp. oregano
1/2 tsp. garlic powder
1/4 tsp. ginger

Cut the tofu into several slices, then place on some paper towels. Put more paper towels on top then add a heavy plate. Leave for 15 minutes, then cut into 1½ inch chunks.

In a small bowl, whisk together the marinade ingredients.

Put the onions, mushrooms, pineapple, potatoes and green pepper in a large bowl. Add the tofu. Pour the marinade over all and toss.

Cover and set in the refrigerator. Marinate 4-5 hours, tossing the ingredients several times.

Thread the ingredients on skewers. Place on a broiler rack or outdoor grill.

Cook until the edges of the fruit are crisp. Turn several times and baste with marinade while cooking.

Spiced Kabobs

1 package low fat, extra firm tofu
1 T. lemon juice
1 1/2 tsp. ginger
1 1/2 tsp. cumin
1 tsp. ground coriander
1/2 tsp. paprika
1/4 tsp. cinnamon
2 medium zucchini, cut in 2 inch pieces
8 cherry tomatoes
1/2 tsp. black pepper

Cut the tofu into several slices and place on some paper towels. Put more towels on top and set a heavy plate on top. Leave for 15 minutes. This will help to firm up the tofu so that it does not fall apart. Cut into 2 inch cubes.

Meanwhile, whisk together the lemon juice, ginger, cumin, coriander, paprika and cinnamon. Add the tofu, cover and refrigerate at least one hour. Loosely thread four skewers alternating tofu with vegetables. Arrange on a broiler pan, or use an outdoor grill.

Cook for about 8 minutes, then turn and cook for 5 minutes more.

Shiskabob Sauce

Use this sweet, tangy sauce to baste skewers made with onions, pineapple, mushrooms, green peppers and tofu.

1 apricot preserves
2 T. orange juice
2 T. prepared mustard
1 T. prepared horseradish

Place all ingredients in a saucepan. Cook over medium high heat until the preserves are melted, stirring constantly.

Stuffed Vegetables

Squash, peppers and zucchini can be stuffed and baked offering a terrific alternative for meat centered meals. Here are several recipes that can easily provide the centerpiece for a meal.

Cranberry Stuffed Squash

Use fresh cranberries when they are in season!

2 large acorn squash
2 cups whole wheat couscous
3 cups water
2 tart apples (Granny Smith or Rome), unpeeled and chopped
1 cup fresh cranberries, or 32 oz. canned whole cranberry sauce
5 T. frozen orange juice concentrate
5 T. maple syrup
1 T. cinnamon
1 tsp. allspice
1 T. orange zest

Preheat the oven to 350°.

Lightly coat a large baking dish with cooking spray, and set aside.

In a medium saucepan, bring the water to a boil. Add the couscous, stir, cover and remove from the heat. Let stand for 5 minutes.

Halve each squash crosswise, and remove fibers and seeds. Place the cut side up in the baking dish.

In a bowl, combine the cooked couscous, apples, cranberries, orange juice concentrate, maple syrup, cinnamon, allspice and orange zest. Spoon the mixture equally into the squash. Any left over stuffing can be placed in a covered casserole dish and baked along with the squash.

Bake until the filling is bubbly and the squash is very soft—about an hour and 15 minutes.

Stuffed Acorn Squash

This dish contains the essence of autumn. The wonderful fragrance of cinnamon wafts through your home while it is cooking. Bulgur has a nice nutty flavor. It is high in fiber and contributes protein. Its chewy texture makes it perfect as a binding medium for other ingredients.

1 cup bulgur
2 cups water
4 medium acorn squash
1 Rome or Granny Smith apple, cored and diced
1 cup organic raisins
3/4 cup orange juice
1/4 cup orange marmalade
1 tsp. cinnamon
1 T. allspice

Preheat the oven to 350°.

Place the bulgur and 2 cups of water in a saucepan. Cover, bring to a boil, reduce heat, and simmer for 15 minutes.

Meanwhile, cut the squash in half and scoop out the seeds. Place cut side down in a baking dish. Add 1/2 cup of water. Bake for 20 minutes.

In a large skillet heat about 1/4 cup of water over medium heat. Add apples, and raisins, and cook, stirring occasionally, four minutes. Stir in the juice, marmalade, cinnamon, and allspice, and cook for 2 minutes.

Remove the skillet from heat. Drain the bulgur and mix it with the skillet ingredients. Remove the baking dish from the oven. Turn the squash so that the cut sides are up. Spoon equal amounts of the filling mixture into the squash. If there is leftover stuffing, it can be placed in a small, covered casserole dish and baked in the oven.

Pour one cup of water into the bottom of the baking dish. Cover with foil and bake for one hour, or until squash is tender. Uncover and bake 5 minutes more.

Rice Stuffed Peppers

Almost everyone enjoys stuffed peppers.
Here the traditional favorite is made without meat.

8 large green bell peppers, stemmed and cored
1/4 cup water
1 onion, diced
2 stalks of celery, chopped
8 oz. mushrooms, chopped
2 cups tomato sauce
3 cups cooked brown rice
1 tsp. thyme
1 tsp. sage
1/2 tsp. basil
1/4 tsp. garlic powder
1½ cups water

Preheat the oven to 375°.

Cook the onions, celery, and mushrooms in the water for about 15 minutes, or until tender. Mix in one cup of the tomato sauce, the rice and seasonings.

Pack the mixture into the raw green peppers, and place them in a large baking dish. Pour the remaining one cup of tomato sauce over the peppers. Add about 1½ cups water to the bottom of the baking dish to prevent the peppers from drying out.

Cover and bake for 45 minutes, then uncover and bake for 15 minutes more.

Variation: Substitute one cup of corn or millet in place of one cup of the brown rice.

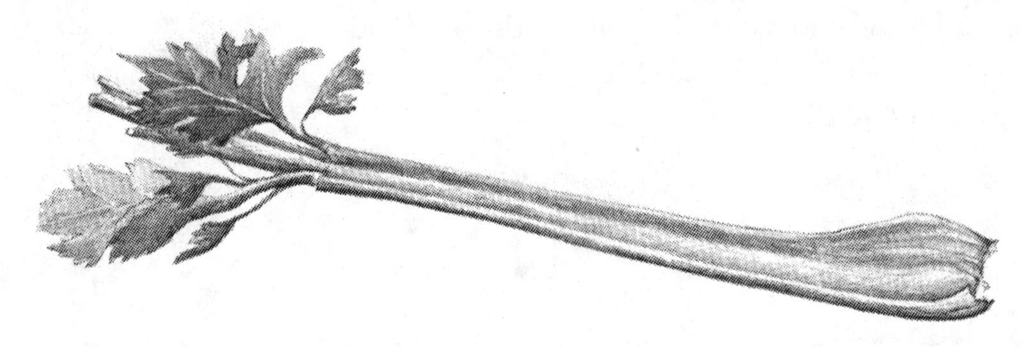

Stuffed Butternut Squash

You can use small pumpkins for this recipe for a colorful change.

4 medium squashes about 1 lb. each
1 medium onion, diced
4 cloves garlic, minced
1 cup cooked wild rice
1/4 tsp. red pepper flakes
1 cup cooked long grain white rice
1/2 cup dry apricots, chopped
1/2 cup organic raisins
1/2 cup minced parsley
1/2 tsp. dried basil

Preheat the oven to 350°.

Halve the squashes and scoop out seeds and fibers. Place the squash cut side up in baking dishes and cover tightly with foil. Bake for 40-50 minutes, or until easily pierced with a knife, but still firm.

While the squash is baking, sauté the onions and garlic in a small amount of water in a soup pot. Add the allspice, and pepper flakes. Then, add the wild rice, white rice, apricots, raisins, parsley, and basil. Heat through.

When the squashes cool enough, scoop out the pulp leaving firm shells about 1/2 inch thick. Chop the pulp and stir it into rice mix. Stuff the squashes, put in baking dishes and cover with foil.

Bake for 20 minutes.

Stuffed Zucchini

A great way to use this prolific summer crop.

4 medium zucchini
2 cloves garlic, crushed
1 medium onion, chopped
1 green pepper, seeded and chopped
1 stalk celery, chopped
8 oz. mushrooms, chopped
1/4 tsp. marjoram
1 tsp. parsley, minced
1 T. Ener-G egg replacer + 4 T. water

Preheat the oven to 350°.

Scrub the zucchini to remove any grit. Bring 6 cups of water to a boil in a soup pot. Boil the zucchini for 10 minutes. Drain and cool. Cut the zucchini lengthwise, scoop out pulp, and dice it. Set aside.

Heat a little water or vegetable broth in a large skillet. Sauté the garlic, onion, green peppers, celery, and mushrooms until tender.

Add the marjoram, parsley and zucchini pulp. Remove from the heat and allow to cool for 5 minutes. Add 1 T. of Ener-G egg replacer to 4 T. of water. Beat well. Fold in the beaten Ener-G mixture with the zucchini mixture. Fill the cavity of each zucchini half with the mixture.

Place in a shallow nonstick baking pan that has been lightly coated with cooking spray. Bake for 30 minutes.

Acorn Squash Stuffed with Quinoa

Quinoa and fruit are made to go together. Find apples, pears and apricots in this fragrant dish.

4 medium acorn squash
4 cups vegetable broth
2 cups quinoa
2 cups apples, cored and chopped
2 pears, cored and chopped
1/2 cup chopped dried apricots
1 T. Sucanat
1 tsp. ground cinnamon
1/2 tsp. ground mace
1/4 tsp. allspice
1/4 tsp. cardamom

Preheat the oven to 350°.

Cut the squash in half lengthwise, and scoop out the fibers and seeds and discard them. Place the halves cut side down, in a baking dish that has been lightly coated with cooking spray. Bake for an hour.

Meanwhile, bring the broth to a boil in a medium saucepan. Add the quinoa, stir and reduce heat to low. Cover and simmer for 20 minutes, or until the liquid has been absorbed. Remove from the heat and let stand for 5 minutes. Fluff with a fork.

Heat a small amount of water in a large skillet. Add the apples, pears, apricots. Cook, stirring frequently, for 5 minutes. Stir in the honey, cinnamon, mace, allspice and cardamom. Cook for 2 minutes. Transfer to large bowl. Add the quinoa and mix well.

Turn the squash cut side up. Divide the quinoa mixture among them. If there is extra stuffing, put it in a casserole dish, cover and bake along with the squash.

Bake for 25 minutes, or until squash is tender.

Potatoes, Rice and Stuffing

Pair rice or stuffing with any dish containing beans for excellent protein in the meal. At holiday time, prepare stuffing in a casserole dish, and serve with lentil loaf for a great celebration meal.

Potatoes deserve their own special place in the world of healthy eating. They are low in calories, and contain protein, iron, phosphorous, thiamin, niacin, B6, copper, magnesium, iodine and folacin. The average potato contains about 11 percent protein, 83 percent carbohydrate, and only 1 percent fat. Most people enjoy eating them.

The potato has a long history. Spaniards brought the first potatoes back from Peru in the 1500s. They quickly became a gourmet treat in Europe. Eventually, the potato traveled back to the Americas with colonists.

The Incas grew hundreds of varieties. Today, only four varieties are grown on a large scale-russet or Idaho, long white, round white and round red—but many other kinds can be found at farmer's markets. Experiment with purple, candy cane, yukon golds and whatever other gems you find.

In general, there are four basic categories to consider—sweet potato, new, baking and all-purpose.

New potatoes are freshly harvested and not fully mature. They are small, thin skinned and good for boiling.

Idaho or russet potatoes are medium to large in size, and have a thicker skin. When cooked, they develop a dry texture that makes them good for mashing. These are used for the traditional "baked potato".

Red potatoes are the most common variety in the all purpose category. They have a waxy texture, and contain less starch. Consequently, they hold their shape better when cooked. This makes them better for stir-frying, or salads.

Sweet potatoes aren't potatoes at all, but members of the morning glory family. They are usually baked, but can be boiled as well.

Always store potatoes in a dark, cool (45-50 degrees) place with a lot of ventilation. If the temperature is too warm, the potatoes will sprout. Never eat a potato that is soft or has sprouted. On the other hand, you can't put them in the refrigerator. The low temperatures will cause the starch to turn to sugar, altering their taste and color.

Methods of Preparation:

Steamed: use new potatoes, and steam for 25-30 minutes. Sweet potatoes can be peeled, cut up and steamed for 25 minutes.

Baked: use Idaho or russet potatoes, pierce skin with a fork, bake at 400° for 60-90 minutes, depending on the size of the potato. Don't wrap in foil; this makes the skin soft and yields a steamed potato, not a baked potato.

Sweet potatoes are commonly baked. Pierce the skin with a fork and place in a 400 degree oven. Bake for 25 and 60 minutes depending on size. Be sure to place foil on the rack underneath them in the oven.

Boiled: use new potatoes, Idaho or russet potatoes. Scrub or peel, cut into even pieces. Cover with cold water. Bring to a boil, turn down the heat and gently boil, covered or uncovered, until tender. Depending on the size of the pieces and the type of potato, this will take between 15 and 30 minutes. Don't over boil- doing so makes waterlogged potatoes. Check the cooking potatoes frequently, and remove them when they become tender. Drain well, then mash if desired.

Potato Salad

Great potato salad doesn't have to be drenched in mayonnaise.

3 lbs. red potatoes
1 medium onion, sliced
1/2 cup prepared mustard
1 cup pickle relish
1 green pepper, seeded and diced
1/2 tsp. dried dill weed
pepper to taste

Quarter the potatoes. Place them in a soup pot. Add water to cover and boil until potatoes are tender—about 20 minutes. Drain and cool. In a small bowl, thoroughly mix the other ingredients together. Toss with the potatoes, coating them evenly. Chill.

Garlic Roasted Potatoes

Watch this dish carefully, and add water if it becomes too dry.

2 lbs. small red potatoes, halved
6 cloves garlic, sliced
1/4 cup fresh parsley, chopped
1/2 tsp. lemon zest
1/2 tsp. salt
1/4 tsp. black pepper
1/4 cup water

Preheat the oven to 425°s. Coat a nonstick roasting pan with cooking spray.

In a medium bowl combine the potatoes, garlic, parsley, lemon peel, salt and pepper. Place the mixture in the pan, along with the water, and bake for 25 minutes, turning the potatoes three times during baking. Add more water to prevent sticking.

Sweet Potato Cakes

Kids absolutely love these!

4 sweet potatoes, peeled and coarsely shredded
1/4 cup whole wheat pastry flour
1 small onion, minced
1/8 tsp. salt
1/8 tsp. pepper
1½ tsp. Ener-G egg replacer + 2 T. of water

Combine all ingredients in a bowl and mix well. Lightly coat a large nonstick skillet with cooking spray. Spoon about 1/4 cup of the mixture onto the hot skillet, and flatten slightly with a spatula. Cook 4 minutes on each side, or until golden brown.

Cranberry Sweet Potatoes

Cranberries shouldn't be confined to Thanksgiving tables. Not only are they delicious, but they have antibacterial and antiviral properties.

6 medium sweet potatoes, peeled and cut into one inch chunks
1/2 cup firmly packed Sucanat
2 T. orange juice
1/2 tsp. salt
1 cup whole berry cranberry sauce
1 T. orange zest

Preheat the oven to 350°.

Place the sweet potatoes in a soup pot with enough water to cover. Bring to a boil and cook for 25-30 minutes, or until tender. Drain and place in a large casserole dish. Combine the Sucanat, orange juice and salt in a saucepan. Heat until it barely begins to boil, stirring constantly. Add the Sucanat mixture and cranberry sauce to the potatoes and toss gently. Cover and place in the oven for 25 minutes, basting with sauce once during cooking. Uncover, baste, and cook for 15 minutes more.

Potato Pancakes

Serve with homemade applesauce

4 T. oat flour
1 cup shredded potatoes, pressed dry
1/4 cup diced onion

Mix the oat flour with enough water to make a pancake batter consistency. Add the onions, potatoes, salt, and pepper. Lightly coat a nonstick pan with cooking spray. Heat the pan over medium high heat. Spoon in the batter to make 4 pancakes. Cook until golden brown, turn over and cook the other side.

Baked Potato Wedges

Say good-bye to greasy fries

2-4 medium Idaho potatoes, scrubbed and cut into wedges
garlic powder, cajun seasoning mix, or any favorite seasoning

Preheat the oven to 400°.

Lightly coat a nonstick baking sheet with cooking spray. Cut the potatoes lengthwise, into wedges, sprinkle with seasoning.

Bake for 25-30 minutes, or until easily pierced with a fork.

Oven Fries

This is a similar recipe to the one above. When the potatoes are cut into smaller pieces, the cooking requirements change.

2-4 Idaho potatoes
garlic powder, cajun seasoning mix or any favorite seasoning

Preheat the oven to 450°.

Cut the potatoes into french fry sized pieces. Place on a nonstick baking sheet, lightly coated with cooking spray. Sprinkle with your favorite seasoning mix. Bake for 15 minutes, then turn over potatoes. Cook for 10-15 minutes more, depending on the thickness of the slices. Do not overcook.

Baked Potato Skins

2-4 Idaho potatoes, scrubbed and pierced with a knife
Oil free Italian dressing
Salt and pepper

Preheat the oven to 450°.

Bake the potatoes for 45 minutes, then cut in half lengthwise, leaving 1/4 inch next to skin. Scoop out the insides and reserve for another use.

Season the skins lightly with salt and pepper, then brush with oil free Italian salad dressing. Broil until lightly browned.

Pineapple Sweet Potatoes

Incredible with Pilgrim's Lentil Loaf

6 medium sweet potatoes
1 cup crushed pineapple
1/4 cup Sucanat
1/2 tsp. cinnamon
1/2 cup water

Preheat the oven to 350°.

Boil the sweet potatoes for 25-30 minutes or until tender. Allow them to cook, then peel, and cut into 1/2 inch slices.

Lightly coat a casserole dish with cooking spray. Alternate layers of pineapple and sweet potatoes, sprinkling each layer with Sucanat. Pour the water over the mixture.

Bake for 30 minutes.

Orange Sweet Potatoes

Excellent with any savory loaf.

6 sweet potatoes, peeled and thinly sliced
8 lemon slices
2/3 cup firmly packed Sucanat
1 T. orange zest
1/2 cup orange juice

Preheat the oven to 400°.

Arrange the sweet potatoes and lemon slices in a large casserole dish lightly coated with cooking spray. Combine the Sucanat, orange zest and orange juice in a small bowl. Drizzle the Sucanat mixture over the potatoes. Cover with foil, and bake for 35 minutes. Uncover, stir well and bake 30 minutes more.

Garlic Mashed Potatoes

You can make wonderful mashed potatoes by using oat milk. Prepare these with the garlic or not, and serve with a healthy gravy.

7 Idaho potatoes, peeled and cubed
4 vegetable bouillon cubes
6 cloves garlic
1/2 cup unflavored oat milk
1/2 tsp. salt
1/8 tsp. pepper

Place the potatoes, bouillon cubes and garlic in a soup pot. Cover with water, and bring to a boil. Reduce heat and simmer hard for 20 minutes, or until potatoes are tender. Drain, reserving 1/4 cup of the liquid. Return the potatoes and garlic to the soup pot. Stir in the salt, pepper and reserved liquid. Add about 1/4 cup of the oat milk, then beat at medium speed until desired consistency is achieved, adding more oat milk as needed.

Garlic Mashed Potatoes and Turnips

The turnips and horseradish provide a tangy, interesting flavor!

6 large baking potatoes, peeled and cubed
3 turnips, peeled and cubed
8 cloves garlic, sliced
1/2 cup unflavored oat milk
4 tsp. prepared horseradish
1 tsp. salt
1/4 tsp. nutmeg
1/4 tsp. pepper
4 T. chopped fresh chives

Combine the potatoes, turnips, and garlic in a soup pot with enough water to cover. Bring to boil then cover and reduce heat. Simmer for 20 minutes, or until vegetables are tender.

Drain well and place in a large bowl. Mash well, and add the oat milk, horseradish, salt, nutmeg and pepper. Beat at medium speed, until desired consistency is achieved, adding more oat milk as needed. Sprinkle with chives.

Sherried Sweet Potatoes

A sweet accompaniment to lentil dishes.

6 large sweet potatoes
5 T. sherry
3/4 cup orange juice
1/2 tsp. nutmeg
2 T. Sucanat
1 tsp. cinnamon

Preheat the oven to 400°.

Bake the sweet potatoes for 50 minutes or until tender. Remove from the oven and allow to cool. Turn down the oven to 350°. Peel the potatoes, cut them into small pieces and place in a large bowl. Mash well. Blend in the sherry, orange juice and nutmeg, and mash again. Season to taste with salt and pepper.

Place into casserole dish that has been lightly coated with cooking spray. Sprinkle with a mixture of the Sucanat and cinnamon.

Cover and bake for 25 minutes at 350 degrees.

Hash Browns

These are excellent for breakfast, or any time. Look in the frozen potatoes area of your market for "potatoes only" options. Read the label to make sure that nothing has been added in. Or, you can use your own coarsely grated and pressed potatoes.

Preheat the oven to 450°.

Lightly coat a nonstick baking sheet with cooking spray. Place the potatoes on the sheet in a single layer. Bake for 15 minutes, turn over and bake for 10 minutes more.

Variation: You can mix together minced onion, diced green or red peppers and the potatoes to have "hash browns O'Brien". You can sprinkle the potato mixture with garlic, paprika, or any favorite spice mix.

Baked Sweet Potato Slices

A surprising and delicious sweet treat.

4 medium sweet potatoes, peeled and cut into 1/4 inch slices
1/4 tsp. salt
1/4 tsp. pepper
1 T. finely chopped fresh parsley or 1½ tsp. dried parsley
1 tsp. orange zest
1/4 tsp. garlic powder

Preheat the oven to 400°.

Combine the sweet potatoes, salt, pepper, and parsley in a large bowl. Toss gently to coat the potatoes. Place the sweet potatoes in a single layer on a baking sheet that has been lightly coated with cooking spray.

Bake for 15 minutes, then turn the slices over. Bake for 20 minutes more, or until slices are tender.

Combine the parsley, orange zest and garlic powder in a small bowl. Mix well. Sprinkle the mixture over the sweet potatoes and serve.

Mashed Parsnips and Potatoes

Garlic becomes very mild when boiled.

6 large baking potatoes, peeled and cut into chunks
4 parsnips, peeled and sliced
12 cloves garlic, halved
2 bay leaf
1 tsp. salt
1/2 tsp. pepper
1/2 cup of unflavored oat milk

Combine the potatoes, parsnips, garlic, and bay leaves in a soup pot. Cover with water, bring to a boil. Cover and reduce heat. Simmer for 25 minutes, or until tender. Drain and discard bay leaves.

Combine the potato mixture, oat milk, salt, and pepper in a bowl. Beat at medium speed until desired consistency is achieved, adding more oat milk as needed.

Sautéed Red Potatoes

8 red potatoes, scrubbed and quartered
1/2 cup vegetable broth
4 garlic cloves, crushed
1/4 tsp. rosemary crushed very fine

Heat a little of the vegetable broth in a nonstick skillet over medium high heat. Sauté the potatoes and the rosemary for 15 minutes, adding more broth as needed. Toss occasionally to make sure the potatoes are evenly cooked.

Add the garlic and sauté 5 minutes more. Sprinkle with a little fresh parsley and serve.

Caramelized Sweet Potatoes

A truly decadent side dish

4 large sweet potatoes
6 T. orange marmalade

Place the sweet potatoes in a soup pot and boil about 30 minutes, or until tender. Allow to cool, then peel and dice.

Melt the orange marmalade in a large skillet over medium low heat. Add the sweet potatoes, and cook gently in the sauce until glazed and brown.

Maple Sweet Potatoes and Apples

Serve this delectable dish with Holiday Lentil Loaf.

6 large sweet potatoes, peeled and sliced into 1/4 inch rounds
6 Granny Smith or Rome apples, cored and sliced
3/4 cup maple syrup
1/2 cup Sucanat
3/4 cup apple cider
1 tsp. pumpkin pie spice

Preheat the oven to 400°.

Arrange the sweet potatoes and apples in a 9 by 13 casserole dish in alternating layers.

In a saucepan, bring syrup, Sucanat, pumpkin pie spice and cider to the very beginning of a boil. Remove from the heat and pour over the sweet potatoes and apples. Sprinkle with a little Sucanat.

Cover the casserole with foil, and bake one hour. Uncover, baste, and bake until sweet potatoes are soft and syrup is thick—about 15 minutes.

Rum-Flavored Sweet Potatoes

6 large sweet potatoes, peeled and thinly sliced
3 large Granny Smith or Rome apples, cored and sliced
1/2 cup Sucanat
1/3 cup honey
1 tsp. allspice
1 T. lemon juice
1½ T. rum extract

Preheat the oven to 375°.

In a small bowl, combine the Sucanat, honey, allspice, lemon juice and rum extract.

Layer the potatoes, apples and Sucanat mixture in a large casserole dish that has been coated with nonfat cooking spray.

Cover and bake for 30 minutes. Uncover and bake for 20 minutes more, or until potatoes are tender.

Potatoes and Herbs

Parsley often meets an undistinguished fate at the side of a dinner plate. Don't judge this delicious herb by its limp restaurant appearances. Fresh parsley is crisp and aromatic. It has excellent blood-purifying qualities as well.

2 bunches of fresh spinach
2 large baking potatoes, peeled and cut into chunks
2 T. green onion, minced
2 T. fresh parsley, minced or 1 T. dried parsley
2 T. fresh dill, minced or 1 T. dried dill
1 tsp. salt
oat milk as needed

Place the potatoes in a soup pot with enough water to cover. Boil for 20 minutes, or until tender. Meanwhile, wash the spinach and remove the stems. Steam for 5 minutes, then chop into fine pieces.

In a large bowl, mash the potatoes and spinach together. Add the green onions, parsley, dill, salt and enough oat milk to achieve desired consistency.

Stuffed Sweet Potatoes

6 large sweet potatoes
6 T. regular molasses
1 tsp. powdered ginger
1 T. chopped green onions

Preheat the oven to 400°.

Pierce the sweet potatoes several times with a knife, then bake for about 50 minutes or until tender. Allow to cool, then scoop out the pulp and reserve the skins.

Combine the molasses, ginger and chives in a large bowl, then add the sweet potato pulp. Blend together, then return the pulp to the potato skins. Bake for 20 minutes, or until heated through.

Note: you can also discard the potato skins and place the mixture in a casserole dish. Bake uncovered for 20 minutes, or until heated through.

Garbanzos, Sweet Peppers and Roasted Potatoes

Easily a main dish.

2 tsp. curry powder
1/2 tsp. salt
1½ pounds Idaho potatoes, cut into one inch cubes
2 cups cooked garbanzo beans (if canned, rinse and drain)
1 large red pepper, cored, seeded and cut into strips
4 T. soy sauce
1 green onion, minced

Preheat the oven to 425°.

Mix together the curry powder and salt. Toss with the potatoes in a large bowl. Transfer to a baking sheet that has been lightly coated with cooking spray. Bake for 20 minutes or until the potatoes are tender. Remove potatoes from oven, and arrange on a platter.

Meanwhile, toss the garbanzo beans and bell peppers with the soy sauce. Spoon over the potatoes and sprinkle with green onions.

Whipped Pineapple Sweet Potatoes

A perfect contribution to a holiday meal. Pineapple contains components closely related to human gastric juices. It's a powerful digestive aid.

6 medium sweet potatoes, unpeeled, cut into chunks
1/2 cup pineapple juice
2 T. chopped pineapple
1/4 tsp. cinnamon
1/4 tsp. nutmeg
1/4 tsp. allspice
pinch each cinnamon, nutmeg and allspice
2 T. regular molasses

Preheat the oven to 350°.

Place the sweet potatoes in a soup pot. Cover with water and boil about 30 minutes, or until tender. Allow to cool, then remove the skins.

In a large bowl, mash the sweet potatoes, add the pineapple juice and whip until fluffy. Add the chopped pineapple and spices.

Spoon into a large casserole dish that has been lightly coated with cooking spray. Spread the molasses over the top, and bake uncovered for about 25 minutes, or until heated through.

Sweet Spiced Rice

Brown rice has a more earthy flavor than white rice. Its texture is chewier, and its nutrients are intact.

1 cup carrots, thinly sliced
3/4 cup apple juice
2 T. lemon juice
2 T. Sucanat
1 tsp. salt
1 cup brown rice
1/2 tsp. cinnamon
1/2 cup organic raisins
5 green onions, sliced
2 apples, sliced and unpeeled

Heat a small amount of water in a skillet over medium heat. Cook the carrots for 5 minutes or until they are just tender. Add 1¼ cups water, the lemon and apple juice, Sucanat and salt. Bring to boil, and stir in the rice, cinnamon and raisins. Simmer covered for 25-45 minutes, or until rice is tender. Stir in the green onions and apples. Cook until heated through.

Lemon Rice

A delicious way to use leftover rice. Lemon zest is the fresh grated peel from a lemon. You can also find it dried in the spice section of the market.

3 stalks celery, chopped
5 green onions, sliced thin
1 cup cooked brown rice
1 tsp. lemon zest
1/4 tsp. salt

Heat a small amount of water in a skillet and cook the celery and onions until just tender. Stir in the rice, lemon zest and salt. Cook until heated through.

Vegetable Rice

This recipe is also good reheated in a skillet like traditional "fried rice". Simply heat a small amount of water in the skillet and add the rice. When the rice starts to stick to the bottom of the pan, add a little more water. You can also add additional vegetables if you like.

1 small onion, chopped
1 green pepper, seeded and chopped
8 oz. mushrooms, chopped
1 tsp. basil
1 cup brown rice
2 cups water

Heat a small amount of water in a skillet and cook the onion, green pepper, and mushrooms for 10 minutes. Add the basil, rice and water. Bring to a boil, reduce heat, and simmer covered until the rice is tender—25-45 minutes.

Wild Rice Pilaf

Wild rice isn't really rice at all, but the seed of grasses growing in the Great Lakes section of America. Much of it is still harvested by the Native Americans who have inhabited the regions for centuries. Using small wooden boats and traditional tools, the rice is gathered by hand.

1/2 cup wild rice
1 tsp. salt, divided
1 cup white rice
1 clove garlic, minced
3 T. orange juice
1 tsp. orange zest
1/4 tsp. pepper
4 green onions, sliced
1 orange, peeled and segmented
1/2 cup organic raisins
2 T. chopped fresh cilantro

Bring the wild rice, salt, and three cups of water to a boil in a saucepan. Reduce the heat, cover and simmer for 20 minutes. Stir in the white rice and simmer covered for 20 minutes more. Meanwhile whisk the garlic, orange zest and pepper together in a bowl. Add the green onions, orange, raisins and cilantro. Add the cooked rice and toss well.

Harvest Stuffing

Excellent with any lentil loaf on the holiday table. It contains walnuts, so reserve it for special meals.

2 large carrots, shredded
2 stalks celery, chopped
1 onion, chopped
1 tsp. sage or poultry seasoning
1/2 tsp. salt
1/4 tsp. cinnamon
1/8 tsp. pepper
10 slices dry whole wheat bread cubes
2 apples, peeled and finely chopped
1/2 cup chopped walnuts
1/4 cup wheat germ
1/2 to 3/4 cup vegetable broth

Preheat the oven to 325°.

In a large bowl, combine the bread cubes, chopped apple, walnuts and wheat germ and set aside. Heat a small amount of water in a skillet over medium high heat. Cook the carrot, celery, and onion until tender. Stir in the sage or poultry seasoning, salt, cinnamon and pepper. Add the cooked vegetable mixture to the bread crumbs. Drizzle with enough broth to moisten and toss. Bake covered for 20-30 minutes.

Wild Rice Stuffing

A personal favorite

1 onion, diced
4 cloves garlic, minced
1 cup wild rice
3½ cups vegetable broth
1/4 tsp. red pepper flakes
1 cup long grain white rice
1/2 cup dried apricots
1/2 cup organic raisins
1/2 cup minced parsley
1/2 tsp. dried basil

Preheat the oven to 350°.

Heat a small amount of water in a soup pot over medium high heat. Cook the onions and garlic until just tender. Add the wild rice, broth, allspice, pepper flakes, and bring to a boil. Cover and simmer for 20 minutes. Add the white rice, apricots, raisins, parsley and basil.

Place in a casserole dish, cover and bake for 10 minutes. Remove the cover and bake for 15 minutes more.

Walnut-Apple Stuffing

A special stuffing that is wonderful served with Pilgrim's Lentil Loaf.

10 slices whole wheat bread cubes
1 onion, chopped
2 tart apples, peeled and diced
10 green onions, minced
2 T. chopped fresh parsley
1/2 tsp. thyme
1/2 tsp. savory
3/4 tsp. seasoned salt
1/2 cup finely chopped walnuts
3 T. organic raisins
ground pepper to taste
1½ cups apple cider

Preheat the oven to 350°.

Place the diced bread on a baking sheet. Bake 10-12 minutes, or until dry and lightly browned. Heat a small amount of water in a skillet over medium high. Cook the onion until just tender. Add the apple and cook for 5 minutes more.

In a medium bowl, combine the bread cubes with the onion and apple. Add the rest of the ingredients, except the apple cider. Toss together. Sprinkle in the cider slowly, stirring to moisten the mixture evenly.

Place in a casserole dish and bake 25-30 minutes, stirring once during cooking.

Sauces

The most familiar sauce to the American palate is gravy. You can still have it! Loma Linda and Hain's both make excellent vegetarian, low fat, gravy mixes. And there are lots of other sauces that are delicious and nutritious. Experiment with the sauces you will find in this section as a start.

Mushroom Sauce

Experiment with different types of mushrooms to achieve different flavors.

2 lbs. of mushrooms, chopped
4 green onions, chopped
1/4 cup all purpose flour
1½ cups vegetable broth
1¼ cups water
1/4 cup dry red wine
2 tsp. tarragon
2 tsp. lemon zest
2 T. lemon juice
2 tsp. balsamic vinegar
1/4 tsp. black pepper

Heat a small amount of red wine in a skillet over medium heat. Add the mushrooms and green onions. Cover and cook for 5 minutes, or until the mushrooms release their moisture.

Put the flour in bowl. Gradually add the vegetable broth, stirring until well blended. Add the water, wine, tarragon, lemon zest, lemon juice, balsamic vinegar and black pepper to the flour mixture. Pour over the mushrooms in the skillet. Bring to a brief boil, then reduce the heat and simmer, uncovered for 10 minutes, or until thickened, stirring constantly.

Orange Sauce for Savory Loafs

This tastes especially good with lentil loaf.

1/4 cup vegetable broth
1/4 cup minced shallots
3 cloves garlic, minced
1 lb. mushrooms, chopped
1/2 cup flour
1 cup orange juice
1 cup water
1 cup vegetable broth
2 T. Sucanat
1 T. chopped fresh rosemary
1 T. chopped fresh parsley
1 T. orange zest
2 T. orange liqueur

Heat 1/4 cup of broth in a skillet over medium heat. Add the shallots, garlic, and mushrooms and cook until all of the liquid has evaporated. Add the flour and stir until it disappears. Whisk in the orange juice, water, and remaining vegetable broth. Cook until smooth. Blend in the Sucanat, herbs, orange zest and orange liqueur, and cook for 2 minutes.

Apricot Sauce for Savory Dishes

You won't miss gravy with a delectable alternative like this. Apricot nectar is located in the juice section of your market.

1 cup apricot nectar
1 T. soy sauce
1/2 cup marsala wine
1 cup vegetable broth
3 cloves garlic, minced
1 tsp. pepper
1 tsp. Sucanat
1 tsp. dried chervil
2 tsp. cornstarch mixed with 1 T. water

Place all of the ingredients in a saucepan and blend well. Cook for 20 minutes over low heat.

Honey Garlic Sauce

This is a wonderful sauce to use over steamed vegetables. There are many ethical honey producers. Try not to buy ordinary honey—it is often gathered by destroying the bees. Honey bees are in serious decline due to pesticide use. Honey is technically an animal product—you may choose not to use it. Never give honey to children under 6 years old.

1 cup of beer
1 cup honey
4 cloves garlic, minced
1 tsp. thyme
1 tsp. sea salt

Place all of the ingredients in a saucepan and blend well. Cook over medium heat, stirring continually, for 5 minutes.

Mushroom Onion Gravy

Great with mashed potatoes.
You can make this gravy with oat or soy milk.

1 package vegetarian dry onion soup mix
1½ cups oat milk
1/2 cup dry red wine
2 T. cornstarch mixed with 4 T. warm water
8 oz. mushrooms, chopped

In a saucepan over medium heat, combine the onion soup mix, oat milk, and wine. Cook for 2 minutes. Add the mushrooms and cook for 2 minutes.

Add the cornstarch, stirring constantly until thickened.

Veggie or Potato Topping

You don't have to load vegetables or a baked potato with butter.
Try this delectable sauce instead.

3/4 cup tomato paste
1 tsp. dry mustard
1 T. Sucanat
1/2 tsp. salt
1 T. vinegar
1 T. horseradish
1 T. chopped onion, chives or herbs

Place all of the ingredients in a small bowl and blend together well.

Brandy Sauce

1 T. Sucanat
1/2 cup apple juice
1/4 cup brandy
1 cup vegetable broth
1 tsp. lemon juice
1/2 tsp. salt
1/4 tsp. allspice
1½ T. cornstarch dissolved in 2 T. of water

Place the Sucanat and apple juice in a saucepan over medium heat. Stir constantly for 1 minute. Add the brandy, lemon juice, salt and allspice and cook for 1 minute. Increase the heat to high, whisk in the cornstarch, cook until thickened, stirring constantly, about one minute.

Marinara Sauce–1

Many people have treasured recipes for marinara sauce that have been handed down through their families. Here are a trio of favorites that you can use to start your own tradition. This is our family favorite when fresh tomatoes are not in season. Sauté broccoli, cauliflower, and zucchini to serve on top of the marinara.

1 onion, chopped
1/2 pound mushrooms, chopped
15 oz. can Italian-style stewed tomatoes
15 oz. can tomato puree
15 oz. can tomato sauce
1/2 tsp. dried basil
1/2 tsp. oregano
2 cloves garlic, minced
2 tsp. Italian seasoning *or* The Spice Hunter 'Italian Pizza Seasoning'
2 green bell peppers, seeded and chopped
2 T. parsley flakes

Sauté the onion, mushrooms, and garlic in a small amount of water for 10 minutes. Add the remaining ingredients. Simmer, uncovered, over low heat for 1 to 2 hours, until thick.

Variation: Add one can of water-packed artichoke hearts, and one-quarter teaspoon red pepper flakes.

Marinara Sauce–2

4 cups tomato sauce
24 oz. tomato paste
1½ cups water
2 onions, chopped
1 tsp. basil
2 tsp. thyme
1 T. + 1 tsp. oregano
2 T. garlic powder
2 tsp. rosemary
1 tsp. pepper
Sucanat to taste

Mix all ingredients together in a saucepan. Simmer for at least 1 hour. The longer this cooks, the better it will taste. Add prepared TVP if you wish to make a more substantial sauce.

Marinara Sauce–3

2 onions, diced
6 cloves garlic, minced
2 28 oz. cans stewed tomatoes
6 oz. tomato sauce
1/4 tsp. pepper
1 tsp. oregano
1 tsp. basil
2 green peppers, seeded and diced
8 oz. mushrooms, chopped
4 medium carrots, sliced thin
8 oz. oil free sun-dried tomatoes
2 cups water

In a small saucepan, boil the water and add the sun-dried tomatoes. Remove from the heat, cover, and allow to stand for 15 minutes. Drain and chop. Combine the sun dried tomatoes, and all remaining ingredients in a soup pot. Bring to a brief boil, then reduce heat, and simmer for at least 1 hour. The longer you cook this, the better it will taste.

Spicy Tomato Sauce

Great with Millet Lentil Loaf

3 medium onions, chopped
5 cloves garlic, minced
6 tomatoes, chopped
4 oz. can diced green chilies
1 tsp. basil
1 tsp. oregano
1 T. Sucanat
1/3 cup red wine

Heat a little water in a skillet over medium high heat. Sauté the onions and garlic until the onion is tender. Stir in the remaining ingredients. Heat to a boil, then reduce heat, cover, and simmer for 1 hour. The longer it cooks, the better it will taste.

Spicy Cranberry Sauce

A fantastic addition to the holiday table.
You won't ever want to eat canned cranberry sauce again!

2 cups fresh cranberries
1 cup Sucanat
1/2 tsp. ginger
1 T. cornstarch
1 firm pear, cored and chopped
1 T. lemon zest
1 T. lemon juice
1/4 cup amaretto

In a large saucepan, combine the Sucanat, ginger, cornstarch and one cup of water. Bring to a boil, reduce heat, and simmer for 5 minutes. Stir in the pear and the amaretto, and simmer for 3 minutes. Add the cranberries and cook until the cranberries pop. Cool to room temperature, and stir in the lemon juice, and lemon zest.

Maple Cranberry Sauce

Be sure you buy real maple syrup. "Pancake syrup" has no connection to the maple tree! Real maple syrup contains a substantial amount of calcium, and imparts a lovely taste.

3 cups fresh cranberries
2/3 cup organic raisins
1/2 cup maple syrup
1/2 cup honey
1/4 cup cider vinegar
1/2 tsp. allspice

Combine all ingredients in a large saucepan. Bring to a boil, reduce heat, and simmer 10 minutes or until the cranberries have popped. Serve warm.

Raisin Sauce

Traditionally served with ham, this is a delicious choice with savory loafs.

1 cup organic raisins
1/3 cup Sucanat
1½ T. cornstarch
1/4 tsp. cloves
1/4 tsp. cinnamon
1/4 tsp. dry mustard
1/4 tsp. salt
1 T. rice vinegar

Combine the raisins and 1½ cups water in saucepan. Boil for 5 minutes. Reduce the heat to a simmer, stir in the Sucanat, cornstarch, cloves, cinnamon, dry mustard, and salt. Cook, stirring constantly until thickened. Stir in the vinegar and cook for about 1 minute more.

Vegetables!

It is common for a vegetarian at a dinner party to be served a few uninspiring vegetables, and a dinner roll. It seems that many people think that is all we eat! Hopefully, you have seen that there are countless ways to combine vegetables, grains, beans, pasta and sauces to make delicious meals. Furthermore, vegetables don't have to be boring. They offer beautiful colors and wondrous flavors when freshly picked, seasoned with herbs and spices and properly cooked.

Vegetables have everything. They are low in calories, fat and cost, yet high in almost everything required for our health.

Vegetables are filled with the phytochemicals that are so essen tial to the prevention of disease and the creation of glowing health. They contain an enormous variety of vitamins, minerals, enzymes and many other substances that contribute to our well-being.

In addition, the fiber found in the stems, leaves, roots and other structural parts of vegetables plays a vital role in good health.

Unfortunately, many of us learned to see vegetables as items that came out of a can. Usually, they were boiled until they were pale, limp, flavorless things that were only saved by loading on the butter and salt. Furthermore, all but the most common vegetables have become unfamiliar. When I shop at a regular supermarket, I often have to help the checkout clerk identify the items from her own produce department. The beautiful array of colorful vegetables once grown in home gardens and country farms are now unfamiliar.

Buy local, organic produce whenever possible. It not only helps your health, but the local economy as well. Try to concentrate on recipes that call for the produce that is currently in season. Items grown out of season are often subjected to processes that leave them nearly devoid of nutrients. If you must buy processed vegetables, get those that are frozen, not canned.

Use a steamer basket to prepare your vegetables whenever you can. Vegetables that are still colorful, and crisply tender have more nutrients, flavor and fiber. simply place the vegetables in the steamer basket over boiling water. Arrange them in a single layer if they are whole, or layer cut up vegetables no more than 2 inches deep. Cover the pan, reduce the heat so that the water continues to boil and begin timing. Make sure your pot doesn't run dry.

Why Organic?

When you eat foods that have been grown organically, you avoid the pesticides and herbicides that are used in typical farming. Pesticide residue penetrates the peel of many fruits and vegetables. Some herbicides and insecticides are absorbed through the roots and leaves of fruits and vegetables. Washing and peeling removes only about 25 percent of such residues.

To be considered organic, crops must be grown without synthetic pesticides, on land that hasn't had synthetic chemicals applied during the last three years.

To be labeled organic, at least 95 percent of the ingredients in prepared foods must be organically grown. The product may contain no artificial additives or preservatives.

Organic food may look a little odd to you at first. It might not appear perfect. In order to look that way, fruits and vegetables are waxed, colored, and dusted with chemicals. Doesn't it make more sense to cut away any blemished parts, than to allow a flood of pesticides into your body?

When you buy organic, you help to support small farmers whose practices support the health of the soil, the cleanliness of the water supply, and whose hearts and hands are still connected to a living Earth.

The sales of organic foods have surged 20 percent in each of the last six years. If your grocery store has no organic products, ask that they begin to carry them. It should be possible to find organic produce, wine, pasta, canned goods, prepared foods, tortilla chips, cereals, and a huge variety of frozen foods in grocery stores.

Vegetables

Artichokes: Remove the stem and cut off the tips of the leaves. Place the artichoke bottom up in a steamer basket and steam about 40 minutes, or until a fork can easily penetrate.

Herbs and Spices: basil, black pepper, chervil, garlic, ginger, lemon, oregano, parsley, shallots. Look for a variety of animal free, no fat sauces in your market. You might try Nayonnaise—a mayo substitute made of tofu. Add some garlic and lemon for a delicious sauce.

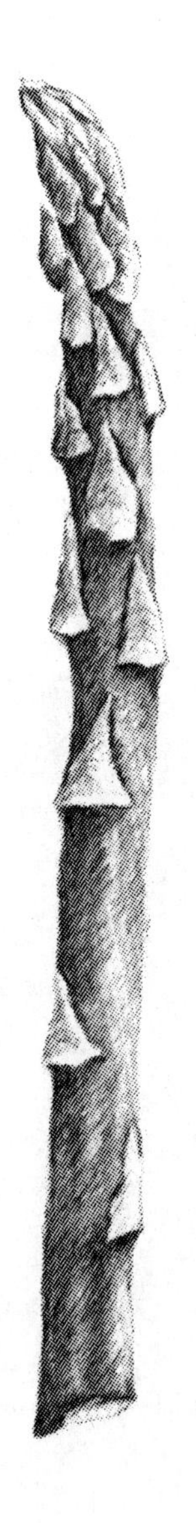

Asparagus: Look for narrow stalks with tight heads. Take one stalk at a time and bend until it breaks. Use the part with the head, and reserve the rest for another use (like a delicious soup). Scrub the stalks with a vegetable brush under running water to remove sand. Steam for 4-6 minutes, or add to a stir-fry.

Herbs and Spices: chives, lemon, lemon balm, nutmeg, orange, parsley, sage, savory, tarragon, thyme

Bell Peppers: These are now available in orange and yellow, as well as the familiar green and red. Peppers must be seeded before using. Simply slice off the top and bottom, and cut the pepper lengthwise on one side, open the pepper until it's flat. Run a knife sideways along pepper to remove the ribs and seeds, then rinse. Bell peppers are delicious in salads, stuffed with grains, or added to a stir-fry dish.

Herbs and Spices: basil, black pepper, chili, dill, garlic, lemon, lemon balm, marjoram, oregano

Broccoli: This vegetable provides some of the most potent anticancer phytochemicals yet discovered. Try to include it as often as possible. Chop the most dense part of the stem away and use the more tender top part of the stem and the florets. Steam 6-9 minutes, add to a stir-fry or use in salads.

Herbs and Spices: basil, black pepper, caraway seed, celery seed, chili, curry powder, dill, garlic, lemon, lemon balm, marjoram, mustard, oregano, tarragon, thyme

Brussels Sprouts: This is another vegetable with active cancer-fighting compounds. Look for small heads with tight leaves. Steam 6-10 minutes, or bake 25-30 minutes at 350°.

Herbs and Spices: black pepper, lemon, maple syrup, nutmeg, onion, orange, parsley, shallots, thyme

Cabbage: Another potent cancer fighter, learn to include it as often as you can- the benefits are enormous. Chop cabbage, discarding the dense stem. Steam 4-6 minutes, or add to a stir-fry. Cabbage made into healthy coleslaw is another delicious alternative. Bok choy is a form of mild cabbage found in many Asian dishes. Try it as another alternative.

Herbs and Spices: allspice, basil, black pepper, caraway, cayenne pepper, chili, dill, fennel seed, ginger, marjoram, nutmeg, onion, sage, savory, soy sauce, vinegar, wine

Carrots: Fortunately, most people like carrots. They are filled with beta-carotene, a potent antioxidant. Eat them raw, or cut them into slices and steam for 8-11 minutes.

Herbs and Spices: allspice, basil, Sucanat, caraway seed, cardamom, chervil, cinnamon, clove, cumin, curry, dill, ginger, marjoram, orange, parsley, sage, savory, maple syrup, tarragon, thyme

Cauliflower: Another warrior in the fight against cancer, cauliflower tastes like mild cabbage. Remove the stem, cut into pieces and steam 6-10 minutes.

Herbs and Spices: basil, black pepper, capers, caraway seed, chervil, chili, chive, cumin, curry dill, garlic, lemon, marjoram, mustard, nutmeg, parsley, savory

Corn: Please don't ever boil this vegetable again! Steamed corn remains bright in color and sweetly delicious. Look for tight, small kernels—try white or blue corn for a change. Steam 10-12 minutes.

Herbs and Spices: basil, chervil, chili, chive, cilantro, cumin, curry, lemon balm, nutmeg, oregano, parsley, sage, thyme, turmeric

Eggplant: This vegetable is a member of the nightshade family. Some people are sensitive to its compounds. If you have joint pain, try eliminating, tomatoes, eggplant and potatoes from your diet. Eggplant can be bitter, so always peel it and soak the slices in salted water for about 15 minutes before using in recipes.

Green Beans: Along with corn, green beans have been the most abused vegetable. Never boil them, and don't use canned green beans. Buy them fresh whenever possible. Just remove the string and slice off the ends. Steam 8-10 minutes, or add to stir-fry dishes.

Herbs and Spices: basil, chervil, chili, chive, cilantro, cumin, curry, lemon balm, nutmeg, oregano, parsley, sage, thyme, turmeric

Green Peas: Steam for 8-10 minutes.

Herbs and Spices: basil, caraway, chervil, chive, dill, lemon, nutmeg, savory, shallot, tarragon, thyme, marjoram

Mushrooms: Many people are only familiar with canned button mushrooms—a taste disaster. Buy fresh, plump, firm mushrooms, or dried varieties. For an exceptional treat, try portobello mushrooms. Their texture and taste can be amazing similar to meat. Many markets now carry a variety of exotic mushrooms—try them and see what you like. Mushrooms are excellent sautéed in a small amount of wine, garlic and rosemary.

Herbs and Spices: balsamic vinegar, black pepper, coriander seed, garlic, lemon, marjoram, gram marsala, nutmeg, parsley, rosemary, shallot, sherry, tarragon, thyme, wine

Onions: Onions can be white, yellow, red or green. Use the red and green ones fresh in salads, or as a topping for chili or burgers. Yellow onions can be added to recipes, sautéed or even baked whole. To bake, simply add ½ cup of vegetable broth to the bottom of a baking dish. Bake at 375 degrees for 1½ hours.

Although you can't actually fry onions without oil, you can achieve something delicious. Chop the onions and cook them in a small amount of liquid. When they just start to stick to the bottom of the pan, add a very small amount of liquid. Allow them to just start to stick, then add liquid. Repeat this process until they achieve the texture and color you want.

Parsnips: This is a delightful, sweet vegetable that looks like a white carrot. In generations past, parsnips were common on the dinner table. You can boil them for 10-15 minutes, then mash them and add spices and a little maple syrup. They're excellent baked—350 degrees for about 50 minutes.

Herbs and Spices: dill, chervil, ginger, mace, pumpkin pie spice

Potatoes: New potatoes can be steamed for 15-30 minutes, depending on size.

Idaho or russet potatoes can be boiled—scrub or peel, cut into even pieces, cover with cold water. Then heat the water to a rolling boil, turn down the heat to medium and boil gently uncovered until tender. Check the potatoes at 15 minutes—don't over cook or they become water logged and mushy. Drain well.

The traditional baked potato is an Idaho or russet. Scrub and pat dry, then pierce the skin a few times with a fork. Bake at 400 degrees for 1-1/2 hours, or more depending on size. Run a knife through the potato to check to see if it's done. Continue to cook if you like the skin more crispy.

Herbs and Spices: basil, caraway, cardamom, cayenne pepper, chives, cilantro, dill, fennel, garlic, mustard, nutmeg, onion, oregano, parsley, rosemary, tarragon, thyme

Spinach: This vegetable is a powerhouse of antioxidants! Eat it as frequently as you can. Spinach is wonderful fresh as a much more nutritious salad than lettuce can offer. You can make a wilted spinach salad by washing fresh leaves, then placing in a skillet over low heat with a small amount of water. Cook until the desired "wilt" is achieved, then add a wonderful oil free dressing. Boiled spinach is the most familiar to most people, but a better result can be had by steaming. Buy fresh or frozen and chop. Steam 6-8 minutes for fresh, or 10-15 minutes for frozen.

Herbs and Spices: basil, black pepper, chervil, chive, dill, garlic, lemon, nutmeg, onion, oregano, parsley, rosemary, shallot, thyme

Squash: Squash comes in two basic categories, hard skinned or winter squash, and soft skinned, often called summer squash.

Winter squash, like acorn and pumpkin, requires cooking: cut off the stem, scoop out all the seeds and string. Cut into halves or quarters, and place cut side down in a baking dish. Bake at 375-400° until tender. Depending on the size and variety of squash, this can take from 45 minutes to 1 ½ hours, or more.

> **Herbs and Spices:** Sucanat, caraway, cinnamon, clove, coriander, curry, ginger, honey, mace, nutmeg, onion, oregano, rosemary, thyme.

Summer squashes are delicious raw, but I think they're even better lightly steamed. Cut them into medium sized pieces and steam. Usually 4 minutes is plenty.

> **Herbs and Spices:** basil, black pepper, chive, cilantro, dill, garlic, onion, parsley, savory, tarragon, thyme oregano, shallots, ginger, chili peppers

Sweet Potatoes: An absolute winner in providing beta carotene. Peel and cut into pieces and steam 25-30 minutes. To boil, place unpeeled in large pot and cover with cold water, boil, covered until tender when pierced 30-45 minutes.

Drain and peel as soon as you can handle them. To bake, pierce the skin with a fork and bake at 350 degrees for 1½ hours. Be sure to put foil on the rack below to prevent a messy cleanup.

> **Herbs and Spices:** cinnamon, allspice, nutmeg, honey, maple syrup, Sucanat, honey

Tomatoes: A member of the nightshade family, tomatoes can provoke inflammation in the joints for some people. If you suffer with pain, try eliminating tomatoes, eggplant and potatoes from your diet.

The tomatoes you can buy in a regular market are so tasteless they're hardly worth eating. Grow your own in the summer. They're easy to produce and full of flavor. Tomatoes can be stuffed and baked, sautéed, eaten raw or dried.

> **Herbs and Spices:** basil, bay leaf, black pepper, chives, dill, garlic, marjoram, onion, oregano, parsley, rosemary, savory, tarragon, thyme

Orange and Ginger Carrots

Carrots are excellent detoxifiers—helping to cleanse and nourish the entire body. This dish provides a subtle and delightful taste difference.

3/4 cup orange juice
3 cups carrots, cut into 1½ inch pieces
2 T. finely chopped fresh ginger root or 1 T. powdered ginger
1 T. honey
1 tsp. orange zest
1/4 cup water

Combine the carrots and orange juice in a medium saucepan. Stir in the ginger, honey, orange zest and water.

Bring the mixture to a brief boil, then reduce the heat. Simmer until the carrots are just tender, about 8 minutes, adding a little water if necessary.

Zucchini, Corn and Tomato Sauté

Zucchini can grow to an impressive size! Choose small, fresh squash for the most flavor.

1 medium onion, chopped
1 green pepper, seeded and cut into strips
3 small zucchini, sliced 1/4 inch thick
1/4 cup water
1 large tomato, chopped
2 cups of freshly cut corn (about 3 ears) or 16 oz. frozen corn kernels
1/4 tsp. oregano
1/4 tsp. marjoram
pinch of crumbled rosemary
1/4 tsp. basil

Using a large skillet, heat a little water and sauté the onion and green pepper for four minutes over medium high heat. Add the spices, corn and 1/4 cup water. Cover and simmer for 7 minutes. Remove the cover, add the zucchini and sauté for two minutes. Add the tomato and sauté for another 2 minutes.

Note: This dish is very easy to season with your favorite spices. Experiment with dill, garlic, marjoram, tarragon, thyme, lemon balm, chervil.

Herbed Baked Tomatoes

Fresh tomatoes are essential the this dish.

4 large tomatoes, diced
1/2 tsp. Sucanat
1/2 tsp. onion powder
1/4 tsp. basil
1/4 tsp. oregano
1/8 tsp. black pepper
1/2 cup unsalted cracker crumbs

Preheat the oven to 350°.

Mix together the Sucanat, onion powder, basil, oregano, and pepper. Add the tomatoes and stir well. Place in a casserole dish that has been coated with cooking spray. Top with the cracker crumbs.

Bake uncovered for 25 minutes.

Variation: Mix the tomatoes with 3 T. vegetable broth, 1/4 cup of fine bread crumbs, 2 cloves of minced garlic, 1 tsp. chopped parsley. Place in a casserole dish and bake for 25 minutes.

Baked Parsnips in Orange

Almost every time I buy parsnips, I have to identify them for the checkout clerk. This vegetable deserves to be rediscovered! It is sweet, almost nutty in flavor. Almost everyone enjoys them.

1 lb. parsnips
1/4 cup orange juice
2 T. Sucanat
1 tsp. orange zest

Preheat the oven to 400°.

Peel the parsnips and slice them about 1/2 inch thick. Place them in a casserole dish. Mix the orange juice, Sucanat and orange zest together and pour over the parsnips.

Cover and bake for 40-50 minutes, adding more orange juice, or a little water during cooking if needed.

Very Simple Green Beans

A delicious option in a pinch.

2 packages frozen green beans
1/4 cup catsup
1/2 tsp. Sucanat

Preheat the oven to 325°.

Thaw the green beans. Place in a small casserole dish. Mix in the catsup and Sucanat. Cover and bake for 30 minutes, stirring once during baking.

Italian Broiled Tomatoes

6 large tomatoes
1/2 cup unsalted cracker crumbs
1/2 cup oil free Italian dressing

Slice the tomatoes in half crosswise. Lightly coat a nonstick cookie sheet with cooking spray. Place tomatoes on the sheet, cut side up.

Combine the crumbs and dressing. Sprinkle over each tomato. Place about 10 inches under the broiler, and cook for about 4 minutes or until golden brown.

Sautéed Zucchini

Marjoram has a flavor like sweet oranges. Folklore contends that it will bring love and happiness.

1 lb. zucchini, scrubbed and sliced thin
1 onion, chopped fine
1 tsp. marjoram
1 tsp. dill

Heat a little water in a skillet and sauté the onion until soft. Add the zucchini and spices. Sauté for 1 minute. Cover and reduce heat. Add a little water if necessary and simmer for 5 minutes.

Note: experiment with the spices you like. Thyme, oregano, shallots, garlic, pepper, ginger, even chili peppers taste good.

Pepper Slaw

Cabbage has probably been cultivated for thousands of years. Its benefits are substantial—stimulating the immune system, cleansing the digestive tract, killing bacteria and stimulating the liver.

1 medium head cabbage, finely shredded
1 cup cider vinegar
1 cup water
1/2 cup Sucanat
1/2 tsp. salt
2 medium green peppers diced fine
1 medium red pepper, diced fine
2 T. celery seed

In a small bowl, combine the vinegar, water, Sucanat and salt. In another bowl, mix the cabbage, peppers, and celery seed. Add in the vinegar mixture, and mix well. Cover and chill for several hours.

Stir-Fried Tomatoes and Peppers

1 green pepper, cut into strips
1 red peppers, cut into strips
16 oz. mushrooms, sliced
2 stalks celery, cut into 1/2 inch slices
2 T. chopped onions
1 clove garlic, crushed
1/4 tsp. oregano
1/2 tsp. black pepper
4 tomatoes cut into wedges
1/4 tsp. Sucanat
1/4 tsp. salt
1/2 tsp. white vinegar

In a large skillet, heat a little water. Add the green pepper, red pepper, mushrooms, celery, onion, and garlic. Sauté over medium high heat until the peppers are just tender. Add the tomatoes, oregano, black pepper, Sucanat, salt and white vinegar. Mix well. Cook for about 5 minutes, stirring constantly.

Green Beans in Apricot Sauce

1 lb. green beans
3 carrots, sliced
1/2 cup apricot preserves, melted
1 tsp. nutmeg
1/2 tsp. salt

Bring about 2 inches of water to a boil in a medium saucepan. Add the green beans and carrots, cover and simmer for 5 minutes. Drain and place in a serving bowl. Toss with the rest of the ingredients.

Savory Green Beans

Vegetarian Worcestershire sauce can be found at your natural food store.

2 packages frozen green beans, thawed
4 T. red wine vinegar
1/2 tsp. prepared yellow mustard
2 T. vegetarian Worcestershire sauce

Preheat the oven to 325°.

Place the vinegar, yellow mustard and Worcestershire sauce in a casserole dish and mix thoroughly. Place the green beans in the dish and toss together with the sauce.

Cover and bake for 30 minutes, stirring once during cooking.

Stuffed Tomatoes

4 large, ripe tomatoes
1 small onion, chopped
2 T. chopped parsley
1 slice whole wheat bread crumbled
1 cup cooked brown rice
1 T. oregano
salt and pepper to taste

Preheat the oven to 350°.

Cut off the stem end of each tomato, and hollow it out leaving a half inch shell. Reserve the pulp. Turn the tomatoes upside down on a rack to drain.

Heat some water in a skillet, and sauté the onion and parsley until the onion is tender. Add the onion mixture, bread crumbs, rice and oregano to the tomato pulp, mix thoroughly and season to taste with salt and pepper.

Fill the tomatoes with the mixture and bake for 20-30 minutes.

Simple Squash

1 lb. small zucchini
1 lb. small yellow crookneck squash
1/2 cup vegetable broth
1/2 cup chopped parsley
2 T. lemon juice
1/4 tsp. pepper
1 tsp. salt

Cut the squash into strips about 2 inches long. Bring the vegetable broth to a boil in a saucepan. Add the zucchini, squash, and 1 tsp. salt. Bring back to a boil, then reduce the heat to low. Cover and simmer for 3 minutes, or until vegetables are just tender. Drain.

Return the vegetables to the saucepan and place over low heat. Stir in the parsley, lemon juice, and pepper.

Sweet and Sour Salad

This is a variation on the simple salad often found in Japanese restaurants.

1 medium cucumber, sliced very thin
1 green or red bell pepper, seeded and chopped fine
1 T. honey or Sucanat
1/4 cup tarragon vinegar
1/2 red onion, sliced very thin

Place the honey and vinegar in a small saucepan and heat over medium heat until aromatic. Add more Sucanat or honey if you wish. Toss with the cucumber, bell pepper, and onion. Place in the refrigerator overnight. The longer the cucumbers marinate, the better they are.

Candied Parsnips

If you've never tried parsnips, here's your chance!

2 lbs. parsnips, peeled and sliced
1½ cups Sucanat
1/2 tsp. nutmeg
1/2 tsp. cinnamon
1/2 tsp. allspice
1/4 cup water

Preheat the oven to 375°.

Lightly coat a shallow baking dish with cooking spray. Mix together the Sucanat, nutmeg and cinnamon. Pour the water in the baking dish, then layer the parsnips, sprinkling the Sucanat mix over each layer.

Cover with foil and bake for 50 minutes. Remove the foil and bake another 15 minutes.

Dutch Mashed Potatoes with Sauerkraut

This is a dish from my childhood. If you enjoy sauerkraut, try it!

6 large baking potatoes, unpeeled, cut into chunks
6 cups of water
1 16 oz. jar of sauerkraut
4 cubes vegetable bouillon
salt and pepper to taste

In a soup pot, bring the water and bouillon cubes to a boil. Put in the potatoes and sauerkraut and boil until tender, but not mushy—about 25 minutes.

Drain the potatoes and sauerkraut, reserving 1 cup of the liquid. Return to the soup pot and mash, adding reserved liquid as needed to achieve desired consistency. Season with salt and pepper.

Cabbage Colcannon

6 large baking potatoes, peeled and cut into small chunks
7 cups of water
4 leeks, thoroughly cleaned and chopped
(use white part only)
1 head of cabbage, shredded
1/4 tsp. black pepper
1/2 tsp. savory
1/2 tsp. salt

In a soup pot, bring the water to a boil. Put in the potatoes, leeks, and cabbage. Boil until the potatoes are tender, but not mushy—about 25 minutes.

Drain the vegetables, reserving 1 cup of the liquid. Return to the soup pot and mash, adding reserved liquid as needed to achieve desired consistency. Add the spices, and mash again.

Stuffed Mushrooms

12 large whole fresh mushrooms
1/4 cup sliced green onion
1/3 cup fine dry whole wheat bread crumbs
1/2 tsp. dried dill
1/4 tsp. salt
1/2 tsp. vegetarian Worcestershire sauce
2 T. balsamic vinegar

Preheat the oven to 325°.

Wash and drain the mushrooms. Remove the stems and chop them into very small pieces. In a skillet over medium high heat, cook the chopped stems and green onion in the balsamic vinegar until tender. Add a little water if needed.

Stir in the bread crumbs, dill, salt and Worcestershire sauce.

Fill the mushroom caps with the mixture.

Coat a nonstick baking sheet with cooking spray. Bake the mushrooms, uncovered for about 15 minutes, or until heated through.

Mushrooms and Onions in Wine

Mild and tasty, pearl onions are tiny white onions.

1 lb. mushrooms, quartered
1 16 oz. can pearl onions, rinsed and drained
2 T. whole wheat flour
1/4 cup chopped parsley
1/2 bay leaf
1/2 tsp. rosemary, crumbled very fine
1/4 cup dry red wine

Heat a small amount of wine in a skillet over medium high heat. Add the onions and rosemary, and sauté for 5 minutes. Add the mushrooms and sauté for 2 minutes. Add the flour, parsley, rosemary, and a little wine. Stir very well and cook for about 3 minutes, or until the onions are tender.

Cole Slaw

A summertime favorite transformed into a healthy treat. You can add a little chopped jalapeño pepper for a spicy alternative.

1 head of cabbage, chopped
1/4 head of red cabbage, chopped
2 carrots, grated
2 T. balsamic vinegar
6 T. cider vinegar
2 T. mustard
1 T. soy sauce
2 T. honey
1/2 tsp. celery seed
1/2 tsp. caraway seed
black pepper to taste

Mix the dressing ingredients together in a large bowl. Add the vegetables and mix well. Refrigerate for at least one hour. To save time, use one package of organic cole slaw mix in place of the cabbage and carrots.

Baked Cauliflower

An unusual way to prepare this valuable vegetable, it makes an interesting presentation on the table.

1 head of cauliflower
1/2 tsp. dill
1 tsp. lemon zest
1 clove garlic, minced
1/2 tsp. cumin
1/4 tsp. salt
1/2 cup water

Preheat the oven to 350°.

In a bowl, mix together the dill, lemon, garlic, cumin, salt and water. Trim all leaves from the cauliflower; cut the stem even with the bottom of the head. Place the cauliflower in a large casserole dish.

Pour the spice mixture over the top and sides of the cauliflower. Cover with foil.

Bake until tender—about 1 hour and 15 minutes.

Cabbage and Corn

Rice vinegar is sweeter and more mild than other kinds of vinegar. Look for it in the Asian foods section, or along side other vinegars.

1/2 cup Sucanat
1/2 tsp. salt
1/2 tsp. dry mustard
1/8 tsp. pepper
1/2 cup rice vinegar
1 small head cabbage, coarsely shredded
2 cups fresh corn or canned
1 green bell pepper, chopped

In a large saucepan, combine the Sucanat, salt, dry mustard, pepper, and vinegar. Bring to a boil. Add the cabbage and stir well. Return to a boil, then cover and simmer until the cabbage is crispy—tender. About 10 minutes. Add the corn and green pepper. Cook for another 10 minutes.

Desserts!

Yes you can eat dessert and be healthy too. The following dessert recipes contain no added fat, and lots of nutritious ingredients. However, if you are trying to lose weight, too much sugar can slow your progress. You may choose to limit how often eat these sweet treats. Some people are especially sensitive to sugar. If your triglycerides are high, sugar may be the culprit. Of course, if you have problems with high blood sugar, use these recipes for very special celebrations.

Chocolate Zucchini Brownies

Yes! Chocolate brownies! Ripe banana provides a substitute for oil.

Wet ingredients:
- **1 cup grated zucchini**
- **1 medium ripe banana, mashed**
- **1 T. water**
- **2 tsp. vanilla**

Dry ingredients:
- **1 cup whole wheat pastry flour**
- **1 cup unbleached flour**
- **1½ tsp. baking soda**
- **1/2 tsp. salt**
- **1/3 cup cocoa powder**
- **2/3 cup Sucanat**

Preheat the oven to 350°.

Place the wet ingredients in a medium bowl. Fold in the dry ingredients. The batter will be stiff.

Place the batter in a baking pan that has been lightly coated with cooking spray. Bake for 25-35 minutes, or until a toothpick inserted in the center comes out clean.

Strawberry 'Ice Cream'

Try growing strawberries in the summer.
There are new varieties that will yield the season through.

- **1 pint ripe strawberries,**
- **2 large *or* 3 small very ripe organic bananas**
- **juice of 1/2 lemon**

Peel ripe bananas, cut into two-inch chunks, coat with lemon juice. Fold them tightly in plastic wrap or wax paper, then freeze. When you're ready to make the ice cream, place the banana and strawberries in the blender and process until smooth.

Dairy Free Pumpkin Pie

This is an unbelievably delicious recipe. No one can tell that the eggs and milk in traditional pumpkin pie are missing. Serve it with the whipped topping recipe at the end of this chapter.

1 package silken, firm tofu (not low fat)
1 tsp. vanilla
1 T. molasses
16 oz. pumpkin puree
3/4 cup Sucanat
1/2 tsp. salt
1 tsp. cinnamon
1/2 tsp. ginger
1/4 tsp. cloves

Preheat the oven to 425°.

Cut the tofu into small pieces and place in the blender. Add the vanilla and molasses. Process until smooth.

In a medium bowl, blend together the pumpkin and Sucanat. Stir in the salt and spices. Add the tofu and mix together well. Pour into a graham cracker pie crust. Bake for 15 minutes, then lower the heat to 350 degrees, and bake for 40 minutes more. Chill for at least 2 hours.

Creamy Banana Smoothies

Bananas are high in potassium, an important ingredient to normal heart function. Include a banana and extra water on hot summer days.

organic bananas
lemon juice
fresh or frozen fruit (blueberries, cherries, peaches, raspberries, strawberries)
granola *or* toasted nuts (optional)

Peel ripe bananas, cut into two-inch chunks, coat with lemon juice. Fold them tightly in plastic wrap or wax paper, then freeze. Pull the frozen bananas out as needed and place in the blender with fresh or frozen fruit and top with granola or toasted nuts.

Hint: The riper the banana, the stronger its flavor, so use the ripest bananas with fruits that can stand up to robust flavor competition, like strawberries.

Apple Pie with Millet Crust

A wonderful recipe to enjoy in the fall.
You can substitute cornstarch for the arrowroot.

1/4 cup pumpkin seeds
2/3 cup millet, rinsed well
1/2 cup apple juice or cider
7 medium Gravenstein apples, grated
1/8 tsp. salt
1/2 to 1 tsp. cinnamon
dash nutmeg
1 T. arrowroot
1/4 cup fresh cranberries, halved

Preheat the oven to 375°.

Place pumpkin seeds in a single layer in a 9-inch pie plate and bake until popped, about 10 to 15 minutes; stir seeds once or twice while cooking. When done cooking, coarsely grind pumpkin seeds in a mortar and pestle or coffee grinder.

Combine pumpkin seeds and millet in a clean bowl. Pour apple juice into a small pot and bring to a boil; remove from heat and pour over seed/millet mixture. Stir well to mix, then pour into pie plate. Use a wooden spoon to push mixture up the sides of the pie plate.

In another bowl, combine grated apples, salt, cinnamon, and arrowroot; mix well Spoon this mixture over the millet crust; smooth with the back of a spoon. Top with halved cranberries, cover with foil, and bake 45 minutes to 1 hour. Let cool completely before slicing.

Banana Oatmeal Cookies

These cookies are a healthy dessert your kids will love.

1 jar baby food prunes
1 tsp. baking soda
1/2 cup Sucanat
1/2 tsp. salt
1½ tsp. vanilla
1 tsp. cinnamon
3 ripe bananas, mashed

1/4 tsp. nutmeg
1½ tsp. Ener-G egg replacer + 2 T. of water
3 cups rolled oats
1 cup whole wheat flour
1 cup organic raisins
1/2 tsp. ground cloves

Preheat the oven to 375°.

Mix the prunes, Sucanat, vanilla and bananas in a large bowl. Whisk egg replacer and water until frothy and add to the mixture. Stir in flour, cloves, soda, salt, cinnamon, nutmeg, and rolled oats. Add raisins. Drop batter by rounded teaspoonfuls 1-inch apart on a nonstick baking sheet. You should end up with about 50 cookies. Bake for 12-15 minutes.

Strawberry Pie

You can use graham cracker or grape nuts pie crust with this recipe for an excellent pie.

1 cup Sucanat
1/2 cup mashed strawberries
3 T. cornstarch
1 T. lemon juice
2 cups sliced strawberries
2 ripe organic bananas, sliced

Add enough water to the mashed strawberries to make 1 cup. Combine the lemon juice, Sucanat, mashed strawberries, and cornstarch in a saucepan. Cook over medium heat until thick. Arrange the sliced strawberries and sliced bananas in the bottom of a pie crust. Pour the mixture over the fresh fruit and chill for at least 2 hours.

Easy Crustless Apple Pie

Another delicious and easy apple pie recipe to try.

5 cups sliced apples
1/3 cup thawed apple juice concentrate
1 tsp. cinnamon
1/2 tsp. ground nutmeg
1/4 tsp. ground cloves
1/2 cup thawed orange juice concentrate
1/2 cup whole wheat pastry flour or other whole grain flour
1/2 tsp. baking powder

Preheat the oven to 350°.

Stir apples, apple juice, nutmeg, and cinnamon in a large saucepan and cook until apples are partially cooked. Transfer to an 8-inch pie plate.

Stir the orange juice, flour, and baking powder together in a small bowl and sprinkle over apple mixture. Bake until crisp and brown, about 45 minutes.

Hot Cocoa

Curl up with a good book and enjoy this treat.

2 cups vanilla flavored oat milk
3 T. Sucanat
1 T. + 1 tsp. unsweetened cocoa
1/2 tsp. vanilla

In a saucepan, combine all ingredients. Beat with a whisk. Over medium heat, bring to just below a boil. Serve steaming hot.

Note: If you wish, you can add 1/2 tsp. of mint extract for a great drink. Peppermint Schnapps is also delicious.

Pineapple Bread Pudding

1/2 cup all purpose flour
1/4 cup whole wheat pastry flour

1 tsp. cinnamon
1/4 tsp. nutmeg
1/3 cup Sucanat
1/4 cup baby food prunes
2 cups fresh pineapple cut into ½ inch pieces,
or 2 cups pineapple canned in its own juice
4 slices whole wheat bread
1/2 cup water

Preheat to the oven to 350°.

Combine both flours, cinnamon, nutmeg, and the Sucanat in a large bowl. Mix well. Add the prunes and mix with a fork until the mixture is moistened.

In another bowl, toss together the pineapple and bread.

Lightly coat a nonstick baking pan with cooking spray. Sprinkle the bottom of the pan with about a 1/2 cup of the flour and spice mix. Cover it with the pineapple mix. Top with the remaining flour and spice mixture. Drizzle the water over all.

Bake uncovered for 40 minutes.

Orange Chocolate Pudding

You can flavor this dessert with anything you like. Khalua, Amaretto, or Mint work well, as do many fruit-flavored extracts. When using something other than an orange flavoring, omit the orange zest.

2 cups vanilla oat milk
1/4 cup Sucanat
2 T. unsweetened cocoa
3 T. cornstarch
1/2 tsp. vanilla
1 tsp. Grand Marnier or orange extract
1/2 tsp. orange zest

In a saucepan, combine the Sucanat, cocoa, orange zest and cornstarch. Add the oat milk, orange flavoring and vanilla. Whisk together well. Cook over medium-high heat, stirring constantly and gently for about 8 minutes, or until thickened.

Pour into four dessert dishes. Chill for at least 1 hour. Garnish with thin slices of fresh fruit if desired.

Chocolate Pie

This is a very adaptable recipe. Use any flavored extract that you like to achieve different flavors. I like a dash of strawberry, or a little coffee liqueur.

2 packages silken firm tofu
3/4 cup honey
3 tsp. vanilla
1/2 cup cocoa powder

Cut the tofu into pieces and place in a blender. Process until smooth. Put the cocoa powder in a bowl, heat the honey, and pour over the cocoa powder. Add the vanilla and stir until smooth. Add the cocoa mixture to the tofu in the blender and process for 1 minute. Pour into a graham cracker pie crust or custard cups and chill for at least 2 hours. Garnish with fresh fruit.

Maple-Cranberry Baked Apples

You can substitute organic raisins for the dried cranberries if you wish.

2½ cups cranberry juice cocktail
1/2 cup maple syrup
1/4 cup firmly packed Sucanat
1 T. lemon juice
2 tsp. grated fresh ginger
1 tsp. cinnamon
1 tsp. cornstarch
1 tsp. vanilla
8 medium Rome or Granny Smith apples, cored
3/4 cup dried cranberries

Preheat the oven to 375°.

Combine everything except the apples and dried cranberries together in a bowl. Stir very well and set aside.

Place the apples in a shallow roasting pan. Fill the centers of the apples evenly with the dried cranberries. Pour the maple mixture over the apples. Bake for 1 hour, or until the apples are tender, basting twice during cooking with syrup from the pan.

Blueberry-Peach Crisp

Absolutely delicious!

5 sliced, peeled fresh or frozen peaches, thawed
2 cups fresh or frozen blueberries, thawed
3 T. flour
3-4 T. Sucanat

Topping:
1/4 cup firmly packed Sucanat
1/2 cup quick cooking rolled oats
2 T. flour
1 tsp. cinnamon
1/2 tsp. allspice
1 jar of baby food prunes

Preheat the oven to 350°.

In a 2 quart baking dish, combine the peaches, blueberries, flour and Sucanat. Toss together well.

In small bowl, combine all topping ingredients except prune puree. Mix well. Cut in the puree with a fork until the mixture is crumbly. Sprinkle over the fruit.

Bake for 30 minutes.

Variations: use bananas and peaches, *or* pears and blueberries.

Cinnamon-Raisin Bread Pudding

2 cups vanilla flavored oat milk
2 T. cornstarch
1/4 tsp. cinnamon
3 T. packed Sucanat
2 tsp. vanilla
4 slices whole wheat bread cut into cubes
1/4 cup organic raisins

In a medium saucepan, combine the oat milk, cornstarch, cinnamon, and Sucanat. Stir to dissolve the cornstarch. Cook over medium heat, stirring until the mixture just comes to a boil. Cook for 3 minutes, stirring constantly. Remove from the heat and stir in vanilla. Add the bread and raisins, and mix well.

Spoon into a baking dish, cover and chill for at least 1 hour.

Apples and Oats

4 large Rome or Granny Smith apples
2 T. cornstarch
1/4 cup maple syrup
2 tsp. lemon juice
1 tsp. ground cinnamon

Topping:
1 cup quick cooking rolled oats
2 T. maple syrup
2 T. baby food prunes
1 tsp. vanilla

Preheat the oven to 350°.

Peel and core the apples. Cut into small chunks. Place in a small casserole dish and toss with the cornstarch. Combine the maple syrup, lemon juice, and cinnamon. Drizzle over the apples. Cover and bake for 20-30 minutes, or until the apples are tender.

To make the topping, Combine all topping ingredients except prune puree in a small bowl. Mix well. Cut in the puree with a fork until the mixture is crumbly. Sprinkle over the apples. Return to the oven and bake, uncovered for 15 minutes, or until the oats are brown and crispy.

Peach Pie

1 grape nuts pie crust or graham cracker pie crust
9 medium fresh peaches
4 T. cornstarch
1 cup water
3/4 cup Sucanat
1 tsp. cinnamon
pinch of salt

Preheat the oven to 350°.

Slice up three of the peaches and place in a blender. Add the cornstarch, water, Sucanat, cinnamon and salt. Puree until smooth, then pour into a medium saucepan. Cook over medium heat, stirring constantly, until the mixture comes to a boil. Continue to cook and stir until the puree is thickened. Allow to cool.

Slice up the remaining peaches, and stir into the cooled mixture. Pour into the pie crust and chill at least three hours.

Whipped Topping for Desserts

Excellent with fresh fruit or pumpkin pie.

1 package silken, firm tofu
2-4 T. honey
2 T. lemon juice
1/4 tsp. vanilla
1/8 tsp. salt
1/8 tsp. almond extract
vanilla flavored oat milk as needed

Place all the ingredients in a blender, and process until very smooth. Add vanilla flavored oat milk a teaspoon at a time if the mixture is too thick to blend well. Place in a covered container, and refrigerate for at least 2 hours.

Graham Cracker Pie Crust

Try this recipe for pumpkin or apple pies.

8 large fat free graham crackers
1/4 cup baby food prunes

Preheat the oven to 350°.

Break up the crackers and place in a blender. Process until you have fine crumbs. You should end up with about 1¼ cups of crumbs. Add the prunes and process until moist and crumbly.

Lightly coat a 9 inch pie pan with cooking spray. Press the crumbs against the sides and bottom of the pan. Bake for 10 minutes. Allow to cool to room temperature, then fill as desired.

Grape Nuts Pie Crust

Especially good for fruit pies.

6 oz. apple juice concentrate (frozen apple juice)
1½ cups grape nuts cereal

Preheat the oven to 350°.

Mix the apple juice concentrate with the grape nuts and let stand for 5 minutes, or until the moisture is absorbed. Press into a 9 inch pie pan, then bake for 10-12 minutes. Allow to cool to room temperature before filling.

Appendix

Steps to Success

Step 1: Check your attitude

When you make the transition to a diet based on unrefined, plant-based foods rather than processed foods, you are embarking on a healthy adventure! You will discover new ways of cooking, shopping, and storing foods while developing new habits and tastes. Be patient and consistent. Soon, you'll begin to see and feel the results that will make your efforts worthwhile.

Make friends with new ingredients. Remember that they are included in the recipes because they offer benefits to your health and taste delicious. The more you are willing to try, the faster you will be comfortable with your new way of eating.

Step 2: Find a good natural foods store or green supermarket

A natural food store is different from a vitamin store. Look in your telephone book, or ask around. Sometimes natural food stores are called health food stores. Look for cooperatives—natural food stores owned by the people who shop in them.

The green supermarket is a wonderful new addition to many communities. It looks like a regular market, but it is stocked with natural and organic foods. Many green supermarkets carry gourmet items, and ingredients from cultures around the world. They are great fun to explore.

In the spring, summer, and early fall, many communities have farmer's markets. Often you will find organic growers—they're a wonderful wealth of information about their products and how to prepare them.

You might look for something called "community supported agriculture," in your area. Local farmers grow the produce, and members receive regular deliveries of fresh, organic food. It is very satisfying to support the hands that till the soil, and the hearts that care about protecting the Earth.

Your regular supermarket should carry most of the ingredients called for in this cookbook. Ask for what you want. As consumers ask for natural, whole, organic products, markets will meet their demand.

If you cannot find items locally, you can order them through the mail. Sometimes it is actually preferable to do it that way. Prices can be much lower, although you usually have to order larger quantities. As you demonstrate to those around you the power of eating this way, your friends and family may become interested in joining together to order items through the mail.

Step 3: Make sure you have the necessary equipment to cook great food

As you gain experience with cooking natural, whole foods, you'll discover different pieces of kitchen equipment that appeal to you. The items listed below are suggestions about what you'll need to get started. Remember, there is always a way to get around not having a particular item. But, having what you need makes things easier and much more enjoyable.

One large nonstick skillet. A "wok skillet" works very well. This is a large pan with high sides that can be used for sautéing vegetables, stir-frying, and many other dishes. Because no oil is used in this type of cooking, the nonstick feature is very important. Be sure that you use Teflon-coated utensils with a nonstick pan. These pans are very safe unless the Teflon begins to chip. By using the correct utensils, you will lengthen the use of your pan. Make sure you replace the pan when chips begin to appear. I've been very happy with a moderately priced line of nonstick cookware called "Tefal."

Two 2-quart saucepans with lids. Get more saucepans as you can afford them. You can never have too many. Again, nonstick is best.

One 2-quart casserole dish with a cover. Corningware makes excellent oven-proof dishes. When doubling a recipe that goes into a casserole dish, don't try to put all of the mixture in one, large dish—use two.

One large, nonstick baking sheet

A soup pot. Sometimes this is referred to as a Dutch Oven, but that is a different thing altogether. A soup pot should hold at least eight quarts. Again, nonstick is best. I like one with a glass lid, so I can keep an eye on things without letting heat escape by lifting the lid. You'll be using this pot for many different things—soups, stews, boiling pasta, cooking beans, and making large batches of sauces.

A blender. Many recipes require the use of a blender. You can work around that, but it is really much better to have one. Hamilton Beach makes an economical blender with an attachable food processor. I've found this piece of equipment to be a wonderful, time-saving device in my kitchen. You'll be chopping up a lot of vegetables, so it is a worthwhile investment.

A variety of knives. Do yourself a favor and buy good knives! I like one that is large and square in shape, and is often called a cleaver. It makes chopping vegetables very easy. Take a little time, go to a store that has a variety of knives, and choose what feels best in your hand. Just make sure your knife is big and sharp enough to do a lot of chopping. You will also need a good paring knife, although I like to use a slightly larger knife usually used to de-bone chicken. Don't try to get by with dull, uncomfortable knives. In the long run, you'll only undermine your efforts in the kitchen.

While we're on the subject of utensils, a company called Oxo makes wonderful utensils. Ergonomically designed, they're easy on your hands and a pleasure to use. They're priced about the same as other utensils. Their potato peeler is an absolute wonder.

Miscellaneous equipment: make sure you have at least three measuring cups, two sets of measuring spoons, three large bowls, and a colander. Also, you'll need a steamer basket. It is used to steam vegetables so that they retain their shape, color, texture, and nutrients; you can obtain a simple basket in the grocery store.

It is important to have a good work surface. Clear off the counters in your kitchen, and use them to prepare food. You'll need a good chopping board. Please choose either tempered glass or heavy plastic. Wood boards are beautiful, but they cannot be cleaned adequately, and often harbor a host of bacteria.

Environmentally friendly cleaning products: choose cleaning products that are not hazardous to your health and the environment. "Citra-Solv" is an excellent product. Made of the acidic oil contained in oranges, it will clean almost anything, and do it safely. It also leaves a delightful orange scent, instead of the chemical fog left by regular cleaning products. Because you dilute Citra-Solv in water, it is economical.

Feeling a little overwhelmed? Remember, you are making an investment in your health. Wouldn't you rather buy equipment with your money than spend it at the doctor's office? Once you stock up with what you need, you won't have to buy anything else for quite a while.

Step 4: Learn to plan ahead

When you plan a weekly menu, you'll dramatically cut your food budget while eating delicious meals! Set aside a little time to draw-up a list of meals for the week ahead and make a shopping list. At first, many of the meals on your menu plan will be unfamiliar. However, remember that the average family only uses about ten favorite recipes over and over again. Start by building a set of recipes that you really enjoy, then simply rotate them. When you're ready, add something new.

Sample Menu Plan

Here is a sample menu plan to help get you started:

Sunday

Loaf, casserole
Potatoes or whole grains
Vegetables and/or green vegetable salad
Dessert

Make good use of your oven on Sundays. Choose from loafs, casseroles, roasted potatoes, baked French fries, whole grain dishes, and roasted vegetables. Make the most efficient use of your time in the kitchen and double a recipe whenever possible, freeze the extra and reheat for dinner or lunch during the week. Serve dinner with either a green or grated vegetable salad on the side and a healthy dessert. Since the oven has already been heated, consider making healthy muffins or breads as well—freeze them for use throughout the week.

Monday

Soup, Stew or Chili
Whole grains, whole grain bread, or potatoes
Vegetables and/or green vegetable salad

Soups, stew and chilies are a great way to experiment with whole foods. Try a variety of grains, beans, and seasonal vegetables to make your own special creations.

Double every soup recipe you make and freeze half. The night before you plan to serve it, move it to the refrigerator to thaw. Add a little water and heat on low. Store soups and stews in individual serving containers for lunches.

Tuesday

Stir-Fry
Whole grains (brown rice, couscous, millet, polenta, quinoa)
Vegetables
Vegetable salad

Stir-fries are a wonderful opportunity to experiment with different grains and local, seasonal vegetables.

Wednesday

Whole grain pasta
Fresh stir-fried vegetables or marinara
Vegetables and/or green vegetable salad
Whole grain bread or rolls

On pasta nights, pick a whole grain and cook up some fresh vegetables with garlic and herbs, or top it with your favorite marinara sauce. Serve with a salad.

Pasta is great as a base for not only Italian dishes, but also Mexican style and Oriental flavors as well. For Mexican style dishes, just add some onions, peppers, cumin, chili powder, cilantro, and black beans. Give it a more Oriental flavor with ginger, bok choy, sprouts, and soy sauce.

Thursday

Soup
Whole grains, whole grain bread, or potatoes
Vegetables and/or green vegetable salad

Once you begin to double each soup recipe, you will usually have two kinds of soups waiting in the freezer for some variety during the week. Or, make a fresh (double) batch for dinner. Serve with whole grain bread and fresh veggies.

Friday

Veggie Burgers or Pizza
Whole grain buns or pizza crust
Fresh vegetables
Vegetable salad
Oven fries or whole grain rolls

Veggie burgers and vegetarian pizza are great transition foods that almost everyone enjoys. You can make your own or purchase pre-made veggie burgers and pizzas.

Saturday

Burritos, Fajitas, Enchiladas, Tacos
Beans
Whole wheat or corn tortillas
Fresh and/or stir-fried vegetables
Chips and salsa

Step 5: Make a Weekly Shopping List

There is no way around it—eating whole, natural foods requires a little planning. However, you can greatly streamline that process by using a shopping list. In the Appendix, you'll find a shopping list that you can photocopy—use it as a starting point to create your own. Organize your shopping list according to the layout of your market. As you change the way you eat, you'll be amazed at how many of the market's aisles become irrelevant to you. Your shopping trips will be much easier and faster. You'll be spending most of your time in the fresh produce section.

Print off a couple dozen copies of the list, and post one on your refrigerator so you can circle the foods you need as you run out.

When you plan your menu, keep your shopping list nearby so you can circle items and the quantity needed. This will eliminate any surprises when it comes time to cook—all your ingredients will be available and there will be no last minute trips to the store. Remember, buy organic whenever possible.

Buy the foods that you use frequently in bulk. This is the least expensive and the most environmentally friendly way to buy staples such as grains, beans, flours, herbs, spices, and pastas, as well as canned foods such as tomatoes, salsas, and beans.

You can get tremendous savings by ordering products through a wholesale food distributor. They also sell frozen and refrigerated products, produce, health supplements, and cleaning supplies. Order on your own, or get together with a few friends and start a food buying club.

Don't waste your money on those small cans or jars of herbs and spices that you find in the supermarket. Most natural food stores, and even some major markets, offer these items in bulk. You simply buy per pound. What costs three to four dollars already packaged can cost a few cents when purchased this way. Herbs and spices lose their flavor over time. Buying bulk usually gives you a fresher product. Or, grow your own herbs. Most of them are very easy to grow during the summer. You can dry and store the extras for use in the other seasons.

Stock your pantry and freezer with healthy convenience foods. These items are meant to be fill-in foods, so save them for when you really need them. You pay for the convenience, but it is a great deal compared to eating out. Although these foods are not fresh from the ground, they are made from foods that are. Check out the freezer section in your natural foods store for a great selection, including *Amy's Entrees, Cascadian Farms, Ken & Robert's,* and *Whole & Natural Foods.*

By the way, consider buying canvas bags to use when you shop. Although you have to make an initial investment, you won't be contributing to the landfill with hundreds of plastic bags. Reuse plastic or paper bags whenever possible. Use cloth string bags for fruits and vegetables, rather than plastic.

How to Cook the Healthy Way

The number one rule of cooking is:
READ THE RECIPE ALL THE WAY THROUGH BEFORE YOU START!

Cooking is much easier if there aren't any surprises!

Get out all of your ingredients before you start cooking. That way, you don't have to send somebody on an emergency run to the grocery store. It also makes cooking less stressful. Everything is right there when you need it.

Measure out the herbs and spices required in the recipe and combine them in a very small bowl. You won't have to stop in the middle of things to do this task. You will get more flavor if you crush them with the back of a spoon or a pestle, which releases their oils.

Clean up as you go. Often, a recipe asks that something cook for five minutes or so. Clean up what you've already used while you're waiting. You'll be glad when there is little to do later. The same thing applies to putting things away.

Let's go over some of the cooking terms you'll find in this book:

Chop: To render the item into small pieces.

Dice: To chop an item into small pieces that are approximately the same size and shape.

Mince: To chop into tiny pieces.

Note: When using a food processor, it is very easy to overdo. Don't pulverize the food into a liquid. Make sure your food retains texture and shape, otherwise it will act as a liquid in your recipe and the results will not be satisfactory.

Seed and chop: Many fruits and vegetables have inedible seeds. Green and red peppers are a good example. To prepare a pepper, chop the top and the bottom off, slice through one side, and lay the remaining part flat in a strip. Using a paring knife, remove the seeds and lighter colored membrane from the strip. Rinse away any remaining seeds. Chop and add to your recipe.

Core and chop: This instruction usually concerns apples or other fruit. Be very careful that you remove all of the seeds from an apple. They contain arsenic!

Drain: This usually means placing cooked food into a colander so that excess liquid will drain away—pasta or boiled potatoes are good examples. Sometimes, this refers to food that has been cooked in a skillet that has excess liquid. Take the entire skillet over to the sink. Tip it slightly, using a knife to protect the food, allow the liquid to drain.

Steam: Many of us grew up on boiled vegetables. These tasteless, limp, pale vegetables required dousing with butter and salt to be palatable. Steaming vegetables leaves them bright, delicious, and slightly crisp. Just put about two or three inches of water in your soup pot. Place the steamer basket in the pot and bring the water to a boil. Place your vegetables on the steamer and cook according to the chart that will be given in the chapter on vegetables. That is all there is to it.

Sauté: This is a term you will see over and over in this book. To sauté means to place some fluid in a skillet, bring it to a high temperature, and cook the food while stirring frequently. Traditionally, sautéing is done with oil. But the added fat and calories are entirely unnecessary.

About 2 tablespoons of liquid is enough to begin. Sauté with vegetable broth, dry sherry, wine, soy sauce, tomato juice, balsamic vinegar, or plain water. Simply follow the recipe, or use a liquid that will compliment the rest of the ingredients in a recipe. The important thing is to not add too much liquid. Cook until the food is to your liking, adding a little liquid only when it is necessary to keep things from sticking to the bottom of the pan.

You can brown onions just fine without oil. Just let the onions begin to stick, and add a tiny amount of liquid. Keep doing this process until they reach the desired color and texture—be careful not to scorch them.

Stir-Fry: This is just another name for sauté. Usually, a stir-fry contains a variety of vegetables that are added sequentially, according to the amount of time that it takes for them to become crispy-tender. For example, broccoli needs a head start over snow peas, so that both will be ready at the same time. The recipes in the stir-fry section give you exact instructions about what to do and when.

Many of your favorite recipes can be adapted for healthy eating.

- Choose one that's already rich in grains, legumes, fruits and or vegetables
- Delete all animal products

    Substitute oat milk, soy milk or rice milk for cow's milk
    Substitute Ener-G egg replacer for eggs
    Substitute TVP, beans or grains for meat

- Substitute whole grain products for refined flour
- Delete all added fats—replace fat with prune puree, applesauce, or mashed banana. Try to match your substitute with the other flavors in the recipe. For example, applesauce would taste good in a recipe based around spices—like spice cake, or carrot cake.
- Use salt to season the food after it is cooked, not while preparing the recipe.

Glossary of Ingredients

Agar—a jelling agent that is tasteless, odorless and colorless made from a sea vegetable. It can be used in place of gelatin (which is made from animal parts). Available in powder, flakes and bars from natural foods stores.

Amaranth—a grain that was once important in the ancient Aztec culture. It has an earthy flavor and sticky texture. Richer in protein than corn and beans, and higher in fiber than wheat, corn, rice or soybeans. Combine with other grains in pilafs.

Arrowroot—a thickening agent that can be evenly substituted for cornstarch. Cornstarch is chemically bleached, while arrowroot is prepared using a natural process. Arrowroot should be used for hot foods, as its texture becomes too glossy when cool.

Artificial sweeteners—many are nonfood chemicals. They have been poorly tested and no one is sure what the long term effects will be. NutraSweet is an amino acid which the body should be able to process effectively. However, there are many studies underway, some with preliminary findings that are alarming. Symptoms in some people have included memory loss, difficulties with vision, impaired muscle coordination, and insomnia. Needless to say, they should be avoided.

Baby food prunes—an incredible substitute for fat in baked goods. You can adapt many of your favorite recipes by using 1/2 as much puree as the margarine, oil, or butter called for. Puree can be found in the baby food section of any grocery store, and is labeled simply as "prunes".

Baking powder—a leavening agent that is used in baked goods that do not have yeast. Be sure to get one that is aluminum free.

Balsamic vinegar—a very rich tasting and aromatic red vinegar made from sweet wine that has been aged. It can be a bit expensive, but it is delicious, and a little goes a long way.

Barley—once very common on dinner tables, barley is a nutritious grain. When it's whole, it's called Scotch or pot barley. Barley with the bran layer peeled off is referred to as pearl barley, and is lower in fiber, protein, fat and minerals. Chewy and nutty-tasting, it makes a great base for soups and stews, or can be used in salads. Barley flour can be substituted for whole wheat pastry flour.

Barley malt—a natural sweetener made from sprouted roasted barley; it is 50 percent as sweet as sugar. It comes in granular form or syrup. It is called a "malt" because maltose is the sugar that occurs when starch in the barley sprouts.

Bifun—a type of quick cooking clear noodle made from potato starch and rice flour. Also known as rice vermicelli. Use in soups, salads and stir-fry dishes.

Black beans—an earthy, mild bean. They are sometimes called turtle beans and are found both canned and dried.

Bok choy—a mild member of the cabbage family. Found fresh in the produce section of the market, it is often used in Asian cooking.

Brown rice—whole rice that contains the bran and the germ of the grain. It is much more nutritious than white rice, and has a full, nutty flavor. It comes in long and short varieties—the short is more tender, with a wetter, heavier quality. White rice contains about only 85% of the protein, and 53% of the minerals, 38% of the vitamins found in brown rice.

Brown rice pasta—substitutes well for wheat pasta. It works well in Asian-style dishes and casseroles combined with beans and vegetables.

Brown rice syrup—made by slow-cooking brown rice until it develops into a thick sweet syrup. Few people have allergies to rice, which makes it an ideal sweetener. It has a light, delicate flavor that compliments most foods.

Brown sugar—white sugar with molasses added. Many people believe that brown sugar is a "more natural" product, but that is incorrect.

Bulgur—has a sweet, nutlike flavor and slightly chewy texture. It is made from whole wheat berries that have been cracked and precooked. It is the base for tabbouleh, and is great in chilies or vegetable salads.

Capers—the tangy buds of a Mediterranean bush, capers bottled in vinegar can be found next to the pickles in the market.

Chicken-like seasoning—found in natural food stores, this vegetarian seasoning imparts a chicken flavor to recipes.

Chick-peas—another name for Garbanzo or Cici beans. A round, nut-flavored bean that is delicious in almost any recipe.

Cilantro—a leafy green vegetable, cilantro adds flavor to many Asian and Mexican dishes.

Corn—referred to as maize in other countries. It is the only grain eaten in its natural, unprocessed form, and the only grain needing to be replanted by humans. However, many people are sensitive to corn. Watch how you feel after eating it—intestinal bloating, feeling mentally foggy or diarrhea may indicate corn is not for you.

Cornmeal—flour made from coarsely ground corn. Cornmeal gives breads a sweet taste and crumbly texture.

Corn pasta—comes in a variety of traditional pasta shapes. It blends well with fresh vegetables, beans, and Italian-style tomato sauces.

Couscous—the ground form of semolina, and a staple in North Africa. It has a texture and taste similar to some varieties of rice. Use whole wheat couscous, which is available in health food stores. Use it as a base for vegetable stew, pasta salads, stuffing vegetables or in desserts.

Curry powder—a combination of spices, curry gives a delightful, spicy flavor to a dish. It comes in either hot or mild and can be added or subtracted to a recipe depending on your preferences.

Date sugar—made by dehydrating and pulverizing dates. The date fruit has a high concentration of naturally occurring sugars. Good for cooking and baking.

Diced green chilies—Available in the Mexican foods section of your grocery store. Or, look for them next to the salsa. Make sure you don't pick up jalapeño peppers by mistake.

1½ teaspoons of Ener-G Egg + 2 tablespoons = one egg. See Eggwhites for amount.

Ener-G egg replacer—a completely egg free product used when eggs are called for in baking or cooking. No preservatives, artificial flavorings or added sugar. Many health food stores carry this product. Or, you can order it directly by calling 800-331-5222, or writing to Ener-G Foods, Post office Box 84487, Seattle, WA 98124.

Fennel bulb—sometimes called "anise". Fennel can be found in the produce section of your grocery store. It looks like a very large white onion, with feathery green leaves coming out of the top.

Fennel seeds—found in the spice section, they impart a slight licorice taste.

15 bean mixture—found in the dried beans section.

Fettuccine—a type of pasta found dried or fresh.

Flax seeds—are high in Omega-3 fatty acids and vitamin E. Grind and add to your cereals, breads and pancakes. Flax seeds also make a good binder for eggless baking. They can also be substituted for cooking oil at a ratio of 3 to 1 in baked goods. For example, 1½ cups of ground flaxseed can replace 1/2 cup butter or cooking oil in a recipe. Baked goods substituting flaxseed meal tend to brown more rapidly.

Cook baked goods at a lower temperature to retain nutrients. Store seeds in the refrigerator or freezer.

Fresh ginger root—a wonderfully aromatic, crisp addition to many dishes, ginger is prominent in Asian cuisine. You can buy the whole root in the produce section. To use, simply cut off the amount you need, peel it, and mince or slice. The root will store nicely in your refrigerator for quite a long time. Ground ginger is also available in the spice section. You may even see crystallized ginger. This is not usually used in cooking, but for garnish, or even as candy.

Fruit juice concentrate—This sweetener, which undergoes little processing, can be found in many products, such as cookies, candy, cereal, and sodas. Usually made from a concentrate of pineapple, pear, peach, or clarified grape juice.

Garam masala—a spice combination similar to curry powder.

Garbanzo beans—see chick peas.

Grated orange peel—you can buy it dried in the spice section, but it is quite expensive. Buy a small tool called a "zester" and grate the fresh fruit instead.

Hoisin sauce—a spicy sauce found in the Asian section of your market.

Honey—After gathering nectar from flowers, the bees return to the hive and process this nectar into honey. The flavor of the honey depends on the flower—sources include buckwheat, clover, orange blossom, wildflower, and sage. To process raw honey, it is removed from the wax comb, then strained or heated and filtered. Many vegans are uncomfortable using honey—it is, after all, an animal product. Commercial hives often use chemicals, smoke, and other harsh methods to drive out the bees so that the honey can be harvested. So, be sure you buy organic honey that has been ethically produced. Honey can also host a variety of bacteria, so should never be given to very young children.

Idaho potatoes—also called russet potatoes, these are the common potatoes used in American cooking. Bake, mash, or boil them.

Jalapeño peppers—a small, hot pepper which can be found fresh in some parts of the country. Look in the section of your grocery store where the pickles are located to find jalapeño peppers in jars.

Kale—a dark green, leafy vegetable similar to spinach.

Kamut—It originated in Egypt more than six thousand years ago. Now grown in Montana, it is a distant relative to wheat, and contains

40 percent more protein than modern wheat. It has a rich buttery flavor and chewy texture. Use in salads and pilafs and as a substitute for rice. Kamut flour is ideal for pasta making and pastries.

Kidney beans—dark red beans with a meaty texture. Often used in chili recipes, they can be found canned or dried.

Leeks—a great vegetable with a mild onion taste. Leeks look like giant, pale green onions. Only the white part is used.

Lemon zest—see zest.

Lentils—one of mankind's oldest foods, lentils are very nutritious, fast and easy to prepare, and blend well with a variety of flavors. They are not available canned, but can be found with other dried beans in the grocery store.

Liquid smoke—found with BBQ sauces in the market, this ingredient provides a delicious smoky flavor to soups or stews.

Maple syrup—made from boiling down the sap from maple trees. It has twice as much calcium as milk and is just as sweet as sugar. Classified by color and flavor, the lighter the syrup color (grade A), the lighter the flavor. The grades of syrup have more to do with taste rather than quality. The darker the color, the longer the syrup boiled.

Millet—a staple food in Africa, China, and India for thousands of years, it has a mild, nutty flavor and fluffy texture. It is excellent in salads, pilafs or tossed with pasta. Combine with vegetables in a spicy curry sauce.

Miso—a fermented paste made from soybeans, sea salt and a special bacteria, miso is a staple in Asian cuisine. It comes in many different and subtle flavors, and can be used as a highly nutritious soup base or seasoning. Miso can be found in some larger grocery stores, many health food stores, and in Asian markets.

Molasses—made from the cooked liquid that is left after the crystallization of sugar. It has a unique flavor that can't be replaced by other products. Light molasses refers to the intensity of flavor, not fewer calories. Regular molasses is full flavored. Blackstrap molasses contains iron, calcium, potassium and B vitamins, but its flavor is nearly unpalatable.

Nutritional yeast—a powder that is very rich in B vitamins and protein, low in calories. It adds a pleasant nutty taste to dinner loaves and vegetable burgers. This is a different substance than the yeast used for baking.

Oats—the only grain endorsed by the FDA as aiding the prevention of heart disease, yet only 5 percent of the U.S. oat crop is consumed by humans. Purée in your blender to make your own oat flour which adds a sweetness to baked goods, making them chewy and moist.

Oat bran—the outer covering of the whole oat, it is an incredible source of fiber. Just 3 T. added to foods supplies the recommended daily fiber intake for adults. Oat Bran can be found in markets and health food stores and is very inexpensive. It can easily be added to casseroles, stews, and spaghetti sauce.

Oat milk—a delicious substitute for cow's milk. You can buy it in natural foods stores.

Orange zest—see zest.

Orzo—a tiny pasta that looks like rice, orzo can be found in the dried pasta section of the market.

Parsnips—one of the forgotten foods in recent decades, parsnips look like white carrots. They are sweet and delicious.

Pepperocini—a mild, Italian pepper found along with the pickles and olives in the market.

Pinto beans—a staple in Mexican cuisine, you can find them canned or dried.

Polenta—made of cornmeal, polenta is often baked and served with camponata or ratatouille.

Portobello mushrooms—enormous mushrooms that have a remarkably meaty flavor and texture.

Prune puree—see baby food prunes.

Quinoa—called the "super grain of the future", quinoa actually has ancient origins. Pronounced "keen-wa", it dates back to the Incas, and is one of the best sources of protein in the vegetable kingdom. Quinoa has a light, nutty and fluffy texture. Try it in salads, soups, stews, pilafs and as a rice substitute. There are more than eighteen hundred varieties that vary in color from pink to orange to green to purple.

Quinoa-corn pasta—a nutritious pasta with a high protein content. The nutty flavor of quinoa blends well with mild sauces.

Red pepper flakes—found in the spice section of your market.

Red potatoes—small potatoes that are excellent boiled or sautéed.

Rice—the most consumed grain in the world. There are four types: long grain, medium grain, short grain and waxy. Extremely versatile, use it in soups, salads, pilafs, or for stuffing vegetables.

Rice milk—made from cooked, fermented brown rice, rice milk has a light, sweet taste, and is low in fat, or fat-free. Use it with cereal or in cooking.

Rice vinegar—a very light vinegar found in the Asian section of your market.

Roasted red peppers—found in jars in the produce section of the grocery store.

Rolled oats—the whole grains of oats that have been run through rollers to flatten them so they will cook faster. Found in the cereal section.

Russet potatoes—also called Idaho potatoes, these are the common potatoes used in American cooking. Bake, mash, or boil them.

Rye—lower in nutrients and proteins than most other grains. Used mainly in breads and hot cereals.

Soy milk—an excellent source of isoflavones and calcium, soy milk can readily be substituted for cow's milk. Look for low fat varieties.

Split peas—found dried.

Soy sauce—a versatile liquid seasoning made from soy beans. However, it is high in sodium. Use versions labeled "lite".

Soba noodles—made with buckwheat flour or a combination of buckwheat flour and wheat flour. Buckwheat is one of the best grain sources of calcium. The hearty texture and distinct taste complements strong-flavored sauces such as sweet and sour, soy sauce or spicy stir-fry sauce.

Sucanat—a granular form of dehydrated juice of organic sugar cane. The acronym, "sucanat" comes from the term "sugar cane natural". In its natural form, sugar cane contains the vitamins and minerals missing from refined sugar. Use as a substitute for sugar in all recipes. Find it in your natural foods store.

Sugar—the most common sweetener. It is a highly refined product made from sugar cane or beets. It contains almost no nutrients. Perhaps most importantly, charred animal bones are sometimes used in the bleaching process of white sugar.

Sun-dried tomatoes—these come soaked in oil, or dry. Use only the dried ones, which can be found in the produce section. You can make your own if you live in an area with plenty of sunshine.

Spelt—a native of southern Europe with a rich and nutty flavor; it is higher in protein than wheat. It is quicker and easier to digest than most grains. Spelt flour is a great substitute for whole wheat flour in bread and pastry recipes.

Stevia—available in powdered or liquid form, this substance comes from a South American plant. It is 300 times sweeter than sugar, and it does not seem to affect blood sugar levels, therefore, it is used by diabetics in many parts of the world. You can find it in your natural foods store.

Taco seasoning mix—your market has a section with many seasoning mixes for a variety of dishes. Many of them are excellent in taste and good for your health. Read the labels.

Tamari—a natural Japanese soy sauce.

Teff—a staple in Africa and rich in iron calcium. It is also grown in Idaho. Use with vegetables, other grains, tofu and fresh or dried fruit. Teff flour can be used in place of whole wheat flour to make pancakes, cookies, and muffins.

Tofu—made from soybeans very much like cheese is made from milk. Tofu is very easy to prepare. It adds protein to dishes without cholesterol or saturated fat. It can be found in your grocery store, and is often kept in the produce department where it can be refrigerated. However, you may have to look in a health food store to find the extra low fat varieties. Mori Nu is a brand of tofu that is hermetically sealed and does not have to be refrigerated. It has an excellent flavor and can be stored for long periods of time. Mori Nu makes a wonderful very low fat product.

Turbinado sugar—the light brown crystalline substance removed from molasses during the first separation. Although it contains traces of nutrients, it is identical to white sugar in the way it is absorbed.

Udon—flat, wheat or rice flour noodles.

Vegetable broth—like bouillon, but derived from vegetables, rather than beef, poultry or fish. It can be found in cubes, or canned. Make sure you check the label for fat content. See the index for two recipes to make your own.

Vinegar—made from many sources with many different flavors. For example, white vinegar comes from alcohol, wine vinegar from wine, cider from apple cider, malt vinegar from barley, and rice vinegar from rice. There are also herb-flavored vinegars like tarragon.

Whole wheat flour—made from whole wheat berries without chemical whiteners, it is higher in protein and other nutrients. Whole wheat pastry flour is lighter and has less bran than whole wheat flour.

Whole wheat pastry flour—whole wheat flour that is lower in gluten. It is better for baked goods that should be finer and lighter than bread.

Wild rice—not really rice, but the seed of a long grass. It is found along with regular rice in the market, and has a mild, nutty flavor.

Winter squash—all of the hard-skinned varieties of squash such as acorn, pumpkin and butternut.

Worcestershire sauce—a flavoring that often contains animal products. Look for the vegetarian variety in your natural foods store.

Zest—often orange or lemon. Refers to the colored skin of the fruit, peeled off with a small tool called a "zester". One medium fruit will yield about 1 T. of zest. Or, you can purchase orange or lemon zest in the spice section of the grocery store. It is usually labeled as orange or lemon peel. Use slightly less of the jarred product than you would of the fresh.

Equivalents

Fluids

Dash	=	2 or 3 drops
1 tsp.	=	1/3 T.
1 T.	=	3 tsp.
2 T.	=	one fluid ounce
4 T.	=	1/4 cup or two ounces
5 1/3 T.	=	1/3 cup
8 T.	=	1/2 cup or four ounces
16 T.	=	one cup
1 cup	=	1/2 pint or 8 fluid ounces
2 cups	=	1 pint or 16 fluid ounces
1 pint	=	16 fluid ounces or two cups
1 quart	=	4 cups or 2 pints
1 gallon	=	4 quarts or 16 cups
1/3 cup	=	5 T. plus 1 tsp.
1/2 cup	=	8 T.

Bread-Crackers-Nuts-Rice

1 slice of bread with crust	=	1/2 cup soft bread crumbs
1 cup fine dry bread crumbs	=	5 slices of bread
1 cup small bread cubes	=	2 slices of bread
1 cup of uncooked cornmeal	=	4 cups cooked
1 cup cracker crumbs	=	12 graham crackers or 20 saltine crackers
1 cup chopped nuts	=	1/4 lb.
1 cup uncooked rice	=	3 cups cooked rice

Fruits-Vegetables

apples — 1 lb. = 3 medium apples or 3 cups sliced apples

apples — 1 cup chopped apple = 1 medium apple

bananas — 1 lb. = 3 medium bananas or 1 1/3 cups mashed banana

cabbage — 1 lb. = 4 cups shredded cabbage

carrots — 1 cup grated carrots = 1 large carrot

celery — 1 cup chopped celery = 2 medium stalks

cranberries — 1 lb. fresh cranberries = 4 cups cranberries

lemon juice — 3 T. = the juice of one medium lemon

lemon zest — 1 tsp. = the scraped peel from 1 lemon

mushrooms — 8 oz. sliced mushrooms = 2 cups raw mushrooms

onion — 1 cup chopped onion = 2 medium onions or one large onion

orange juice — 8 T. = the juice of one medium orange

orange zest — 2 tsp. = the scraped peel from 1 orange

peaches — 4 cups sliced peaches = 8 medium peaches

potatoes — 1 lb. = 3 medium potatoes or 2¼ cups diced potatoes

potatoes — 1 lb. raw unpeeled = 2 cups mashed

raisins — 16 oz. package = 3 cups loosely packed raisins

sweet potatoes — 1 lb. of sweet potatoes = 3 medium sweet potatoes

tomatoes — 1 lb. = 3 medium tomatoes

tomatoes — 2 cups canned tomatoes = 16 oz. can

tomato juice — 1 cup = 1/2 cup tomato sauce with 1/2 cup water

Seasonings

1/2 tsp. dried herbs = 1 T. fresh

1/8 tsp. of garlic powder = 1 clove of garlic

Beans

2½ cups beans = 1 cup dried

1 lb. dry = 2½ cups dry = 7½ cups cooked

14 oz. can = 1½ cups drained beans

Sugar Substitutions

Barley malt:	Replace 1 cup sugar with 1¼ cup barley malt minus 1/4 cup of other liquid ingredients.
Brown rice syrup:	Replace 1 cup sugar with 1 to 1¼ cup rice syrup.
Date sugar:	Replace 1 cup sugar with 2/3 cup date sugar.
Honey:	Replace 1 cup sugar with 1/2 cup honey minus 1/4 cup of other liquid ingredients.
Maple syrup:	Replace 1 cup sugar with 1/2 - 3/4 cup maple syrup minus 1/4 cup of other liquid ingredients.
Molasses:	Replace 1 cup sugar with 1/2 cup molasses minus 1/4 cup of other liquid ingredients.
Sucanat:	Replace 1 cup sugar with 1 cup Sucanat.

Fat Substitutions

You can replace oils or animal fats with baby food prunes, apple sauce, or ripe mashed banana. In baking, substitute these ingredients one for one. In other words, one cup of oil can be replaced by one cup of applesauce, etc. Try to match your substitute with the other flavors in the recipe. For example, applesauce would taste good in a recipe based around spices—like spice cake, or carrot cake.

Spices

Allspice combines taste of cloves, cinnamon and nutmeg—and juniper berry

Basil sweet, spicy, mint-licorice flavor used often in Italian cooking

Bay Leaf aromatic, woodsy, pleasantly bitter, often added to soups and stews

Capers the buds of a Mediterranean bush, it's sold pickled in vinegar

Caraway distinctive sharp, tangy taste found in pumpernickel bread

Cardamom mild, pleasant ginger flavor used in desserts

Cayenne very hot pepper

Chili Powder commercial mix of ground chili peppers, cumin, oregano and other herbs. Chili powder provides the heat in chili and Mexican dishes. It can be adjusted up or down according to your taste.

Chervil delicate herb with subtle celery-parsley taste

Chives very mild onion taste. Often used dried.

Cinnamon warm, sweet, aromatic, often used in breads and desserts

Cloves pungent, spicy, hot

Coriander pleasant lemon-orange flavor

Cumin warm, distinctive, bitter—used in Mexican cooking

Curry combination of many spices, warm, fragrant, exotic, combinations vary from very mild to very hot

Dill delicate licorice flavor

Fennel seeds slight licorice flavor

Fines Herbs French herb blend of parsley, chives, tarragon

Ginger has a sweet, hot zing—you can buy fresh or powdered, dried or candied

Mace strong, spicy sweet

Marjoram sweeter, milder cousin to oregano

Nutmeg	sweet, nutty
Oregano	pungent, robust marjoram taste—used in Italian cooking
Paprika	mild, sweet pepper
Parsley	crisp herb with celery flavor—fresh or dried
Rosemary	strong piney scent both sweet and savory
Sage	musky flavor, strong aromatic, pungent, astringent—a classic flavor of Thanksgiving
Savory	sweet smelling, tangy tasting, peppery
Tarragon	mild licorice flavor
Thyme	sweet, minty, with a tea like flavor
Turmeric	use as substitute for saffron, aromatic, warm, mild. It also makes tofu scrambles yellow like scrambled eggs.

Grain Cooking Times

Rinse all grains prior to using them.

Grain (1 cup)	Water (cups)	Cooking Time (minutes)	Yield (in cups)
Amaranth	3	25	2½
Barley flakes	2	15-20	2½
Barley, pearled	3	45-60	3½
Barley, whole	3	120-180	3½
Buckwheat	2	15-20	2½
Cornmeal	4	20-25	3
Kamut groats	3	35-45	2½
Millet	2¾	30-40	3½
Oat groats	4	60	3
Oats, rolled	1½	10	2½
Oats, steel cut	4	40-45	3
Polenta	1	15	2½
Quinoa	2	15	3½
Rice, basmati	2	45	3
Rice, brown	2	45-50	3-4
Rice, long-grain	2	15	3-4
Rice, medium/short	1¾	15	3
Rye berries	3½	60	3
Rye, cracked	3	45	3
Spelt	1½	35	2
Sorghum, whole	2½	45-50	3
Teff, whole	3	15	3
Triticale, berries	3½	60	2½
Triticale, flakes	2	20	2½
Wheat, berries	3½	60	2½
Wheat, bulgur	2	30	2½
Wheat, couscous	2	15	3
Wheat, cracked	3	20	2½
Wild Rice	2	50	2-2/3

Cooking Times for Beans

The following cooking times are for soaked beans (except for split peas, black-eyed peas and lentils, which do not need to be soaked). Cooking time may vary with the size, quality, and freshness of the beans.

Overnight Soaking Method: Place beans in a bowl and add enough water to cover beans by 3 inches. Soak overnight, drain, and cook as directed.

Quick Soaking Method: Place beans in a pot and add enough water to cover beans by 3 inches. Bring to a boil over medium heat. Boil 2 minutes. Remove from heat, cover, and let stand 2 hours. Drain and cook as directed.

Bean (1 cup)	**Water** (cups)	**Cooking Time** (mins./hours)	**Yield** (in cups)
Aduki Beans	3	2 hours	2
Anasazi Beans	4	1½ hours	2
Baby Lima Beans	2	1½ hours	1¾
Black Beans	4	1½ to 2 hours	2
Black-eyed Peas	3	45 minutes	2
Chickpeas	4	2½ to 3 hours	2½
Fava Beans	3	3 hours	2
Garbanzos	4	2½ to 3 hours	2½
Great Northern	3½	2 hours	2
Kidney Beans	3	1½ to 2 hours	2
Lentils	3	30 to 45 minutes	2¼
Mung Beans	2½	1½ hours	2
Navy Beans	3	2½ hours	2
Pink Beans	4	1½ hours	2
Pinto Beans	3	2½ hours	2
Red Beans	3	3 hours	2
Soybeans	4	2 to 3 hours	3
Split Peas	3	30 to 45 minutes	2¼

Two Easy Recipes for Homemade Vegetable Broth

Throw in all your leftover veggies, except those with a strong, distinctive taste like cabbage.

1.

Add:

4 quarts water
1 T. oregano
2 tsp. marjoram
2 tsp. thyme
2 tsp. garlic powder
1 tsp. onion powder
1/2 tsp. pepper

Bring to a boil, reduce heat and simmer for 2 hours. Strain. This can be kept in a tightly covered jar in the refrigerator for about eight days. Or, put the broth in ice cube trays in your freezer. Then, it will be ready to use on demand.

2.

3 carrots
1 turnip
2 stalks celery
2 onions
3 quarts water
2 tsp. salt
6 sprigs fresh parsley
1 bay leaf
1 tsp. thyme

Chop all of the vegetables, but do not peel them.
Place the water, salt, parsley, bay leaf and thyme in a soup pot along with the vegetables. Bring to a boil, reduce heat and simmer for 2 hours.

Strain out the liquid and discard the vegetables.

This will make about 2½ quarts of broth.

This can be kept in a tightly covered jar in the refrigerator for about eight days. Or, put the broth in ice cube trays in your freezer. Then, it will be ready to use on demand.

Food Safety and Storage

- Buy small quantities of foods that contain natural oil (grains, wheat germ, popcorn, freshly ground flours) and store them in the refrigerator.
- Always label and date stored leftovers.
- Store your whole food basics in all-glass preserve jars with metal clasps and rubber seals. They come in a variety of shapes and sizes to accommodate your storage needs.
- When you purchase herbs and spices, write the date on the outside of the jar. Replace those that are over a year old. Whole seeds can last up to two years.
- Store your herbs and spices that contain natural oils, such as cayenne pepper, chili powder, curry powder and paprika, in the refrigerator.
- Store your vegetables properly, sealed in airtight bags or containers, and eat them promptly. Root vegetables such as potatoes, carrots, turnips, onions, winter squash and cabbage store well for long periods of time in a cool, dark place.
- Leafy greens, celery, carrots, peas, radishes, broccoli and cauliflower should be kept refrigerated in a sealed bag or container. Cucumbers, beans, eggplant and summer squash can be left uncovered. Fresh peas and beans should be stored in their pods and not shelled until just before cooking.
- Let fruits ripen at room temperature and handle as little as possible. Keep the fruit covered, otherwise vitamins will be lost to the light and the air. Once the fruit is mature, eat it or refrigerate it.
- Store vegetables and fruits in separate areas. Fruits emit methane as they ripen which speeds up the deterioration of any vegetables in the vicinity.
- Dry beans will keep in a cool, dry storage area for a long time—years, if needed.
- Store half-used cans of broth or tomato sauce in an ice-cube tray in the freezer. Pop out a cube as needed.
- To freeze and store berries or cherries, spread fruit out separately on wax paper-lined trays in freezer. When frozen, transfer to bags. This is a great summer snack.

Sample Weekly Shopping List

Photocopy, post in your kitchen, and mark off what you need.

Fresh produce

Apples
Asparagus
Avocado
Bananas
Beans (Green, Yellow)
Beets
Berries
Broccoli
Cabbage (Green, Red)
Carrots
Cauliflower
Celery
Chard
Cherries
Collard Greens
Corn
Cucumbers
Fresh Herbs
Garlic
Ginger Root
Grapefruit
Grapes
Jicama
Kale
Leeks
Lemons
Lettuce
Limes
Melon
Mushrooms
Nectarines
Onions (Red, Yellow, Shallots)
Oranges
Parsnips
Peaches
Pears
Peas (Shelling, Snow)
Peppers (Green, Hot, Red, Yellow)
Pineapple
Potatoes (Red, Russet, Sweet)
Radishes
Salad Mix
Scallions
Spinach
Sprouts
Summer Squash
Tomatoes (Cherry, Slicing)
Turnips
Winter Squash

Canned/Bottled Goods

Applesauce
Bottled Juices
Bottled Water
Canned beans—black, pinto, kidney, white, garbanzo, refried
Green Chilies
Marinara Sauce
Pearl onions
Oil Free Salad Dressing
Salsa
Soy Sauce
Tomatoes—stewed, diced, puree, sauce, whole, paste
Vinegar—rice, balsamic, wine

Flours and Grains

Brown rice flour
Cornmeal
Oat flour
Whole wheat flour
Whole wheat pastry flour
Amaranth
Barley
Bulgur
Couscous
Kamut
Millet
Oats (Bran, Quick, Rolled)
Pancake mix
Popcorn
Quinoa
Rice (Brown, wild)
Spelt
Teff
Wheat Bran

Pasta

Amaranth
Brown Rice
Corn
Polenta
Quinoa
Soba
Udon
Whole Wheat

Dried Beans

Black
Fifteen Bean Mixture
Garbanzo
Kidney
Lentils
Lima
Pinto
White
Split Peas

Cooking Items

Arrowroot powder
Baby food prunes
Baking Soda
Baking powder
Bouillon Cubes
Cooking spray
Cornstarch
Ener-G egg replacer
Extracts
Flax seeds/flax seed oil
Honey
Maple syrup
Molasses
Raisins
Stevia powder
Sucanat
Vanilla

Prepared Foods

Condiments: catsup, mustard, Worchestershire sauce, Tabasco sauce, capers, pickles
Egg free bread—whole wheat, sourdough, multi-grain
Fruit preserves
Frozen foods—potatoes, entrees
Frozen veggies—broccoli, corn, green beans, mixed, peas, potatoes, spinach
Frozen Fruits—apple/orange juice concentrate, blueberries, strawberries
Low fat Tortillas—whole wheat, multi-grain
Oat, rice, soy milk
Oil free tortilla chips
Rice cakes

Herbs and Spices

Allspice, basil, bay leaf, black pepper, cardamom, cayenne pepper, chili powder, Chinese 5 spice, cinnamon, chives, coriander, cumin, curry powder, dill, dry mustard, fennel seeds, garam masala, garlic powder, ginger, Italian seasoning blend, mace, marjoram, nutmeg, oregano, paprika, pumpkin pie spice, red pepper flakes, rosemary, sage, salt, sea salt, tarragon, thyme, turmeric

Household and Personal Care Items

Bath soap
Citra-Solv or other natural cleaner
Dental floss
Dog/cat food
Dish soap
Dish washer soap
Kleenex
Laundry soap
Light bulbs
Mouthwash
Paper towels
Storage bags
Shampoo/conditioner
Toilet paper
Toothpaste

Fast Meal Ideas

Beans, rice and veggies of all varieties in tortillas

Black beans and rice with salsa

Freezer goodies from previously made meals

Fruit and Tofu Smoothie

Granola, oat milk and fruit

Fruit juice with soy protein powder, fresh berries and ice cubes- blend into a delicious shake

Organic fruits or veggies with healthy dip

Oat milk shake—one cup oat milk with 1/2 cup apple juice and 2 bananas

Pasta with prepared sauce

Prepared products from Amy's, Lundberg Farms, Yves, or Nile Spice

Scrambled tofu

Soup—Nile Spice Soup cups, or Fantastic Foods Soup cups

Steamed red potatoes, with sautéed peppers, onions, mushrooms and tofu

Steamed vegetables with oil free salad dressing

Stir-fry of any kind

Tostadas—refried beans, brown rice, assorted veggies and salsa

Veggie Burgers and whole wheat buns

Veggie Burgers with Vegetarian Chili

Veggie Hot Dogs

Whole wheat bread or pita pocket with bean spread and veggies

Resources

Books

Ageless Body, Timeless Mind : The Quantum Alternative to Growing Old—Deepak Chopra, 1993

Diet for a New America: How Your Food Choices Affect Your Health, Happiness and the Future of Life on Earth—John Robbins, 1987

Diet for a Poisoned Planet—David Steinman, 1990

Diet for a Small Planet—Frances Moore Lappe, 1971

Dr. Dean Ornish's Program for Preventing Heart Disease—Dean Ornish, MD 1996

Gaia : A New Look at Life on Earth—James Lovelock, 1987

Healing with Whole Foods—Paul Pitchford, 1993

Living Healthy in a Toxic World—David Steinman & R. Michael Wisner, 1996

Spontaneous Healing—Andrew Weil, MD, 1996

Peace, Love and Healing: Bodymind Communication and the Path to Self-Healing: An Exploration—Bernie Siegel, 1990

The Complete Book of Natural Foods: A Sane and Sensible Guide to Improving the Quality of the Food You Eat—David Carroll, 1985

The Dancing Wu Li Masters—Gary Zukav, 1994

The Green Kitchen Handbook—Annie Berthold-Bond, 1997

The McDougall Plan—John McDougall MD, 1985

The Non-Toxic Home—Debra Lynn Dadd, 1986

The Safe Shopper's Bible—David Steinman & Samuel Epstein, 1995

The Tao of Physics—Fritjof Capra, 1981

Who Dies?—Steven Levine

Newsletters & Journal

A Real Life
Box 400, 245 8th Avenue, New York, NY 10114
One year (six issues) $30.00
Subscription information can be faxed to (212) 229-1876

Mothers & Others for a Livable Planet
40 W. 20th Street, New York, NY 10011
(212) 242-0010

The Vegetarian Journal
P.O. Box 1463, Baltimore, MD 21203
Yearly membership (six issues)
(410) 366-VEGE

Organizations and Websites

EarthSave International—founded in 1988 by John Robbins, author of Diet for a New America. The organization educates, inspires and empowers people to shift toward a plant-based diet centered on fruits, vegetables, grains and legumes—foods that are healthy for people and the planet.

www. EarthSave.org

444 NE Ravenna Blvd, Suite 205
Seattle, WA 09105
Information: (206) 524-9903

Greenpeace

Perhaps the world's most familiar environmental organization, it is independent and non-political, dedicated to the protection of the environment by peaceful means. It depends entirely on the support of individuals to carry out nonviolent campaigns to protect the world we live in. Involves 2.5 million people in over 158 countries who have chosen to demonstrate their concern for our planet.

www.greenpeace.org

People for the Ethical Treatment of Animals (PETA)

With more than six hundred thousand members, PETA is dedicated to establishing and protecting the rights of all animals. PETA works through public education, cruelty investigations, research, animal rescue, legislation, special events, celebrity involvement, and direct action.

www.peta-online.org

501 Front St.
Norfolk, VA 23510
Phone: 757-622-PETA (7382)
Fax: 757-622-0457

Physician's Committee for Responsible Medicine (PCRM)

Founded in 1985, PCRM is a nonprofit organization of 5,000 physicians and 100,000 laypersons, including Drs. Neal Bernard, John McDougall, Dean Ornish and Andrew Weil. PCRM promotes preventative medicine through innovative programs, and higher standards for ethics in research. It consistently challenges research generated by special interests, and offers the public a wider view.

www.pcrm.org

5100 Wisconsin Ave., Suite 404
Washington, D.C. 20016
Phone: 202-686-2210

The Vegetarian Resource Group

Health professionals, activists, and educators work with businesses and individuals to bring about healthy changes in schools, the workplace, and community. Registered dietitians and physicians aid in the development of nutrition-related publications and answer member and media questions about vegetarian diets. Their website contains recipes, nutritional information, and more.

www.vrg.org

PO Box 1463
Baltimore, MD 21203
Phone: (410) 366-8343

Veggies Unite!

An online "cookbook" which features a collection of more than 1,300 vegetarian and vegan recipes. Also, discussion forums, cookbook reviews, event listings, a composting guide, answers to frequently asked questions, and links to dozens of vegetarian, animal rights, and environmental sites.

www.vegweb.com

Mail Order Companies

Arrowhead Mills
Box 2059
Hereford, TX 79045
(800) 829-5100

Beans, grains, flour, flax seeds, etc.

Bio-Earth, Inc.
5233 Maudelayne Dr. South
Mobile, AL 36693
(334) 660-1445

Garden resources

Frontier Herb and Spice
(800) 786-1388

Herbs, spices, coffee filters

Gardens Alive!
5100 Schenley Place
Lawrencebur, IN 47025
(812) 537-8650

Organic gardening supplies

Garden Spot Distributors
438 White Oak Road
New Holland, PA 17557
(800) 858-4308

Beans, grains, flours, pastas, date sugar, flax seeds, maple syrup, etc.

Gifts Organic
18 East 41st Street, #801
New York, NY 10017
(800) 651-4438
www.gifts.organic.com

Gold Mine Natural Food Company
3419 Hancock Street
San Diego, CA 92110-4307

(800) 475-FOOD (3663)

Grains, flours, noodles, beans, sea vegetables, kitchen cookware, etc.

Harvest Direct
P.O. Box 988
Knoxville, TN 37901-0988
(800) 835-2867

Soyfoods, vegetarian foods, camping foods, cookbooks, etc.

Mountain Ark Trading Co.
799 Old Leicester Hwy.
Asheville, NC 28806
(800) 643-8909

Grain, flours, beans, sea vegetables, soy sauce, miso, kitchen cookware, etc.

Natural Lifestyles Supplies
16 Lookout Drive
Asheville, NC 28804

(800) 752-2775

Grain, flours, beans, miso, herbs, kitchen cookware, etc.

Nontoxic Environment
(800) 789-4348

Household products, water filters, cleaning products, etc.

Nature's Spirit Herbs
164-A Coffee Pot Drive
Sedona, Arizona 86336
888-802-5674
Fax (520) 204-5975

A large selection of organically grown herbs in bulk

Pangea
On-line ordering: www.pangea.com

Cruelty-Free, Vegan Products

Paradise Farm Organics
1000 Wild Iris Lane
Moscow, ID 83843
(800) 758-2418
Fax (208) 882-3655
www.paradise@moscow.com

Beans, grains, backpacking, supplies, sea vegetables, etc.

Peaceful Valley Farm Supply
(916) 272-4769

Organic gardening supplies

Taylor's Organic Gardens
1 West Katharine Avenue
Seaville, New Jersey 08230
800-925-2279
www.taylorgardens.com

Another great selection of organically grown herbs.

Tieraona's Herbals
112 Hermosa Dr. SE
Albuquerque, NM 87108
800-553-4165

This is a wonderful resource for tinctures. Made from organically grown herbs, prepared without heat, she offers many combinations that can be used to support healing from specific ailments. Dr. Tieraona Low Dog is a trained physician, native American healer and midwife.

Walnut Acres Organic Farms
Penns Creek, PA 17862
(800) 433-3998
Fax (717) 837-1146
www.walnutacres.com

Granola, mixes, fruit, vegetables, etc.

Whole Food Distributors

Azure Standard
79709 Dufur Valley Road, Dufur, OR 97021
(541) 467-2230

Blooming Prairie Cooperative Warehouse
(800) 323-2131
Illinois, Indiana, Iowa, Kansas (Northern), Minnesota, Missouri, Nebraska, North Dakota, South Dakota, Wisconsin, Wyoming

Federation of Ohio River Cooperatives
(888) 936-9648
Indiana, Kentucky, Maryland, North Carolina, Pennsylvania, South Carolina, Tennessee, Virginia, West Virginia

Hudson Valley Federation
(914) 473-5400
New York, New Jersey, Connecticut, Pennsylvania

Mountain People's Warehouse
12745 Earhart Avenue, Auburn, CA 95602
(800) 679-8735 / Fax (916) 889-9544
Call to request a credit application, catalog & current sales catalog
Minimum order is $500
Arizona, California, Colorado, Hawaii, Idaho (Southern), Montana, Nevada, New Mexico, Oregon, Utah, Wyoming

Mountain People's Northwest
(800) 336-8872
Alaska, Idaho (Northern), Washington

Northeast Cooperatives
(800) 321-2667
Connecticut, Maine, Massachusetts, New Hampshire, New York, Pennsylvania, Rhode Island, Vermont

North Farm Cooperative
(800) 236-5880
Illinois, Indiana, Iowa, Michigan, Minnesota, Missouri, Montana, North Dakota, Ohio, South Dakota, Wisconsin, Wyoming

Ozark Cooperative Warehouse
(501) 521-4920
Alabama, Arkansas, Florida, Georgia, Kansas, Louisiana, Mississippi, Missouri, Oklahoma, Tennessee, Texas

Recipe Index

Sandwich Spreads and Dips 87

Soups, Stews and Chilies 95

Burritos, Enchiladas and Fajitas 143

Skillet Dinners 149

Pasta Dinners 163

Stir-Fry Recipes 169

More Great Meals 183

Special Healing Programs

The medical model offers only one approach to healing. It has become clear to many that medicine is not enough. By integrating natural methods of healing, the medical process can be greatly enhanced, or sometimes even eliminated. Natural approaches can serve to restore health, not simply control symptoms. When you learn to help yourself, the results can be miraculous.

The following tape programs will be available in the fall of 2001.

Natural Answers to Cancer

Cancer is one of the most complicated disease processes in the human body. However, we all have an army of cancer-fighting systems within us that can be called into action. Our own immune system can be the most powerful, effective cancer eliminator. Even if we choose to include medical treatment, we need to marshal our own forces to win the fight. If you or someone you love has cancer, now is the time for action. Put your hands on the resources you will need to make good decisions about your healing process.

This tape series will show you how to use supplements, natural practices, herbs and foods to give yourself the very best opportunity to heal. Learn why cancer gets started in the body and how you can help to turn off the switch that controls the disease process. Gain vital information that will allow you to be a partner in your own healing. Understand the dynamics of pain, and how you can diminish or even eliminate this symptom. Learn how you can dramatically enhance the effects of conventional cancer treatment—and what your alternatives are.

The diagnosis of cancer is one of life's major wake-up calls. Be sure you respond in the strongest way possible. Your life may depend on it.

Natural Answers to Heart Disease

Your heart is the most important muscle in your body—every 24 hours it pumps 2,000 gallons of blood through 60,000 miles of blood vessels, making sure that oxygen and nutrients arrive to the 300 trillion cells of your body. Each year brings new diagnostic procedures, new drugs and new surgical techniques to address the ever-increasing rates of heart disease and stroke. This new technology has helped many to survive heart attacks and strokes, but it has done little to prevent disease or to restore people to full health.

In this tape series, understand why heart disease develops and how you can actually reverse it and reclaim your health. Learn which specific vitamins, herbs, foods and natural practices can prevent heart disease. Create a future for yourself that is free of cardiovascular disease.

Natural Answers to Menopause

Aptly labeled the "silent passage," countless women have quietly suffered the symptoms of menopause. Most women believe that this suffering is an inevitable part of life, or that they must take the risks associated with hormone replacement therapy in order to control the symptoms. Yet, cross-cultural studies have found that only 8 percent of Asian women suffer menopausal symptoms, while 58 percent of American women do.

This tape series will provide you with specific dietary, supplement, herbal and natural practices that can make this life transition easier. Learn how you can eliminate mood swings, hot flashes and night sweats with a natural substance that has proven to be just as effective as hormone replacement with none of the risks. Understand what you can do about controlling your increased risk for cardiovascular disease. Gain the information you need to enhance your sexual desire and fulfillment. Learn how you can prevent osteoporosis and slow the aging process.

Natural Answers to Weight Loss

Now you can support your new healthy eating habits with the power of self-hypnosis. A natural and dynamic method for overcoming well-entrenched habits and self-defeating behaviors, these tapes have already changed the lives and eating habits of thousands of individuals. Contains four unique programs: "Permanent Weight Control", "Making Your Body Work for You", "Controlling Emotional Eating" and "A Twelve Minute Weight Loss Boost." Fill your mind with the successful new behavior patterns and watch your excess weight drop away.

Programs can be ordered from:

Windover Press
967 E. Parkcenter Blvd.
Suite 306
Boise, Idaho 83706
(800) 359-4492
www.KitchenintheClouds.com

Printed in the United States
2644